Papers of the Forty-Fifth Algonquian Conference

Actes du Quarante-Cinquième Congrès des Algonquinistes

PAPERS OF THE ALGONQUIAN CONFERENCES
ACTES DU CONGRÈS DES ALGONQUINISTES

45

Papers of the Forty-Fifth Algonquian Conference

Actes du Quarante-Cinquième Congrès des Algonquinistes

EDITED BY Monica Macaulay, Margaret Noodin, and J. Randolph Valentine

MICHIGAN STATE UNIVERSITY PRESS | EAST LANSING

∞ The paper used in this publication meets the minimum requirements of ANSI/NISO Z39.48-1992 (R 1997) (Permanence of Paper).

Michigan State University Press
East Lansing, Michigan 48823-5245

Printed and bound in the United States of America.

26 25 24 23 22 21 20 19 18 17 1 2 3 4 5 6 7 8 9 10

Paper ISBN: 978-1-61186-224-9
PDF ISBN: 978-1-60917-510-8

Book design by Charlie Sharp, Sharp Designs, East Lansing, MI
Cover design by Erin Kirk New
Cover detail of a quill box is used courtesy of Julie L. Loehr.

Michigan State University Press is a member of the Green Press Initiative and is committed to developing and encouraging ecologically responsible publishing practices. For more information about the Green Press Initiative and the use of recycled paper in book publishing, please visit *www.greenpressinitiative.org*.

Visit Michigan State University Press at *www.msupress.org*

CONTENTS

PREFACE

The Forty-Fifth Algonquian Conference, held in Ottawa, Ontario, October 18–20, 2013, was organized by Éric Mathieu of the University of Ottawa. He would like to thank Brandon Fry, whose help was crucial in making this conference happen; graduate students Jumanah Abusulaiman, Julie Barette, Paul Melchin, Kate Riccomini, Suzanne Robillard, Basile Roussel, Vesela Simeonova, Nova Starr, and Tharanga Weerasooriya; the Aboriginal Resource Centre at the University of Ottawa for its generous contribution to the dinner, and Manon Tremblay especially; and for administrative help, Jeanne D'Arc Turpin, Donna Desbiens, and Maurice Bélanger.

In addition to the papers published here, the following papers were presented at the conference:

Morgan Baillargeon (Canadian Museum of Civilization): Hiding Symbols of Power

Heather Bliss (University of Victoria), Rose-Marie Déchaine (University of British Columbia), and Tomio Hirose (Kanagawa University): A Comparison of Locative PPs in Blackfoot and Plains Cree

Chantale Cenerini (University of Regina): The Relational Inflection: Definition and Modern Use in Swampy Cree

Avelino Corral Esteban (Universidad Autónoma de Madrid): Coordination, Subordination, and Cosubordination in Cheyenne

David J. Costa (Miami University): Enclitics and Sentence Particles in Miami-Illinois

Danielle E. Cyr (York University): Mi'gmaq Place Names and Migration Routes

Regna Darnell (University of Western Ontario): Intergeneration Trauma and Embodied Metaphor in First Nations Narrative

Brent Delaine (McGill University): Watch and Learn: Assessing the Efficacy of a Narrative Ojibwe-Teaching Video Series to Support Adult Language Learning

Christian DiCanio and D. H. Whalen (Haskins Laboratories): Phonetic Patterns of Arapaho Vowels

Lynn Drapeau (Université du Québec à Montréal): Relational Verbs in Montagnais (Innu)

David A. Ezzo (Erie Community College): Montagnais and Southern New England Religion: A Brief Overview

George Fulford (University of Winnipeg): What Cognitive Linguistics Can Tell Us about Cree Stem Formation

Brandon Jacob Fry (University of Ottawa) and Michael David Hamilton (McGill University): Long-Distance Agreement in Mi'gmaq and Ojibwe: Towards a Comparative Study

Claude Gélinas and Yves Bouchard (Université de Sherbrooke): An Epistemological Framework for Indigenous Knowledge

Inge Genee (University of Lethbridge): Prolegomena to a New Dictionary of Blackfoot

Ives Goddard (Smithsonian Institution): Southern Unami Texts: Editing Variation

Arthur Haines (Delta Institute of Natural History) and Conor McDonough Quinn (University of Maine–Orono): Recovering Natural History Designata in the Northeast: Interdisciplinary Efforts in Ecological Linguistics

Kerry Hardy (independent scholar): Fox Island Lifeways: Pre-Contact Human Ecology in Penobscot Bay, Maine

Meredith Johnson (University of Wisconsin–Madison): *Wh*-scope Marking in Menominee

Marie-Odile Junker (Carleton University), Mimie Neacappo (Carleton

University), and Linda Vistor (Cree School Board): Building a Thematic Dictionary for East Cree

Marie-Odile Junker (Carleton University), Delasie Torkornoo (Carleton University), and J. Randolph Valentine (University of Wisconsin–Madison): Relational Databases for Cree, Innu, and Ojibwe Dictionaries

Renée Lambert-Brétière (Université du Québec à Montréal): Variation and Change in Conjunct Third-Person Plural Marking in Innu

Carol-Rose Little (Cornell University): Evidentiality in Mi'gmaq

Jean-François Lozier (Canadian Museum of Civilization): Revisiting the St. Lawrence Algonquians' Experimentation with Sedentism

Yuliya Manyakina (McGill University): The Role of *-ew* in Mi'gmaq

Éric Mathieu (University of Ottawa): Parameters and Clusters in Algonquian

Gretchen McCulloch (McGill University): Mi'gmaq *-asi* as a Middle Voice Marker

Cherry Meyer (University of Chicago): Basic Word Order and Information Structure in Ojibwe

Lori Morris (Université du Québec à Montréal): An Analysis of the Lexical Development of Innu Preschoolers

Anna Parenteau (University of Manitoba): Ojibwe/English Code-Switching on Facebook

Hubert Pineault (Université de Montréal): Research-in-Progress on the Problem of Definition of the Band and the Theoretical Conception of Leadership and Propriety

Claire Owen (Carleton University): "I speak, therefore I am"—Perceptions of the Role of Language in the Construction of Algonquian Cultural Identities

Barnett Richling (University of Winnipeg): The Best Laid Schemes: F. W. Waugh's Labrador Innu Fieldwork, 1921–22

Christopher Roy (Temple University): Rev. Peter Paul Osunkherhine and Rev. Edwin Benedict: 19th-Century Abenaki Kinship, Politics, and Protestantism, On- and Off-Reserve

Kevin Russell (University of Manitoba) and Tanya Slavin (SOAS, London): The Prosody and Syntax of the Plains Cree Verbal Complex

Allan L. Sherwin (McGill University): The Effective Herbal Therapy of Algonquian Women

Tanya Slavin (SOAS, London): Possessive Noun Incorporation and the Left-Edge Requirement in Oji-Cree

Kathleen Strader (University of Manitoba): Michif Discontinuous Elements
Jimena Terraza (University of Ottawa): Ditransitive Constructions in Ojibwe: A Typological Perspective
Natalie Weber and Martina Wiltschko (University of British Columbia): Multiple Locative Adjunction Sites in Blackfoot
D. H. Whalen (Haskins Laboratories), Emily Moline (University of California, Davis), Christian DiCanio (Haskins Laboratories), and Lisa Conathan (Yale University): Phonetic Observations on Glottal Stop in Arapaho
H. C. Wolfart (University of Manitoba): Two Cree Renditions of a Pre-Victorian Kunstmärchen
Arok Wolvengrey (First Nations University of Canada): *Iyaw*: Whoever Talks about (Cree) Interjections!?
Fanny York (Université du Québec à Montréal): The Use of Innu Intransitive Posture Verbs in Static Localization

We are grateful for the work of our graduate student editorial assistants, Samantha Litty and Bryan Rosen; to the Graduate School of the University of Wisconsin for funding the editorial assistant position; and to all of our anonymous reviewers. Thanks also to the editors at Michigan State University Press.

East Cree Nominalizations: Negotiating Category

Solveiga Armoskaite and Marie-Odile Junker

Bliss, Ritter, and Wiltschko (2016; henceforth BRW) propose a typology of Algonquian nominalizations based on Blackfoot data. Following their call to verify the typology across Algonquian, we show how East Cree facts complement a Blackfoot-based view. Comparing the East Cree data with neighboring languages Innu (Drapeau 1979) and Naskapi (Jancewicz 1996), we conclude that nominalization in Algonquian is subject to cross-linguistic and cross-dialectal variation. Specifically, we compare and contrast the behavior of independent order verb forms (with nominalizer suffix *-suu*/*-siu*) with the behavior of conjunct participles (affixed with *kaa . . . -t*/*-ch*/*-k*).

The paper is organized as follows: we first introduce the typology proposed by BRW. Then we show how some East Cree data match the proposed typology, and

This work was partially funded by SSHRC grant #856-2009-0081 awarded to the second author. Data on Cree participle inflection was gathered during a Cree grammar workshop held in September 2011 at Carleton University by the second author. We thank our research partners, the Cree consultants from Cree Programs, Cree School Board. We also thank Hélène St-Onge for checking the Innu standard orthography we applied to Drapeau's examples and Mimie Neacappo for additional data. We also thank our anonymous reviewers for comments and suggestions. All remaining errors are our own.

how some East Cree data diverge from it. Focusing on the conjunct participles, we first submit them to language-internal categorization tests. Then we discuss the extent to which morphosyntactic category tests available for Blackfoot, Innu, or Naskapi apply to East Cree. The tests reveal that East Cree conjunct participles are verbs, while they may be INTERPRETED as either verbs or nouns in particular contexts. Finally, we sketch out a proposal that allows for categorial ambiguity in the interpretation of East Cree participles.

East Cree Nominalizations Typology

Based on Blackfoot, BRW propose a typology for Blackfoot nominalizations that distinguishes between four types, each identified by a different morphological marking, input, and referent semantic role correspondence. Strikingly, each type of nominalization in Blackfoot corresponds to a particular form of stem and, moreover, a particular thematic role, as Table 1 summarizes.

Even though the proposed typology is for Blackfoot, BRW state that their ultimate goal is to determine whether these parameters are sufficient to characterize the full range of nominalizations in other Algonquian languages. Herein lies our interest. We use BRW's study to contemplate nominalization in East Cree. However, the BRW typology captures East Cree facts only in part, as summarized in Table 2.

Abstract and Concrete (Instrument) nominalizations are attested and match up with their Blackfoot counterparts. For example, the Blackfoot nominalizer *-hsin ~ n* is similar to East Cree *-win*, while the Blackfoot nominalizer *-a'tsis* serves the same end as East Cree *-kan*/*-kin*, as the comparison between Table 1 and Table 2 sums up. Examples are given in (1a, b).[1]

(1) a. chiskutimaachaa-win [ECN]
teach.VAI-**NOMZ**
'teaching'

b. sináákssiiksi [Blackfoot]
sinaaki-**hsin**-istsi
write.VAI-**NOMZ**-IN.PL
'writings' (Frantz 2009:116)

TABLE 1. Nominalization Typology Based on Blackfoot, following BRW 2016

TYPE	MARKING	INPUT	REFERENT
Abstract	*-hsin ~ n*	[Stem (Adv)/(N)-[Root V]—AI/II Final] [Intransitive verb stem]	PROCESS/RESULT
Instrument	*-a'tsis*	[Stem [Root V]—AI/II Final] [Intransitive verb stem]	INSTRUMENT
Bare	—	[CP independent VAI . . .]	ACTOR
		[CP independent VTI . . .]	ACTOR
		[CP independent VTA-*a* . . .]	GOAL
		[CP independent VTA-*ok* . . .]	ACTOR
		[CP independent VTA-*yii* . . .]	ACTOR
Conjunct	*-hp*	[CP conjunct . . . linker . . . linker . . . *-hp*]	TIME
		[CP conjunct . . . linker . . . *-hp*]	TIME/LOC/INSTR
		[CP conjunct . . . Object . . . *-hp*]	OBJECT

TABLE 2. East Cree Nominalization Based on Blackfoot Typology

TYPE	MARKING (ECS/ECN)*	INPUT	REFERENT
Abstract	*-win*	VAI stem	PROCESS/RESULT
Instrument (Concrete)	*-kan*/*-kin*	VAI, VTI stem	INSTRUMENT†
Bare	—	—	—
Actor	*-suu*/*-siu*	independent VAI stem	ACTOR
Conjunct	*kaa* . . . *-t*/*-ch*/*-k*	conjunct VAI, VII, VTI stem	ACTOR, or THEME, or INSTRUMENT

* ECS = East Cree Southern dialect; ECN = East Cree Northern dialect

† Some animate ***-kin*/*-kan*** forms have Actor referents, but with an instrument connotation, for example:

(i) chisheuchimâuâpachihâkan *na*	'Indian agent, civil servant'
uchimâhkân *na*	'chief'
wîchiâpatisîmâkan *na*	'co-worker' (Visitor et al. 2013, Topic: People/Career)

Given the clear parallels in the two languages, we will not dwell on the similarities. For the purposes of this study, we will focus on the differences.

The so-called Blackfoot bare nominalizations, as in (2) below—where just a verbal stem on its own could be used as a noun—are not attested in East Cree.

(2) áakso'kaawa. [Blackfoot]
áak-yo'kaa-wa
FUT-sleep-3SG
(i) 'He will sleep.' (ii) 'One who will sleep.' (Wiltschko 2013:198)

Wiltschko (2013) uses such examples to argue that Blackfoot bare stems are category neutral and may be interpreted as either verbal or nominal. Given the absence of such forms in East Cree, we can only note the interesting gap.

Where East Cree diverges from Blackfoot most is in the contrast between independent *-suu*/*-siu* forms versus conjunct *kaa . . .* forms. Both can be ACTORS/AGENTS as can be seen in (3a–b). Unlike Blackfoot, the conjunct participle *kaa . . . -t*/*-ch*/*-k* forms do not match with a particular thematic role in East Cree, in the sense that they can play roles other than AGENT/ACTOR as exemplified with inanimate participles in (4).[2]

(3) a. chiskutamaache-**suu**
teach.VAI-**NOMZ**
'teacher'

b. kaa-chiskutamaache-**t** [ECS]
PV-teach.VAI-**3.IIN**
'teacher'

c. chiskutimaachaa-**siu** [ECN]
teach.VAI-**NOMZ**
'teacher'

(4) a. kaa-kaawaa-ch
PV-be.rough.VII-0.CIN
'scouring pad'

b. kaa-chiyipipiyi-ch [ECN]
PV-close.VII-0.CIN
'zipper'

c. kaa-kwaapihaamaasunaaniwi-ch
PV-be.flexible.VII-0.CIN
'buffet'

d. kaa-tushtupiyi-ch
PV-pass.food.VII-0.CIN
'Jell-O'

In the remainder of the paper, we explore the *kaa*... conjunct participle forms addressing the following questions: How can one establish the category of *kaa*...? How do *kaa*... forms relate to *-suu*/*-siu* forms? What does a careful look at these forms tell us about cross-linguistic variation in nominalization across Algonquian?

TABLE 3. The Shape of East Cree Participles

INDEPENDENT INDICATIVE NEUTRAL VERB	CONJUNCT INDICATIVE NEUTRAL VERB	PARTICIPLE
ECS		
chiskutamaache-u teach.VAI-3.IIN 'S/he teaches'	kaa chiskutamaache-t preverb teach.VAI-3.CIN '(the one who) teaches'	kaa-chiskutamaache-t preverb-teach.VAI-3.CIN 'teacher'
ECN		
iskwaahtawiipayi-u go.up.VII-0.INN 'It goes up'	kaa iskwaahtawiipayi-ch preverb go.up.VII-0.CIN 'that which goes up'	kaa-iskwaahtawiipayi-ch preverb-go.up.VII-0.CIN 'elevator'

The Shape of East Cree Conjunct Participles

East Cree conjunct participles, in both dialects, consist of a verbal stem preceded by a preverb (usually *kaa*)[3] and a third-person conjunct suffix (like *-t* or *-ch* in the examples given in Table 3). Almost any Conjunct Indicative Present third-person verb form can be used to refer to what is usually translated by an English noun, and offers a flexible device for neologism. A general spelling convention is to write in one word the lexicalized form or participle (preverb+inflected conjunct verb).

Note that verbs of distinct transitivity and animacy may be the basis for participle formation.[4]

Tests for Categorial Disambiguation

The fact that East Cree conjunct participles are translated into English as nouns does not mean that they are, in fact, nouns. To ascertain their categorial affiliation, we submit the conjunct participles to category tests. We apply a set of tests that are both language-internal and based on related Algonquian languages, namely Blackfoot and Innu.

In line with BRW, we assume that category tests must be language-specific. However, comparing category tests across related languages is nonetheless useful. Such a comparison provides insights into typological variation across Algonquian. Moreover, it disperses a plausible assumption that related languages may behave uniformly with respect to categorization. Then the questions of what categorization patterns there are and how the differences arise become interesting.

To the best of our knowledge, there is only one language-internal test that distinguishes conjunct participles from inherent verbs in East Cree: the use of the locative suffix. In (5a–b), the locative suffix is used on a noun; in (5c–d),[5] the locative suffix is seen on a conjunct participle.

(5) a. aaskaahiikin
house
'a house'

b. waaskaahiikin-**ihch** [ECN]
house-**LOC**
'in a house'

c. kaa-chisikaah-kisu-t
PV-[(?)-burn. VAI]-3.CIN
'a cigarette'

d. kaa-chisikaahkisu-**yihch**
PV-cigarette-**LOC**
'on the cigarette'

Thus, with respect to this Cree-specific test, conjunct participles behave like nouns because the locative suffix is not found on verbs. While the locative can be affixed to a noun expressing a destination (6a), it cannot be affixed to a verb describing a destination, as in (6b). The desired meaning may be expressed in a paraphrase, as in (6c):[6]

(6) a. Utiwaa-**hch** nit-ispihyaa-n. [ECN]
Ottawa-**LOC** 1-fly.to.VAI-1.IIN
'I fly (by plane) to Ottawa.'

b. *nit-ispihyaa-n chimuwin-**ihch.**
1-fly.to.VAI-1IIN it rains.VII-**LOC**

c. nit-ispihyaan anitih muush aah chimuwih-ch.
1-fly.to.VAI-1.IIN there always PV rain.VAI-1IIN
'I am flying (by plane) to where it is always raining.'

We now turn to other tests that could potentially help to establish the categorial affiliation of East Cree conjunct participles.

BRW used two tests to verify and establish nounhood in Blackfoot: grammatical number and co-occurrence with demonstratives. Drapeau (1979) concludes that only three tests were in favor of nounhood for Innu participles: possessive affixation, diminutive suffixation, and denominal derivation. For number and obviative, she argued that Innu participles inflect like verbs. Jancewicz (1996) used most of Drapeau's diagnostics to reach the same conclusions for Naskapi participles. In what follows, we examine which diagnostics are applicable to East Cree.

Number is an inconclusive test for the Northern dialect of East Cree, since the suffix for third-person plural (3PL) is the same for nouns and conjunct verbs, thus not allowing for a noun-verb disambiguation, as in Innu and Naskapi. In the Southern dialect of East Cree, however, the suffix for 3PL (VAI) is different between nouns and conjunct verbs, and the participle clearly bears the verbal plural suffix, as shown in Table 4. We take this to mean that East Cree conjunct participles are grouped with verbs rather than nouns.

TABLE 4. Number in Southern and Northern East Cree

	VAI CONJUNCT *'when s/he sleeps'*		NA *'child'*	NAP *'singer, the one who sings'*
Northern				
3	aah PV	nipaa-t sleep.VAI-3.CIN	awaashish child	kaa-nikimu-t PV-sing.VAI-3.CIN
3PL	aah PV	nipaa-**ch** sleep.VAI-**3PL.CIN**	awaashish-**ich** child-**PL**	kaa-nikimu-**ch** PV-sing.VAI-**3PL.CIN**
Southern				
3	e PV	nipaa-t sleep.VAI-3.CIN	awash child	kaa-nikamu-t PV-sing.VAI-3.CIN
3PL	e PV	nipaa-**twaau** sleep.VAI-**3PL.CIN**	awaash-**ach** child-**PL**	kaa-nikamu-**twaau** PV-sing.VAI-**3PL.CIN**

The second diagnostic that BRW apply is demonstratives that modify nouns without occurring pronominally otherwise. This diagnostic does not work for East Cree. As observed by Junker and MacKenzie (2003), ALL East Cree demonstratives can be used pronominally, illustrated here with *uuch* 'these':

(7) a. niwaapamaauch **uuch** atimuch.
I.see.them **these** dogs
'I see these dogs.'
b. niwaapamaauch **uuch.** [ECS]
I.see.them **these**
'I see these ones.'

Drapeau (1979) claims that the possessive suffix is a nominal marker.[7] In her Innu example below, the conjunct personal suffix of the participle has been dropped and replaced by a possessive suffix (*-im*). Furthermore, a personal prefix, normally only allowed on independent verbs or on nouns, is now present on the conjunct form.[8]

(8) a. **ka**-piminuesh-t
PV-cook.AI-3.CIP
'a cook'
b. **ni-ka**piminuesh-**im** [Innu]
ne+[ka.pemenwe.śi]+em
1-[cook]-POSS
'my cook' (Drapeau 1979:223, example (34))

East Cree participles also take the possessive suffix, but, crucially, they also drop the preverb *kaa*, only allowing the personal prefix on the bare stem, as illustrated below.

(9) a. **kaa**-nishtuukaate-t
PV-three.wheeler-3.CIN
'a three-wheeler'
b. **ni**-nishtukaate-**m** [ECS]
1-three.wheeler-**POSS**
'my three-wheeler'

c. ***?ni-kaa**-nishtuukaate-**m**
1-PV-three.wheeler-**POSS**

d. **u**-nishtukaate-**m-h**
3-three.wheeler-POSS-OBV
'his/her three wheeler'

The fact that the conjunct preverb *kaa* has to be dropped for possessive forms (9b, d) has not been previously observed for related languages.[9] Possessive prefixes are the same for nouns and verbs except in the third person. Nouns usually take the third-person personal prefix, but verbs do not. Here, the stem (stripped from *kaa*) behaves like a noun stem, in taking the prefix *u-*, as shown in (9d). A verb in the third person would not bear such a prefix, as shown in (10).

(10) a. nipaau-u.
sleep.VAI-3
'She/he sleeps.'

b. ***u**-nipaau-u [ECS/ECN]
3-sleep.VAI-3

The nominal status of these (bare) possessed forms is further confirmed by the fact that obviative (nominal) morphology can be added to the possessive form, as in (11).

(11) a. ukapiminueshiminua [Innu]
u+[ka.pemenwe.śi]+em+**elu**
3-[cook]-POSS-OBV
'(He sees) her cook' (Drapeau 1979:223, fn. 14)

b. ni-nishtukaate-m-**h** [ECS]
1-three.wheeler-POSS-OBV
'(She sees) my three-wheeler'

However, given that the preverb *kaa* is dropped in these possessive constructions in East Cree, and that just a stem is used, are we still dealing with the *kaa* conjunct participles, or with a new formation for possessive constructions? We thus conclude that the possessive test is not available for East Cree.

Modification by diminutive suffixes is another nounhood diagnostic for Innu, where there is a different suffix for verbs (*-sh*) and nouns (*-ss*). The *kaa* forms take the nominal suffix *-ss* (Drapeau 1979:224). However, as noted by MacKenzie (1996), the diminutive suffix *-sh* is attested across verbal and nominal categories in East Cree with no difference between verbs and nouns, as in (12):

(12) a. atim(u)
dog.NA
'dog'
b. atimu-**sh**
dog.NA-**DIM**
'puppy'
c. ni-nipaa-n
1-sleep.VAI-1
'I sleep.'
d. ni-nipaa-**sh**-in
1-sleep.VAI-**DIM**-1
'I take a nap.'

Thus, the diminutive test is of little use in East Cree because the diminutive itself turns out to be a category-neutral functor.

The process of derivation of a verb is the third diagnostic for Innu.[10] A noun stem is recategorized as an animate intransitive verb if a verb final suffix *-u* (13b) is added. The same derivational process is attested with Innu participles (13c) (adapted from Drapeau 1979:223):[11]

(13) a. mus
'moose'
b. ni-mus-u-n.
1-moose-VAI-1
'I am a moose.'
c. nikapiminueshiun. [Innu]
ni-[ka.piminue.shi]-u̥-n
1-[cook]-VAI-1
'I am a cook.'

TABLE 5. East Cree Participle Behavior in Obviation: Verbal

	VAI CONJUNCT *'when s/he sleeps'*		NA *'child'*	NAP *'singer, the one who sings'*
Southern				
3′(PL)	e	nipaa-**yuuh**	awaash-**a**	awaash-**a**
	PV	sleep.VAI-**OBV**	child-**OBV**	child-**OBV**
Northern				
3′(pl)	aah	nipaa-**yichh**	awaashish-**h**	kaa-nikimu-**yichh**
	PV	sleep. VAI-**OBV**	child-**OBV**	PV-sing.VAI-**OBV**

In East Cree, denominal verb formation does not use the *kaa* form (14c); that is, Innu-like forms as in (13b) are simply not attested. Given that *kaa* is dropped, it is impossible to tell if the base in (14b) is a verb or a noun.

(14) a. kaakischihtaat.
'winner'
b. ni-[kischihtaa.si]-u-n
1-[winner]-vai-1
c. *ni-[**kaa**.kischihtaa.si]-u-n
1-[winner]-vai-1
'I am a winner.'

TABLE 6. Summary of Nounhood Tests Available for Innu, Naskapi, and East Cree (Northern and Southern) Conjunct Participles

	BLACKFOOT	INNU	NASKAPI	ECN	ECS
Number	N	V	n/a	n/a	V
Demonstratives	N	n/a	n/a	n/a	n/a
Possessive	n/a	N	N	n/a	n/a
Locative	n/a	N	N	N	N
Diminutive	n/a	N	n/a	n/a	n/a
Obviation	n/a	V	V	V	V
Derivation	n/a	N	—	n/a	n/a

Note: N = noun; V = verb; n/a = test not available; — = no data

Lastly, there is an obviation diagnostic, used both by Drapeau (1979) and Jancewicz (1996).[12] Like Innu and Naskapi, East Cree participles pattern like verbs in their obviative morphology, as shown in Table 5. The rightmost column illustrates that the obviation marking on the conjunct participles (NAP: 'singer') is consistent with the verbal marking of obviation in the leftmost column. The marking of obviation on inherent nouns (NA: 'child') differs, as presented in the middle column.

Running the battery of diagnostics across the related Algonquian languages shows the variation in the applicability of the diagnostics and in the behavior of conjunct participles. Table 6 summarizes the contrasts.

Like neighboring languages Innu and Naskapi, East Cree participles exhibit mixed verbal and nominal properties, but are even more limited in their nominal properties. They bear clear nominal morphology only in the locative, in the rare case when this inflection is semantically possible.[13] Otherwise, they inflect like verbs, or resort to stripping down to a bare stem for taking on nominal possessive morphology.

Complementary Nominalization Patterns

At this point we take a broader look again at nominalization patterns and see how they complement each other. Cases where several forms coexist can help shed light on inflectional behavior.

Names of Professions

For names of professions, both a *kaa-* (conjunct participle) and a *-suu*/*-siu* (independent verb) form sometimes coexist. There is a slight meaning difference,

TABLE 7. *kaa-* . . . and . . . *-suu* Parallel Forms (ECS)

nikamu-suu kaa-piminuwe-t*	'cook'	piminawe-suu kaa-nikamu-t	'singer'
wepihaakune-suu kaawepahaakune-t	'snowplow operator'	wepahiiche-suu kaa-wepahiiche-t	'sweeper'

*There is a tendency to spell the verb stem with the vowel coalescence *a* > *u* before *w*, (see *miskaweu* > *miskuweu* in the conjugation guide), but the stem is the same.

TABLE 8. Naskapi, Innu *kaa-*. . . with Equivalent . . . *-suu/-siu* Forms in East Cree

ENGLISH	NASKAPI	INNU	EAST CREE
surgeon	kaamaatiswaawaat	kamatishauesht	maachishichaasiu (ECN)
police officer	kaamaakunuwaast	kamakunuesht	maakunuwesuu (ECS)
cook	?	kapiminuesht	piminuwesuu (ECS)

Source: dictionaries of East Cree (Junker et al. 2012), Innu (Mailhot et al. 2013), and Naskapi (MacKenzie and Jancewicz 1994).

described by speakers as follows: the participle (form in *kaa-*) focuses more on the action, 'the one who . . . ', thus understood as a headless relative clause (in line with Drapeau 1979:241 on Innu participles), while the *-suu*/*-siu* form is about 'who this person is'. The *-suu*/*-siu* form itself can behave either as a noun or an AI verb in the independent mode: 'she/he is a . . . '. Some examples are given in Table 7.

Notice that whenever the forms coexist in the same dialect, the possessive will always be based on the *-siu*/*-suu* form. In elicitation contexts during a workshop on Cree morphology, when asked for possessive forms of the participles, speakers have gone back to substitute the entire *-siu/-suu* form paradigm for all the forms, including singular, plural, obviative, and locative, giving us a *-siu/-suu* form paradigm instead.

Across languages or dialects, it is often the case that a participle in Innu or Naskapi will have an equivalent *-suu/-siu* form in East Cree. Some examples are given in Table 8.

The patterns of preference for one process of nominalization over another across languages remain to be determined.

The Limited Use of Nominalizations

What transpired from paradigmatic elicitation sessions with different speakers is that nominalizations can have limited use, compared to regular nouns.

One test for nounhood for nominalizations was denominal verb derivation. However, this is not a preferred way of speaking. When asked for the denominal verb based on the *-suu* form 'governor' *tipeyihchichesuu*, ECS speakers indicated their preference to revert to the base verb *tipeyihchicheu* 'to govern', as quoted below (with interlinear glosses added):

(15) Q: How would you say (Possessed form on the nominalization) "my governor"?
A: nitipeyihchichesiim [ECS]
ni-tipeyihchichesi-im
1-govern.VAI-POSS
Q: and "I am the governor"?
A: nitipeyihchichesiyun . . . I would rather say 'I govern': nitipeyihchichen.
ni-tipeyihchichesiyu-n ni-tipeyihchiche-n
1-be.governor.VAI-1 1-govern.VAI-1

Even when the denominal verb derivation on a nominalized form is widely accepted, it only goes so far. We observed that when asked to put such independent verbs into a conjunct form, speakers revert to the base verb. In the Northern dialect, only the *-siu* form *chiskutimachaasiu* is in use for 'teacher', not the participle form. The denominal verb in (16a) is not possible in the conjunct with *kaa-* (b); one has to revert to the basic verb (c): 'the one who teaches'.

(16) a. chiskutimachaasiu-u [ECN]
be.teacher.VAI-3INN
'She/he is a teacher.'
b. *kaa chiskutimachaa-siu-t
PV be.teacher.VAI-3CIN
'the one who is a teacher'
c. kaa chiskutimaachaa-t
PV teach.VAI-3CIN
'the one who teaches'

The observed limitations can be summarized as follows: the denominal *-suu*/*-siu* forms cannot be put in the conjunct, while the *kaa-* forms revert to a bare (noun) stem when the possessive is put onto it.

Lexical and Clausal Nominalizations

Thus far we have only considered lexical nominalizations. Many expressions fully memorized by speakers actually include a noun and a conjunct verb modifying it as a relative clause, but they have been excluded from dictionaries so far. Drapeau

(1979:276) gives a long list of these clausal nominalizations.[14] One of her examples, adapted to standard orthography, is given in (17):

(17)	ka-shutshetshishi-t	aueshish	[Innu]
	PV-be.strong.VAI-3CIN	animal	
	'lion'		

For clausal nominalizations, nominal inflection goes on the noun and verbal inflection on the verb, as demonstrated by Drapeau (1979). Now, many participles (lexical nominalizations), as in (18), are synonymous with a clausal equivalent, such as those in (19). In (19), a head noun *awen* 'person' is modified by a relative clause, in the same conjunct form as the participle (*kaa-nikamu-t* versus *kaa nikaamut*). However, *awen kaa nikamut* is not a clausal nominalization per se, since it is neither memorized nor put in the lexicon:

(18)	ni-waapam-e-u	[kaa-nikamu-t].	[ECS]
	1-see.VTA-DIR-3	[PV-sing-3.CIN]	
	I see the one who sings'/ 'I see a singer.'		

(19)	ni-waapam-e-u	[awen	[kaa	nikamut]].	[ECS]
	1-see. VTA-DIR-3	[person	[PV	sing-3.CIN]]	
	'I see a person who is singing.'				

The (formal) parallelism between, on the one hand, lexical and clausal nominalizations and, on the other hand, participles and relative clauses modifying an overt noun further supports the verbal status of participles.

Empirical Generalizations

We have shown that East Cree participles straddle the line between verbal and nominal interpretations, even more than their equivalents in neighboring languages Innu and Naskapi, because they drop the preverb *kaa-* once nominal morphology is the only option. They are similar to verbs in that they are relative clauses, but these same clauses may have a nounlike distribution and interpretation. Thus, they manifest properties of two categories. How can we best account for the behavior of East Cree participles? The next section sketches out the approach we take.

Proposal

We take a generative perspective, specifically the Principles and Parameters framework in its Minimalist incarnation (Chomsky 1995, 2000). At the heart of the discussion on categories is an often overlooked problem: there are no clear, universally agreed upon criteria on what constitutes the basis for the categorization of parts of speech and what insights into language are thereby gained (Rauh 2010:4). As has been seen in the discussion of East Cree facts, we assume that morphosyntactic restrictions determine categorial affiliation in East Cree. Next, we assume that category neutrality is allowed by Universal Grammar (UG). It has been argued for quite a while that UG allows for category neutrality at root level (Armoskaite 2011; Borer 2005; Marantz 1997; among many others). Recently, empirical and theoretical arguments have been put forth allowing for category neutrality at the clause level, too (cf. Baker 2011; Malchukov 2006; Wiltschko 2013). Given our morphosyntactically grounded view of categorization, category neutrality would entail that a particular linguistic string passes ALL tests for ALL categories. In a way, the categorial tests themselves are neutralized because they apply without contrast (for example, Lithuanian category-neutral roots pass tests for nounhood, verbhood, and adjectivehood; see Armoskaite 2011 for more details); conversely, some functors may be category neutral and apply across categories—for example, East Cree diminutive as discussed by example (12). However, East Cree conjunct participles are verbal: conjunct is a verb-based clause typing. Moreover, based on the scant morphosyntactic characteristics—number and obviation—conjunct participles pattern as verbs, too. The only nominal morphosyntactic property is their ability to take on a locative suffix, to be addressed shortly. Thus, given the empirical generalizations presented so far, we posit that East Cree conjunct participles are verbs, but allow for category-neutral BEHAVIOR. That is, we distinguish between CATEGORY NEUTRALITY PROPER and CATEGORY-NEUTRAL BEHAVIOR.

We further propose that this category-neutral behavior at the clause level of East Cree conjunct participles can be explained by their relative clause status (cf. Drapeau, for Innu, 1979:241). The antecedent of a modifying relative clause is optional in East Cree, as shown in (20):

(20)	ni-waapam-aa-u	(awen)	kaa	nikimut.	[ECS]
	1-see.VTA-DIR-3	person	PV	sing-3	
	'I see (a person) who is singing.'				

Thus, we are faced with a clause that may be interpreted as a nominal argument only optionally. What remains to be addressed is the one environment that requires obligatory nominal interpretation: locative. So how can one reconcile the conjunct participles' categorial status of verb with a locative suffix that pertains to nouns? We propose that locative licenses a zero nominalizer.

We have shown in the section on nounhood tests that there are hardly any properties that would distinguish nouns from verbs in East Cree. For example, diminutive is category neutral; all demonstratives can be pronominal; and number is category neutral in one dialect, while it is verbal in another. This is, at best, inconclusive or else supports the verbal view of participles. Moreover, the syntactic status of nouns in Algonquian is debated. For some languages, it has been argued that nouns are adjuncts (e.g., Hirose 2003 for Plains Cree; Junker 2004 for East Cree; among others). For other languages, it has been claimed that there exist argument-like rather than adjunct-like nouns (e.g., Bliss 2013 argues for DP arguments in Blackfoot; Bruening 2001, 2009 argues for DP arguments in Passamaquoddy). We take this to mean that in the Algonquian language family there is cross-linguistic variation in how prominent nouns are in a particular language. Meanwhile, we argue that for East Cree the scarcity of noun specific properties combined with functors pertaining to both verbal and nominal domains results in behavior that is category neutral. In other words, while these conjunct participles are not deprived of category—they are verbs—they can be interpreted as category neutral. In particular contexts—for example, when they serve as objects for a transitive verb—they may be perceived as EITHER nouns or verbs.

We know that the locative suffix attaches to inherent nouns and does not favor verbs (see discussion on examples (5)–(6)). We take this to mean that the locative suffix (i) is not a derivational morpheme per se (or else it could derive deverbal nouns, which is not the case), and (ii) selects for the category noun. The participial constructions with locative thus could have the structure in (21) (cf. Citko 2004), with a zero-marked nominalized head. The participial constructions without a locative would have the structure as in (22):

(21) [$_{NP}$ ø$_N$ [$_{CP}$ kaa-chisikaahkisu-**yihch**]] [ECN]
PV-cigarette-LOC
'on the cigarette'

(22) [$_{NP}$ awen$_N$ [$_{CP}$ kaa nikamu-t]] [ECS]
person PV sing-3.CIN
'a person who is singing'

The presence of this structure can only be argued for based on the presence of a locative functional head. In line with Carstens (2008), we argue that locatives license an empty noun head. Carstens (2008), in the case of Bantu, bases the licensing on rich overt noun class agreement morphology facts. East Cree does not have the same kind of rich noun agreement morphology. In fact, as we have insisted, manifesting nounhood tests is problematic in general. However, we can posit this zero head as it is in line with the above-mentioned selection facts: in the absence of an overt *n* head, we posit a covert *n* head.

In addition, positing a zero nominalizer is in line with language-internal facts. As we have discussed above (see under example (6)), there is a considerable subset of data that indicates that the lack of such zero nominal heads results in acategorial derivation. Namely, East Cree has a lexicalized but structurally transparent set of particles that are roots merged with locational suffix *-hch*.

(23)
aanaa**hch**	'on the bottom'
tihku**hch**	'on top of a surface (touching)'
waapinuutaa**hch**	'on the east side'
nipichistiku**hch**	'on the floor'
saaku**hch**	'last spring'

Crucially, these lexicalized entries are INDECLINABLE as either verbs or nouns. Under our approach, the fact that they are indeclinable falls out: locative suffixes select for a (c)overt nominal head. In the absence of such a head, derivation results in an acategorial entry, that is, in INDECLINABLE particles.

Conclusion

As a response to BRW's call, we explored conjunct participle nominalizations in East Cree. In the process, we compared a number of diagnostics for nounhood across Blackfoot, Innu, Naskapi, and East Cree. We have shown that East Cree conjunct participles are predominantly verbal, while they may be interpreted as category neutral at times. We proposed that while conjunct participles are verbs, their category-neutral behavior may be expected given their language particular properties. We argued that the locative suffix licenses a zero nominalizer.

We conclude that nominalization in Algonquian is subject to cross-linguistic variation, and that patterns of nominalization need to be explored further (cf. Déchaine and Wiltschko 2014). The best analysis of the conjunct participles would be in line with Drapeau's (1979) suggestion that these are relative clauses. If the nounlike distribution of participles in East Cree is due to their headless relative clause status, then in order to understand East Cree nominalization patterns, we need to reveal the properties of these clauses. Another promising direction would be to study the clausal uses of other 'nominal' formations like the Actor forms.

Our speaker consultant preferences and judgments also gave us pause with respect to alternative interpretations of one and the same utterance. How does one deal with strings for which speakers CONSISTENTLY offer alternative interpretations? What methodological tools are available to us? What view can one take of the (apparent) discrepancies? At times, it may be important to seriously consider Boas's observation that "the true difference between languages is not in what may or may not be expressed but in what must and must not be conveyed by the speakers" (cited by Jacobson 1990:326). We all know that there is more than one way to convey the same content in a language, but some ways are more appropriate than others. If you were to point to someone as your daughter's former teacher, what would you say in English versus in Cree? The contrast in (24) versus (25) illustrates the distinct strategies as discussed with a bilingual consultant (Ruth Salt, personal communication).

(24) *English strategy*
He used to be my daughter's teacher. This is my daughter's former teacher.

(25) *East Cree strategy*
He used to teach my daughter. This is the one who used to teach my daughter.

The question is then: what are the language-specific reasons that drive the choice of one structural strategy over the other? We hope to have provided here the first element of an answer.

NOTES

1. Abbreviations: 1 = first person; 2 = second person; 3 = third-person animate; 3′ = third-person animate obviative; 0 = third-person inanimate; 0′ = third-person inanimate obviative; AN = animate; CIN = conjunct indicative neutral; CP = complementizer phrase; DIM = diminutive; ECS = East Cree Southern dialect; ECN = East Cree Northern dialect; IN = inanimate; INN = independent indicative neutral; OBV = obviation; LOC = locative; PERS = person; N = noun; n/a = not applicable; NAP = nominal animate participle; NIP = nominal inanimate participle; NOMZ = nominalizer; PL = plural; PASS = passive; POSS = possessive; PV = preverb; V = verb; VAI = intransitive verb with an animate subject; VII = intransitive verb with an inanimate subject; VTA = transitive verb with an animate object; VTI = transitive verb with an inanimate object; 1>3 first-person subject acting on a third-person object; X = passive proximate person.

   The surface sound changes are due to Blackfoot phonology, which has no bearing on the discussion of nominalizers.
2. The *kaa* form is not attested as a participle for the Northern dialect, except as a verb.
3. While most lexicalized forms will be preceded by the preverb *kaa*, it is possible to have nominalizations with other preverbs:

   (i) e-niishukaapuu-naanuu-hch
   when -getting.married.VAI-PASS-X.CIN
   'a wedding anniversary'
4. As shown in the example in note 1, Passive or Indefinite Actor forms may also be used. For a detailed study of the bases for participle formation, see Jancewicz (1996).
5. The *y* in the locative ending is an epenthetic segment.
6. The *n* of the stem becomes *h* in the conjunct form.
7. The (possessive) suffix -(*i*)*m* is attested across verbal and nominal categories in East Cree. Many nouns take an -(*i*)*m* suffix in the possessive. The suffix tends to appear on nouns that are not usually possessed, that is, 'a duck', as opposed to 'a book':

(i) a. **ni**-shiishiip-**im**
1-duck-POSS
'my duck'

b. **chi**-shiishiip-**im**
2-duck-POSS
'your duck'

In EC, this suffix is found both on some nouns and some verbs, right after the stem for marking disjoint reference (Junker 2003, 2008), casting doubt on its exclusive nominal status. The suffix shows up on dependent nouns (inalienable nouns that always require a personal prefix) denoting body parts:

(ii) a. nishkashii
ni-shkashii
1-nail
'my (own) nail'

b. nuushkashiim
ni-u-shkashii-**m**
1-3-nail-**POSS**
'my nail (but not my own, originally someone else's)'

The suffix also shows up on transitive animate verbs as in (iii), including conjunct forms as in (iv):

(iii) a. wâpam-e-u u-tem-h.
see.VTA-DIR-3 3-dog-OBV
'She/he sees his/her own dog/s.'

b. wâpam-**im**-e-u u-tem-iyû-h.
see. VTA-**POSS**-DIR-3 3′-dog-OBV.POSS-OBV
'She/he sees his/her (someone else's) dog.'

(iv) a. aa wâpam-aat
PV see.VTA-DIR-3CIN
'when he loves her'

b. aa wâpam-**im**-aat
PV see.VTA-DIR-3CIN
'when he loves her (son)'

While *-im* does not show up on VAI and VTI, which instead carry a relational suffix, because of its presence on transitive animate verbs (VTA), the nominal status of *-im* is questionable; it cannot serve as a proof of nounhood.

8. The first line of the Innu examples gives the current standard orthography, as used in the online Innu dictionary Mailhot et al. (2013), with morpheme breaks.
9. A few EC (Mistissini) speakers, located closer to Innu dialects, consider (9c) somewhat acceptable.
10. Such constructions are not discussed by Jancewicz (1996) for Naskapi.
11. In Drapeau's original transcription, (13c) is *ne-[ka.pemenwe.śi]-u-n.*
12. "Due to the fact that they [...*kaa* nominalizations...] continue to take verbal plural and obviation markers, they have not completely lost their verb-like-ness" (Jancewicz 1996:29).
13. In elicitation, speakers always have to add *aayihtaayihch* 'it is there' to make the form with the locative plausible. It does not come as naturally as other forms: *kaa-chisikaahkisu-yi-hch aayihtaayihch* 'It is there on the cigarette'.
14. Clausal nominalizations were called "phrase-words" by Bloomfield (1933).

REFERENCES

Armoskaite, Solveiga. 2011. The destiny of roots in Blackfoot and Lithuanian. PhD thesis, University of British Columbia.

Baker, Mark. 2011. Degrees of nominalization: Clause like constituents in Sahka. *Lingua* 121:1164–1193.

Bliss, Heather. 2013. The Blackfoot configurationality conspiracy: Parallels and differences in clausal and nominal structures. PhD thesis, University of British Columbia.

Bliss, Heather, Elisabeth Ritter, and Martina Wiltschko. 2016. Blackfoot nominalization patterns. In *Papers of the Forty-Fourth Algonquian Conference*, edited by Monica Macaulay, Margaret Noodin, and J. Randolph Valentine, 1–22. Albany, NY: SUNY Press.

Bloomfield, Leonard. 1933. *Language*. New York: Holt.

Borer, Hagit. 2005. *In Name Only*. Oxford: Oxford University Press.

Bruening, Benjamin. 2001. Syntax at the edge: Cross-clausal phenomena and the syntax of Passamaquoddy. PhD thesis, MIT.

———. 2009. Algonquian languages have A-movement and A-agreement. *Linguistic Inquiry* 40:427–445.

Carstens, Vicky. 2008. DP in Bantu and Romance. *The Bantu-Romance Connection: A Comparative Investigation of Verbal Agreement, DPs, and Information Structure*, edited by Cécile de Cat and Katherine Demuth, 131–165. Amsterdam: John Benjamins.

Chomsky, Noam. 1995. *The Minimalist Program*. Cambridge, MA: MIT Press.

———. 2000. Minimalist inquiries: The framework. In *Step By Step: Essays on Minimalist*

Syntax in Honor of Howard Lasnik, edited by Roger Martin, David Michaels, and Juan Uriagereka, 89–155. Cambridge, MA: MIT Press.

Citko, Barbara. 2004. On headed, headless and light headed relatives. *Natural Language & Linguistic Theory* 22:95–126.

Déchaine, Rose-Marie, and Martina Wiltschko. 2014. Micro-variation in agreement, clause-typing and finiteness: Comparative evidence from Blackfoot and Plains Cree. In *Papers of the Forty-Second Algonquian Conference*, edited by J. Randolph Valentine and Monica Macaulay, 69–102. Albany, NY: SUNY Press.

Drapeau, Lynn. 1979. Aspect de la morphologie du nom en montagnais. Thèse de doctorat, Université de Montréal.

Frantz, Donald G. 2009 [1991]. *Blackfoot Grammar*. Toronto: Toronto University Press.

Hirose, Tomio. 2003. *Origins of Predicates: Evidence from Plains Cree*. Routledge Outstanding Dissertations in Linguistics.

Jacobson, Roman. 1990 [1959]. Boas' view on grammatical meaning. In *On Language / Roman Jacobson*, edited by Linda R. Waugh and Monique Monville-Burston, 326–331. Cambridge, MA: Harvard University Press.

Jancewicz, Bill. 1996. Nominalizations in Naskapi. In *Papers of the Twenty-Eighth Algonquian Conference,* edited by David H. Pentland, 181–199. Winnipeg: University of Manitoba Press.

Junker, Marie-Odile. 2003. East Cree dependent nouns and disjoint reference. *Algonquian and Iroquoian Linguistics* 28:11–13.

———. 2004. Focus, obviation and word order in East Cree. *Lingua* 114:345–365.

———. 2008. Ghost arguments: Obviative *-im* and relational verbs. Paper presented at the Fortieth Algonquian Conference, University of Minnesota.

Junker, Marie-Odile, and Louise Blacksmith. 2001. Nouns with locative inflection, in East Cree interactive reference grammar. http://www.eastcree.org/cree/en/grammar/southern-dialect/nouns/inflections-locative/.

Junker, Marie-Odile, and Marguerite MacKenzie. 2003. Demonstratives in East Cree. In *Actes du trente-quatrième congrès des Algonquinistes* edited by Christopher Wolfart, 201–216 Winnipeg: University of Manitoba Press.

———. 2013. East Cree word formation. *East Cree Interactive Reference Grammar*, edited by Marie-Odile Junker. http://www.eastcree.org/cree/en/grammar.

Junker, Marie-Odile, Marguerite MacKenzie, Luci Bobbish-Salt, Alice Duff, Ruth Salt, Anna Blacksmith, Patricia Diamond, and Pearl Weistche. 2012. *The Eastern James Bay Cree Dictionary on the Web: English-Cree and Cree-English, French-Cree and Cree-French (Northern and Southern Dialects)*. http://dictionary.eastcree.org/.

MacKenzie, Marguerite. 1996. Diminutive suffixes in Cree dialects. Paper read at the

Twenty-Eighth Algonquian Conference, University of Toronto.

MacKenzie, Marguerite, and Bill Jancewicz, eds. 1994. *Naskapi Lexicon*. Schefferville, Quebec: Naskapi Development Corporation.

Mailhot, José, Marguerite MacKenzie, and Marie-Odile Junker, eds. 2013. *Innu On-line Dictionary*. www.innu-aimun.ca/dictionary.

Malchukov, Andrej. 2006. Constraining nominalization: Function/form competition. *Linguistics* 44:973–1009.

Marantz, Alec. 1997. No escape from syntax: Don't try morphological analysis in the privacy of your own lexicon. In *Proceedings of the Twenty-First Annual Penn Linguistics Colloquium*, edited by Alexis Dimitriadis, Laura Siegel, Clarissa Surek-Clark, and Alexander Williams, 201–225. Pennsylvania Working Papers in Linguistics 4.2. Philadelphia: University of Pennsylvania, Penn Linguistics Club.

Rauh, Gisa. 2010. *Syntactic Categories*. Oxford: Oxford University Press.

Visitor, Linda, Marie-Odile Junker, and Mimie Neacappo, eds. 2013. *Eastern James Bay Cree Thematic Dictionary* (*Southern Dialect*). Chisasibi, QC: Cree School Board.

Wiltschko, Martina. 2013. Patterns of nominalization in Blackfoot. In *Cross-linguistic Investigations of Nominalization Patterns*, edited by Paul, Ileana, 189–214. Amsterdam: John Benjamins.

A Look at the Mathevet Nipissing Manuscript

George F. Aubin

In this paper, I discuss the three-page manuscript on Nipissing written by the Sulpician Jean-Claude Mathevet. You might well wonder: Why discuss a manuscript that is only three pages long? Among the many reasons are the following. First, it is a manuscript written by an individual who is considered to be one of the more competent of the early writers of manuscripts. Second, the manuscript in question is on Nipissing, a language closely related to Algonquin, but, if some of the data in this manuscript are accurate, not completely coterminous with it, at least not in the mid-eighteenth century. In addition, one must also consider the fact that there are few manuscripts extant on eighteenth-century Nipissing. To the best of my knowledge, there is only one early Nipissing manuscript in the Sulpician Archives in Montreal, and only one additional early Nipissing manuscript in the Newberry Library in Chicago.[1] It is, of course, entirely possible that there are other early Nipissing manuscripts in both places that I may have missed. Nonetheless,

I would like to express my special thanks to David Pentland for his valuable assistance and instructive comments as I worked my way through earlier versions of this paper. I would also like to thank the two reviewers, whose criticisms and suggestions were much appreciated. As usual, I alone am responsible for any shortcomings that remain.

because of these very real limitations, my discussion will stay very close to the data in the manuscript that I think I understand, avoiding many of the problems posed by the data that I do not understand well.

The Mathevet Manuscript

The Mathevet Manuscript is stored in the Newberry Library in Chicago. During the Algonquian Conference of 2012, I took digital photos of this manuscript in the Reading Room of the library; the photos are the basis of this paper. Because these are digital photos, I was able to manipulate them in various ways in order to clarify as much as possible various aspects of the manuscript. It is also important to point out that the three manuscript pages I include herein as an appendix are MY TRANSCRIPTIONS of the manuscript and NOT PHOTOGRAPHS of the manuscript.

History

The Mathevet Manuscript was given to the Newberry by James Pilling, who accepts its attribution to Mathevet and who makes the following comments on it in his *Bibliography of the Algonquian Languages* on page 346:

> [Words, phrases, and sentences in the Nipissing language.] Manuscript; a fragment consisting of 2 ll, the verso of the first of which is blank, 4^0, in the possession of the compiler of this bibliography. In poor condition. French equivalents frequently appear. At the top of the first page are the terms "Passion, Resurrection, Sur la perfection," etc.

The Newberry gives the following summary of the same manuscript:

> Fragment from around 1750 containing words, phrases, and sentences in the Nipissing language, compiled by Father Jean Claude [*sic*] Mathevet, a Sulpitian [*sic*] missionary at Lac des Deux Montagnes in Oka, Québec from 1746–1781. Headings at the top of page [1], possibly topics of sermons, include "Passion," "Resurrection," "Sur la perfection," "Divers moyens pour se bien comporter," "Enfer," "Patience," and

> "Regrets d'un incroyant à la veille du depars," the latter followed by a year—1798—in which the sermon may have been given by one of Mathevet's successors.[2] Words and sentences in Nipissing are followed in some cases by translations or comments in French.

The Newberry also adds:

> Pilling, James Constantine, 1846–1895, former owner.

A further note states:

> Some loss of text due to deterioration.

General Outline of the Manuscript

The manuscript is comprised of two leaves, with the back of the first leaf blank and the second leaf written on both sides: three pages in all. The general outline of the manuscript is as follows. Pages 1 and 3 are similar in that there are words, phrases, and sentences in French following some, but certainly not all, of the Nipissing examples. Page 2, on the other hand, has no French equivalents at all, yet in my opinion it seems to be somewhat easier to read (but not necessarily to understand) than the other two pages.

Page 1

Perhaps the most important thing to notice on page 1 (see appendix) is that approximately the bottom third of the page is in Mohawk, as I have indicated, and NOT in Nipissing, as was pointed out by David Pentland. In addition, there are four short sentences in the upper left of page 1, which I have indicated by an asterisk, that are also in Mohawk. Curiously, Mathevet makes no mention of these facts at all. So we are left with an apparently unsolvable mystery: why is there Mohawk data in a manuscript otherwise dedicated entirely to Nipissing?

Turning to other matters on page 1, all of the edges of the page are irregular, with the irregularity of the right edge impinging on the readability of several letters.

The name "Mathevet" is penciled in on the top left in the upper corner. It is not at all obvious what the number 16 and the number 9 refer to, and the reason for the circle in the middle of the upper part of the page is equally unclear. Further, in the middle of the page on the left side, seven lines are preceded by what are apparently numbers, though they are written somewhat strangely and are often difficult to interpret; an eighth number may have been lost in a crease in the manuscript. An additional problem is posed by the three occurrences in the upper right corner of what appears to be *Nid* (which most likely has nothing to do with the word 'nest'), but exactly what these are, what they mean, and why they are here are not at all evident.[3]

Page 2

Here again, all four sides of page 2 are irregular. On the left side toward the middle of the page, there may be some letters or words missing, but this is not entirely clear. By way of contrast, on the bottom right, in spite of a large fold, little appears to have been lost. The two characteristics that stand out here are the following: first, there is not a single example of French anywhere on the whole page; second, this page appears to me to be the clearest of the document, with a fairly readable penmanship and relatively few problems of interpretation. The Newberry suggests in its comments alluded to above that several of the words on page 1 might be sermon topics. The same could also apply to page 2, with several of the paragraphs perhaps constituting a summary of a possible sermon: paragraphs one and three begin with *jes8s* ('Jesus'), paragraph four has *marie* ('Mary') as the second word, paragraph five ends with *kimanit88i8ining* ('In /Of/ With God'), and paragraph six begins with *kikichi manit88in* ('Great God').

Page 3

Page 3 is much like page 1. Here again, all four sides of the page are irregular, and once again, particularly on the right side, several letters and/or words have been lost. Once again, we find in the upper right corner several occurrences of the mysterious *Nid*. (But why are there TEN occurrences of the word on this page?)

My Transcriptions

For each page of the manuscript, I have included my own transcription of the page. My reading of each page was arrived at by blowing up each digital photo, and using contrast, color, and several of the other tools available to change aspects of the photo, all the while carefully studying each word and each letter. Nonetheless, in spite of this attention to detail, certain items proved resistant to my efforts; they are underlined in my transcriptions. On page 1 and page 3 of the manuscript there are also letters that are almost, but not quite, completely obliterated: these unreadable letters are represented in my transcriptions by a capital "X." It is important to point out that it was extremely difficult at times to differentiate between certain letters: ⟨s⟩ and ⟨t⟩, ⟨a⟩ and ⟨e⟩, ⟨q⟩ and ⟨g⟩, initial ⟨i-⟩ and initial ⟨j-⟩, as well as several others, and final vowels were at times very difficult to distinguish one from another. Because of all of these difficulties, I may well have made errors in my readings of various letters at times. Further, since there are no French translations at all on page 2, I have analyzed as many words as possible in the twenty-three lines of text on this page in the section below entitled "Some Linguistic Considerations."

The Dating of the Manuscript

The date given for this particular short manuscript is about 1750. Since we apparently have limited Nipissing resources at our disposal to use to compare with the Nipissing of the manuscript, we are forced to examine the French used by Mathevet. There is one feature in his French that indicates that the manuscript was, in general terms, probably written before the late eighteenth and early nineteenth centuries: the use of ⟨oi⟩ in 'seroit', 'francois', and 'francoise' on page 3. The ⟨oi⟩ spelling in these forms was changing quite generally to ⟨ai⟩ in the late eighteenth century and was changed more or less officially in the early nineteenth century; it remains ⟨ai⟩ today (Didot 1868:19, 155–156). There is one other spelling, apparently incorrect: the ⟨rs⟩ in the singular 'dépars' on page one, which is written instead of the expected 'départ'. It was common, but not required (note 'Regrets' on the preceding line), to drop the ⟨-t⟩ of the singular before the ⟨-s⟩ of the plural in nouns, another usage that disappeared in the late eighteenth and early nineteenth centuries, after which time ⟨t⟩ was retained (Didot 1868:16, 18–19). These two characteristics of the manuscript lead to the conclusion here that the general date of about 1750 is, in all probability, substantially accurate.

Some Linguistic Considerations

Turning now to some linguistic considerations, first notice that in three cases on page one, toward the middle of the page, Mathevet gives both the Nipissing and the Algonquin equivalents of a particular form: Nip: *passa8angak*, Alg. *Ping8a8an-gahigan* 'sucre en Cassonade'; Nip. *missi8echigan*, Alg. *pit̲ig8a 8anguinigan* 'sucre en pain'; Nip. *Sibiskagamisigan*, Alg. *iskabagamisiga̲n̲* 'Sirop'. The three Nipissing forms given here are quite different from their corresponding Algonquin forms, and it does not seem that there is any easy way to predict either one from the other, since they use different derived stems although sharing some morphemes, as one reviewer suggested. In the first pair, there is little similarity at all between the Nipissing form and the Algonquin form. The same can be said of the second pair even if both the Nipissing form and the Algonquin form end in *-igan*. The third pair, however, appears to show a closer resemblance between the Nipissing form and the Algonquin form, with the Algonquin form apparently dropping the initial *sib-* of the Nipissing form and adding *-ba-* before the first *-ga-*. But if *isk-* is NOT a shortened form of *sibisk-*, as one reviewer suggested, even here there is little similarity. It seems to me that Mathevet is suggesting that, in spite of some similarities between the two dialects, Nipissing may at times be quite different from Algonquin, at least circa 1750 in the Nipissing dialect with which he is concerned. To the contrary, another reviewer suggested that the main reason these three words were listed was precisely because they WERE different in the two dialects given that, in the reviewer's opinion, the lexicons of the two dialects were largely identical. Until we know more about Nipissing vocabulary versus Algonquin vocabulary in the mid-eighteenth century, it is difficult to evaluate these various claims (but see (1)–(23), below, for some possibly relevant data).

With respect to the ⟨r ~ l⟩ question, the Nipissing in this manuscript seems to be quite generally in an ⟨l⟩ dialect. There are also several examples with ⟨r⟩, almost all of them in the Mohawk section, where, of course, ⟨r⟩ is expected. In further support of the claim that the Nipissing parts of the manuscript are generally in an ⟨l⟩ dialect, there is only one possible example of ⟨r⟩ on page 2, in the unclear and poorly written word 'm̲a̲r̲ie', and on page 3, there is not a single example of ⟨r⟩.

The following linguistic changes occur often, but not always, as we move from the Nipissing of the manuscript to Algonquin:

- Nip. l > Alg. n always
- Nip. p, t, k > Alg. b, d, g sometimes, and
- Nip. b, d, g > Alg. p, t, k sometimes
- Nip. 8 > Alg. o ~ w
- Nip. tch > Alg. tc ~ dj
- Nip. g, z > Alg. [ž] (often written as ⟨j⟩)
- Nip. h > Alg. Ø / V_V, often but not always

There are also a number of spelling changes that often occur from Nipissing to Algonquin:

- Nip. ⟨gh, gu⟩ > Alg. ⟨g⟩
- Nip. ⟨ch⟩ > Alg. ⟨c⟩ ([š] for both)
- Nip. ⟨ss⟩ > Alg. ⟨s⟩
- Nip. ⟨age⟩ > Alg. ⟨aje⟩

Turning now to specific cases, I deal with each line of page 2 in Table 1, listing first the Nipissing unglossed form, and then indicating related forms in Algonquin, with glosses and sources for each of the latter.

It is reasonably clear from an examination of all of these forms that Nipissing and Algonquin are certainly quite similar. One of the ways that this is manifested is not only in the similarities between the shorter words, of which there are many, but perhaps more strikingly in the similarities between several of the LONGER WORDS, as in these examples from several of the preceding sections: (4) *elabighis*; (5) *p8ala8i8tosin*; (6) *chawelimichil*; (7) *nig8ta8asingua*; (12) *pag8selim*; (13) *8enijanissigik*; (16) *manit88iwin* and *nitapelimon*; (19) *biskalelindal*; and (22) *kitibelindam8lil*; among several others.

Finally, to illustrate some of the difficulties one encounters when dealing with this Nipissing manuscript, I now turn to two of the verb forms on page 3 of the manuscript: *nigaki8iaguinenaban nip88anbanen*, 'Ce serait dommage que je fûs mort' ('It would be too bad if I had died'). In spite of Mathevet's gloss, *nigaki8iaguinenaban* certainly appears to be a PERSONAL verb form beginning with the personal prefix *ni-* followed by the *-ga-* 'immediate future' form and *-ki-* 'past', then ending with

TABLE 1. Nipissing and Algonquin Cognates

LINE	NIPISSING	ALGONQUIN	GLOSS	SOURCE
1	jes8s	Jezos, obv. *-an*, dim. *-ens*		Cuoq 133
	n8osseX	n'ose	'ô mon père'	Cuoq 290
	nitala8i	nita-	'on sait, on peut faire l'action du verbe'	Cuoq 283
	kikelindis	kikénindis	'I know myself'	Bar b187
	ezi	eji	'Voy. IJI dont il est l'augment temporel'	Cuoq 99
			'. . . it signifies 'as; in such a manner; in a certain way; so; like' . . . '	Bar b149
	m8skineskag8ian	moski-	'découvert indécemment'	Cuoq 241
		ki moskinagos	'couvre-toi'	Cuoq 241
	patat88ini	patatowin	'péché'	Cuoq 331
	kel8ek	enowek	'malgré cela; assez'	Cuoq 102
	songa	songan	'(être) bien; fort; solide'	Cuoq 373–374
	kitamaguisi8in	gackitamage	'acquérir, pouvoir obtenir'	Cuoq 105
2	k8etissian	kakwet	'chercher à savoir, à faire'	Cuoq 142
	na		'particule interrogative'	Cuoq 243
	kitchi	kitci	'grand; beaucoup'	Cuoq 174–175
	8tissian	nind otisik	'j'arrive chez lui'	Cuoq 313
3	ki	2sg	'2e p. s. du pr. de l'ind.'	Cuoq 158
	pass8limil	pas, o{long a in *pas*}	'être sec; séché'	Cuoq 330
	kil	kin	'you' 'pronom isolé de la 2e p. s.'	Cuoq 165
	ka	ka+participe présent	'celui qui'	Cuoq 135
	nita-	(See 1, above)		
	cha8elinghen	nita-caweninge	'. . . tout miséricordieux'	Cuoq 83
	kitchi	(See 2, above)		
	pindiken	pindike	'entrer'	Cuoq 342
	niteing	o tehing	'. . . in corde suo'	Cuoq 395
4	Mitchi		'grand; gros'	Cuoq 233–234
	8lichichiton	oniciciton	'améliore-le; embellis-le'	Cuoq 304
	elabighis	enabigis	'en ~ de grâce; je vous en prie'	Cuoq 100
	ghitimakelindel	gitimagenim	'aie pitié de lui'	Cuoq 108
	ninta	nindaha	'je l'envoie . . . '	Cuoq 277
	ezi	(See 1, above)		
	tehen	teh	'coeur'	Cuoq 396
	izitehichil	ijitehehicin	'faites-moi avoir le coeur'	Cuoq 396

LINE	NIPISSING	ALGONQUIN	GLOSS	SOURCE
5	ka	(See 3, above)		
	cha8elinghen	caweninge	'N.-S. est plein de miséricorde'	Cuoq 83
	mit8nelimiahil	mitonenim	'pense à lui'	Cuoq 235
	ka	(See 3, above)		
	napitc	ka napitc	'nullement; pas du tout'	Cuoq 135
	keg8l	kekon	'toute chose; toutes les choses'	Cuoq 141
	ki	(See 3, above)		
	p8ala8it8sin	pwanawitosin	'. . . ne vous est impossible'	Cuoq 162
6	chawelimichil	cawenimicin	'faites-moi cette grâce'	Cuoq 89
	elabighis	(See 4, above)		
	nipatat88in	(See 1, above)	'mon péché' (?)	
	kassihama8ichil	kasihamaw	'essuie-le lui'	Cuoq 147
7	jes8s	(See 1, above)		
	n8sse	(See 1, above)		
	ontchita	ondjita	'sérieusement; exprès'	Cuoq 303
	ki	(See 3, above)		
	saki hig8s	sakihigos, i	'être aimable'	Cuoq 361
	nig8ta8asingua	ningotawasingwa	'qu'ils sont heureux!'	Cuoq 278
	wakoing	wakwing	'du ~ au ciel'	Cuoq 38
8	ka	(See 3, above)		
	iapilchik	—		
	kakik		'toujours'	Cuoq 141
	missis	misi	'grand'	Cuoq 231
	kingik	—		
	ki	(See 3, above)		
	wabamig8k		'they are seen' (?)	
	8it8ka8elimichil	witokaw	'aide-lui'	Cuoq 444
9	kakik	(See 8, above)		
	kitchi	(See 2, above)		
	ali	ani	'commencer à; se faire à'	Cuoq 47
	debisat8\a/ian	débissaton	'I put ~ procure enough of it'	Bar b106
	eli	eni-onâgoshig	'toward evening'	Bar b114
	elêmin	—		
	ondage	ondaje = oom daje	'ici'	Cuoq 301
	aking	aking	'sur la terre'	Cuoq 141
	8akoing	(See 7, above)		
	gaie	gaie	'et; aussi'	Cuoq 107
	nil	nin	'moi'	Cuoq 276
10	kitchi	(See 2, above)		
	kissis	—		
	ki	(See 3, above)		
	8abamilan	minwabaminagos	'avoir bonne mine'	Cuoq 229

LINE	NIPISSING	ALGONQUIN	GLOSS	SOURCE
11	kichit8a	kitcitwa {de kitci towa}	'considérable, important'	Cuoq 177
	marie	mani	'Marie'	Cuoq 205
	ninquinan	gwi, ningwi	'mon camarade (d'homme)'	Cuoq 110, 279
	a8ihichil	awihicin	'. . . prêtez-moi . . . '	Cuoq 226
	kite	kitenimowin	'pride'	Bar a199
		nin kiténima	'I think him proud'	Bar b196
	kig8issis	kigwississ	'thy son'	Bar a237
	8e8ilint	wewenint	'bien; comme il faut'	Cuoq 433
	aking	(See 9, above)		
	kitchi	(See 2, above)		
12	akihak	—		
	kitchi	(See 2, above)		
	cha8elanitch	cawenim	'aie pitié de lui'	Cuoq 83
	songa	(See 1, above)		
	pag8sselim	pagosenim	'prie-le'	Cuoq 318
	8akoing	(See 9, above)		
	kitchi	(See 2, above)		
	8isalakimak	wisagizi VAI	'be bitter'	N&N 146
13	nesh	neshangaa VII	'be limber; be slack'	N&N 95
	8enijanissigik	wenidjanissingig	'like one's own child'	Bar a48
	8assa	wasa	'loin'	Cuoq 425
	kipakila8ak	kip-	'fermé; bouché; enfermé'	Cuoq 170
	kihian	—		
	g8tch	kawin ningotci	'nowhere'	Bar a182
	kitachamimim	acam	'donne-lui à manger'	Cuoq 10
		acamim	'vous voulez me donner à manger'	Cuoq 116
14	epitch=	epitc gackenindang	'tant il est triste'	Cuoq 102
		apitci/ apitc	'bien; beaucoup; quand; tant que'	Cuoq 59–60
	=cha8elimiang	ningi cawenimik	'il a eu pitié de moi'	Cuoq 187
	pakei=	pakeia	'le fleuve se divise en deux branches'	Cuoq 321
	=elindama8ichil	windamawicin	'dis-le moi'	Cuoq 197
	ondage	(See 9, above)		
	aking	(See 9, above)		
	entag8guil	—		
15	songa	(See 1, above)		
	achit=	—		
	=enimicin		{part of cawenimicin: faites-moi cette grâce}	Cuoq 89
	kimanit88i8ing	Manitowiwining	'en Dieu'	Cuoq 282

LINE	NIPISSING	ALGONQUIN	GLOSS	SOURCE
16	kikitchi	kitci	'grand; beaucoup'	Cuoq 174–175
	manit88i8in	kije Manitowiwin	'Divinité'	Cuoq 158
	songa	(See 1, above)		
	nitapelimon	nind apenimon	'j'espere'	Cuoq 57
		apenim, o	'espérer; avoir confiance'	Cuoq 57
	kitcha8elingigue8ining	—		
	song	ni song aiamia	'je suis bon priant'	Cuoq 130
17	minchimelimichil	mindjimenim	'retiens-le dans ton esprit'	Cuoq 220
	mika8elindam8chichil	wani mikaw, i	'perdre connaissance'	Cuoq 424
	g8etch	kawin gwetc	'pas beaucoup'	Cuoq 110
	elelimi8anen	mi ma eneniminang	'ce que demande de nous Jésus'	Cuoq 405
	kitchi	(See 2, above)		
18	tipahigalilan	tipaigan	'mesure'	Cuoq 402
	8it8ka8elimichil	wid, widj, widji	'association, accompanying'	Bar b411
		widokawenima (nin)	'I assist his thoughts, his mind'	Bar b414
19	songa	(See 1, above)		
	kitchi	(See 2, above)		
	sakihilan	nind anisitok ketci-sakihinagok	'J'aime mes très chères filles'	Cuoq 51
	biskalelindal	piskanenindan	'allume-la (chandelle)'	Cuoq 347
		sibisk	'flexible; visqueux; tenace'	Cuoq 367
	ninte	nindeh	'mon coeur'	Cuoq 269
	kitchi	(See 2, above)		
	eka	ekakanatek	'ce qui est carbonisé'	Cuoq 27
		egacinonjicitc	'le plus petit'	Cuoq 15
	Liskihilan	niniskan	'I encumber it'	Bar a87
		niskikân	'I encumber it'	Bar b302
	songitches	—		
20	ka8iehil :	—		
	kinitchike	winanitcike	'où l'on dépèce un fauve tué à la chasse'	Cuoq 440
	tibelindan	ni tibenindan	'elle est à moi'	Cuoq 399
	kakina	tout, tous	'collectif'	Cuoq 141
	missi	mici	'grand; gros; brin de poil, ~ bois'	Cuoq 215
	keg8l	keko	'quelque chose'	Cuoq 399
	ki	(See 3, above)		
	pesik8	pejik	'un'	Cuoq 332
		pêjik	'Un,e'	Lemoine
	manachihil	manacigan	'manacigan'	Cuoq 12
		manashigan	'bass-fish'	Bar b216
	kakik	(See 9, above)		

LINE	NIPISSING	ALGONQUIN	GLOSS	SOURCE
21	tibelimichil	tebenimin	'domine mi!' (Latin vocative)	Cuoq 399
	8ssam	osâm	'too; too much; very much'	Bar b333
	nitagassitehe	—		
	manguitehe=	mangidéé	'I have a large heart'	Bar a131
	=ska8ichil	—		
	keg8la	kegona pitcimagak ki tibeningewin	'adveniat regnum tuum'	Cuoq 153
	kisakihilan	aimer	'to love'	Cuoq 361
22	apitch	(See 14, above)		
	sakihig8ssin	sakihigos,i	'être aimable'	Cuoq 361
	nihiau	ni iaw	'mon corps'	Cuoq 114
	nipimatissi8in	pimatis, i	'être vivant; vivre sur la terre'	Cuoq 68
		kakike-pimatisiwin	'la vie éternelle'	Cuoq 141
	kitibelindam8lil	ki tibenindamonin	'être le maître' (?)	Cuoq K.M.D.W.
	elielelimi8anen	—		
		enenimatc	'celui que tu penses'	Cuoq 70
		anin enenimătc [*sic*]	'que pensez-vous de lui?'	Cuoq 101
23	mi	employé avec	'gwetc' 'merci'	Cuoq 110, 217
		migwetck [*sic*]	'thanks'	Bar b 235
	kakik	(See 8, above)		
	ke8is	nicikewis, i	'être seul'	Cuoq 270
	tian	i kij patatiân	'parce que j'ai péché' {1ère p. sg. conj.= patat+ian}	Cuoq 133 Cuoq 133

Notes: In the third and fourth columns, comments enclosed in { } are explanatory notes. The general format of the last column is "Source page." *Cuoq* refers to Cuoq 1886, *Bar* to Baraga 1992 [1878, 1880], *Lemoine* to Lemoine 1909 (which lacks page numbers on the relevant page), and *N&N* to Nichols and Nyholm 1995. Baraga is divided into two parts: the first is English-Ojibwe and the second is Ojibwe-English. Both start pagination at "1," so *a* is used to refer to the first part and *b* is used to refer to the second part. Thus an entry like *Bar a48* means that the form is found on page 48 of the English-Ojibwe part of the Baraga dictionary.

the 'past tense' marker in *-aban*, preceded by the *-ne(n)-* of 'die'. The verb here is most likely *wiiakine* 'cause harm to (by dying)' ['causer du dommage en mourant'] (Lemoine 1911:202). Mathevet's translation of this form, "Ce serait dommage . . .", as an IMPERSONAL conditional verb form, although idiomatic and perhaps not unusual given the context, is nonetheless somewhat misleading. A translation closer to the original Nipissing, in which this verb is treated as a PERSONAL verb form, would be along the lines of: 'I would perhaps have caused (them) harm . . . ' ('Je (leur) aurais peut-être causé du dommage . . . ').

Nip88anbanen, the second verb form, is much clearer. It begins with the verb *nip8-* 'die' followed by the first-person singular dubitative marker *-8anbanen*. Mathevet translates this as ' . . . que je fûs mort' (' . . . if I had died'). In this case,

Mathevet's gloss is accurate, with, however, one caveat. The verb 'fûs' here, from the verb 'être', is problematic: is it a misspelling for a passé simple or a misspelling for an imperfect subjunctive, neither of which has a circumflex accent in the first-person singular? Because a supposition of the type Mathevet uses here is often indicated in French by a simple 'que' followed by the subjunctive (Grevisse 1959:1038), it appears to be a misspelling of 'fusse', the first-person singular of the imperfect subjunctive, the more elegant and often preferred form here of the auxiliary verb 'être', which, along with the past participle 'mort', makes the full verb a pluperfect subjunctive. It should also be pointed out that the interpretation and analysis of the two verbs discussed here is an interpretation and analysis that can apply, apparently, to either Nipissing or Algonquin. This is quite unlike what one finds with the three examples given earlier by Mathevet, in which the differences between the two dialects are often considerable. Exactly where the two dialects are similar and where they are different is a determination that will, of course, require further work and additional data.

Conclusion

To conclude these remarks on Nipissing, I think I have shown that this manuscript, in spite of its small size, is clearly of some interest to Algonquianists. Although it is very difficult to deal with in places, because it is a manuscript by Jean-Claude Mathevet and because it is one of an apparently small number of manuscripts on early Nipissing, it gains an importance that is greater than its modest size would seem to warrant.

Appendix. Mathevet's Short Nipissing Manuscript

[Page 1]

Nid kaiacha8atissi Nid
Mathevet 16 passion ka8i kika apitch Nid
resurrection nep8tch : il est mort de vieillesse Nid
*tsi ki 8ague ou je vai Sur La perfection 9 88aiek8 askan pimatiss i8in
*tsi ki tage d'ou je viens
Divers moyens pour se bien comporter) il est arrivé au bout de la vie
*iahake8e je suis rendu au bout) ni8aiek8ah aton mikan je vai au bout du chemin
*iague8e je puisse arriver Regrets d'un mourant h p ni8aie k8askan kitigan je vai au bout du champ
a la veille du dépars 1798
enfer
ni nil8elim 8 na =nitapelim8na kélna 8kam onsapi 8ugan ten88an n8zan
ni nil8na je Le soutiens patiance O aiagama pi8abik8an kegapîcek
depuis qu'il me Comde
ni nil8kag8nan il estnre tip de Limit. elelimi lag8g8l eleli mileg8l
soutien
Nip: passa8angak . alg. ping8a8angahigan sucre en Cassonade
nip. missi8echigan .. alg pitig8a 8ang uinigan sucre en pain .. | on appelle aussi La terre
86 | qu'on a c oagulé pitig8
16 nip. Sibiskagamisigan .. alg iskabagamisigan Sirop | 8anguini gems
116 Sinsibak8at Sucre = Les algonkins des trois rivieres l'appellent chi8ens
——
kalaque achamichil pa8iz8atch . donne moy Les miettes au moins
32 —
250 ketna a8eni8i est ce qu'il est qq chose . ka8il nita8eni8isi je ne sai rien
ka8il kita8eni8isin anaban, n8enaie k en kikiski jelimiganan
64
metilîsi Cela ne sent vg du tabac avanté . des oignons trop ireXX
460
XX nit8alimitag8s je suis Las de parler ———
[*Mohawk words begin here and continue for the rest of the page*]
issu genton je parle de toy . issi g8enton ie parle de vs autres . riton je parle de luy, ki ton keton d'eux ou d' elles. ii gatatiton je parle de moy . ii iag8atatiton ns parlons de ns .
ne kiton je parle de cela . ne renton il parle de cela : tossa neXXXrakonhag ne parle pas de cela .
ne ienni il dit cela de toy . nesennî elle dit cela de toy . gonienni je dis de toy g8enni XXX
—
jah ken non8enton te ietsiri8a8asse nationtakassi tsi iagoniagon, ki etnïenha
i'onnerag8at em iagosteniaron ni iemX aonguenonatsentan X qa8ennigo arc onnen iag XXX
onnen iontatenak8asatenni nontatienha, 8aageratsi arc 8ationtakassi ; ag8e gaX XXX.
Sontie 8ha : nahe em tiontateri8a8ass8 ne ienon8a nen, iah ne he Dkari 8aieri .
hietsi ia tsennonniatenni, hietsi ienha ne iahte ietsiri 8a8assu ——]

[Page 2]

patat88ini

jes8s n8ssX nitala8i kikelindis ezi m8skineskag8ian / kel8ek songa \ kitimagui si8in

~~gaie patat88in~~, k8 etissian \ na / kitchi ~~einueXXi 8i~~ an \ 8tissian / , —

ki pass8limil kil ka nita cha8elinghen kitchi pindiken niteing

~~Kitchi 8lichichit8a~~ \ Mitchi 8lichichiton / elabighis ghitimakelindel / ninta ~~8lichi chil~~ \ ezi tehen izitehichil

————————

ka cha8elinghen mit8nelimiahil , ka napitch keg8l ki p8ala8it8sin

Cha8elimichil elabighis nipatat88in kassihama8ichil ________

jes8s n8sse ontchita ki saki hig8s, nig8ta8asingua 8akoing

ka iapilchik , kakik missis kingik ki 8abami g8k : 8it8ka8elimichil

kakik kitchi ali debisat8 \ a / ian \ eli elêmin / ondage aking 8akoing gaie nil

kitchi kissis \ ki / ~~Kakiki~~ 8abamilan .

[k]ichit8a marie ninquinan a8ihichil kite kig8ssis 8e8ilint aking kitchi

akihak, kitchi cha8elanitch songa pag8sselim, 8akoing kitchi 8isalakimak

nesh 8enijanissigik 8assa kipakila8ak , kihiau g8tch kitachamimim

epitch cha8elimiang ; pakeielindama8ichil , ondage aking entag8guil,

songa achitelimichil kimanit88i8ining

kikichi manit88i8in songa nitapelimon , kicha8elingigue8ining song

minchimelimichil , mika8elindam8chichil g8etch elelimi8anen, kitchi

tipahigalilan 8it8ka8elimichil

songa kitchi sakihilan biskalelindal ninte, kitchî eka Liskihilan songhitches —

ka8i ehil : kinichike tibelindan kakina missi keg8l, ki pesik8 manachihil kakik ___

tibelimichil ___ 8ssam nitagassitehe manguiteheska8ichil , keg8la kisakihilan

apitch sakihîg8ssin ; nihiau , nipimatissi8in kitibelindam8lil ; elielelimi8anen

mi kakik ke8is tian ———

[Page 3]

Xn8a kitianakig je suis tres miserable Nid Nid

Nid Nid Nid

Xig8na on me L'a vole ni kis ling8a8an — Nid Nid

kichi mons assin —— gahan je L'ai couvert avec dela Cendre Nid Ni

[J]e sens Le vent du boulet de canon Nid

8l88e skagon

nigaki8iaguinenaban nip88anbanen ka8il La8i kalig8kegon kilan8elindiss8 8ini X

Ce seroit dommage que je fûs mort ne differez pas vre conversion

Ziz8la8enigan parfum sing.

manij8ssel sing. pl.

ilileg8ban pl | 8kakika mitchilin

manij8ssa

iliLag8ban ce qu il vs a dit ————

iliL eg8ban ce que je vs ai dit 8ankipigik ka 8kis il a fait XXX

ali aka8ata k 8ssinan kitchi niganetch qd il n'est pas parti

Suis notre pere pakitamichil Cesse de mXX

ali aka8ata , k8ss inan naganetch qd il est deja parti

8l8skan aki 8t8L8askan aki il est heureux qd il entrprend qq chose v. g. La XXX

kakina missi keg8l 8t8l8askan gaie aki gaie nipi

nimichep8al —

fume en nageant en travaillant | ni nipeka8a je luy fais ses XXX
| kinip ek8l

pakitelindam8chichil aking entag8gil detache moi {?}

ka nisabi tchimesimên ns ne nagêons pas fort

Ki g8tan na kitchi p8k8achibiton kip8i crains tu de Casser ton aviron

engig8t ki kiki ching8as elelin dag8ssin

ontchita 8il ka ki michagasimîn ala8i izaiang8ban

ka8il al8tch izi tchi mesita mama8i 8ik8ap8ieta nageons en semble

Me mitig8si 8ik8a p8ieta nageons a La francoise = nageons fort

Memitig8si m8ta parlons francois

a \ ki / k8ka \ Li / biss8 il s'enrhume 8nissinandan son suc

Nitapiss8ma = kakek ni8aL8Ca

NOTES

1. One Nipissing manuscript is in the Sulpician Archives in Montreal listed as ASSM manuscript 85. The other Nipissing manuscript is in the Newberry Library in Chicago listed as Ayer manuscript 1976.
2. Given the date of 1798 here, this form must have been written by someone else since Mathevet died on August 2, 1781.
3. The puzzling term *nid* shows up several times in this manuscript as well as in other manuscripts gathered together into Manuscript 43. These include two examples of *nid* repeated seven times, one example of it repeated eight times, and one example of it repeated sixteen times. It is often written in the margins, and, if it is within the text, it is seldom on the line, often slanting upward or downward, and sometimes rather sloppily written. Nowhere have I found any indication of the reason for its use or what it might be intended to symbolize. One reviewer makes the reasonable suggestion that it may well be a religious abbreviation, a sort of personal prayer inserted as a devotional act, perhaps for [*ora pro*] *nobis, iesu domine.*

REFERENCES

Baraga, Frederic. 1992 [1878, 1880]. *A Dictionary of the Ojibway Language.* St. Paul: Minnesota Historical Society Press.

Cuoq, Jean-André. 1886. *Lexique de la Langue Algonquine.* Montreal: J. Chapleau et fils, Imprimeurs-Éditeurs.

Didot, Ambroise Firmin. 1868. *Observations Sur L'Orthographe Ou Ortografie Française Suivies D'Une Histoire De La Réforme Orthographique Depuis Le XVe Siècle Jusqu'À Nos Jours. Deuxième Édition.* Paris: Typographie De Ambroise Firmin Didot. Imprimeur-Libraire De L'Institut De France.

Grevisse, Maurice. 1959. *Le bon usage.* Gembloux, Belgium: Éditions J. Duculot.

Lemoine, Georges. 1909. *Dictionnaire Français-Algonquin. Chicoutimi.* G. Delisle, Imprimeur, Bureaux du journal "Le Travailleur."

Nichols, John D., and Earl Nyholm. 1995. *A Concise Dictionary of Minnesota Ojibwe.* Minneapolis: University of Minnesota Press.

Pilling, James Constantine. 1891. *Bibliography of the Algonquian Languages.* Smithsonian Institution Bureau of Ethnology. Washington, DC: Government Printing Office.

Rhodes, Richard A. 1985. *Eastern Ojibwa–Chippewa–Ottawa Dictionary.* Berlin: Mouton.

Syntagmatic Phenomena in the Northern East Cree Verbal Template

Vincent Collette

Many polysynthetic languages of North America exhibit word structures of astonishing complexity, and the description and analysis of these languages have always been a serious challenge for field linguists. Since the pioneering work of Bloomfield, the complex verbal morphology of some Algonquian languages has been described using a template of position classes in order to capture the arrangement of grammatical affixes (see Bloomfield 1958 [Ojibwa], 1962 [Menominee]; Wolfart 1973 [Plains Cree]; Sherwood 1986 [Passamaquoddy]; Bakker 2006 for a critical overview). The essence of the method is well known and straightforward. It is assumed that complex inflection—that is, a word minus its stem—is made up of affixes that have a strict relative ordering. After a careful examination of all the verbal and nominal paradigms, a numbered position is assigned to each of the affixes. In a verb template of eight suffixal positions, for instance, a suffix of position 5 will always precede any suffix of position 6 to 8, while a suffix of position 2 will follow a suffix of position 1, and so forth. Finally, a position

I would like to thank all my Cree consultants who have taken the time to teach me their complex language, especially Noah, Nancy, and Romeo Sheshamush. Many thanks also to Kevin Brousseau for providing me with some useful comments. All errors are mine.

8 suffix will invariably be word-final. For further explanations on the method, see Bloomfield (1962:101) and Nida (1949:205–207), among others.

Considered traditionally as a tool for the description of languages exhibiting complex morphological systems, templatic morphology has received sustained theoretical attention since the mid-1980s, and a set of specific identificational criteria has been put forth in order to circumscribe the essence of templatic morphology. This is usually done by comparing templatic morphology with layered, or scope-governed, morphology (Simpson and Withgott 1986; Spencer 1991; Rice 2000; Stump 2006; Nordlinger 2010). Here is a list of the criteria encountered in the literature:

1. Templatic morphology may contain zero morphemes, while layered morphology does not (for example, impossibility to have zero morphemes in derivation).
2. Templatic morphology is incompatible with headed structures, or semantic scope relations, while layered morphology is compatible.
3. Templatic morphology is not constrained by any principle of adjacency, while layered morphology is.
4. Templatic morphology does permit an inner morpheme to be chosen on the basis of an outer morpheme, while layered morphology does not.
5. Templatic morphology encodes at least one verbal argument, which is not necessarily so for layered morphology.
6. Templatic morphology displays multiple exponents (one meaning for many forms scattered in the word), while layered morphology does not.
7. Templatic morphology exhibits a lack of functional unity—that is, affixes expressing different grammatical categories belong to the same position, and affixes expressing the same grammatical categories belong to different positions.

Since these two types of morphological patterning are diametrically opposed, as the preceding criteria indicate, it has been proposed that templatic morphology may in fact constitute a morphological type on its own, along with the ones traditionally identified by the Neogrammarians of the nineteenth century (Simpson and Withgott 1986; Nordlinger 2010). However, this proposition is not accepted by every linguist working on polysynthetic languages. For instance, a polysynthetic language like Slavey (Athabaskan), which had been traditionally described using the techniques underlying templatic morphology (Kari 1989), has been recently reanalyzed by Rice (2000) using a set of universal principles of semantic/syntactic scope. The lesson to be drawn here is that no single ordering principle can account on its own for all combinations of morphemes in a given language. In my dissertation on the grammatical morphology of Northern East Cree (NEC) (Collette 2014), I show that the ordering of grammatical suffixes is in large part unmotivated and unpredictable. In other words, the relation between the different positions is not meaning-governed but rather strictly form-governed (Manova and Aronoff 2010:113), and the relative ordering has to be morphologically stipulated. However, in other parts of the template the ordering is motivated by linguistic factors (semantic) and extralinguistic factors such as iconicity (Haiman 1980, 1983). In the last section, I introduce the concept of iconicity, as used in linguistics, in order to explain why two morphemes of the same position can appear together in the same word.

In what follows, I describe three identificational criteria of templatic morphology found in the verbal morphology of NEC: multiple exponence, optionality, and suffix permutation. Moreover, I provide a description of the internal structure of the independent person/number inflections in order to show that the relative order of these suffixes is motivated by iconicity.[1]

Northern East Cree

NEC is an Algonquian language belonging to the Cree-Innu-Naskapi-Atikamekw continuum (often called the Cree-Montagnais-Naskapi continuum), a chain of dialects expanding from the Rockies to the Atlantic Ocean in Canada. NEC is spoken in four communities along the east coast of James Bay and the southeast coast of Hudson Bay. The data presented here were collected during my fieldwork in the northernmost community of Whapmagoostui (formerly known as Great-Whale River), with a small set of speakers eight to sixty-nine years old. I present here elicited data (FN; 2011 fieldnotes) as well as sentences taken in vivo (marked with the code GWR 2011). The orthography is that of the Cree School Board except for double vowels such as *aa*, which I have replaced with *â*.

The NEC verb is inflected for person/number, obviation (or second third person), direction, aspect (which indicates also temporal reference), tense (neutral/preterit), mood, or the reality of a proposition as perceived by the speaker (Trask

TABLE 1. Northern East Cree Verbal Template

POSITIONS	GRAMMATICAL CATEGORIES
prefix	local persons (independent)/complementizer, negation
preform	aspect (temporal reference)
preverb	modality
preverb	modality
Verb Stem	
position 1	obviation (of the direct object)
position 2	direction
position 3	obviation
position 4	*HT* preterit/delayed imperative
position 5	number of local/nonlocal persons
position 6	mood (evidentiality)
position 7	*P* preterit
position 8	third singular
position 9	third plural/0pl/obviation
position 10	mood

1993). The last category can also express evidentiality (the source of knowledge of the speaker) in some contexts.[1] The verbal template, which is shown in Table 1, has ten suffixal positions, one set of prefixes for speech-act participants and three preverbal positions.

The simplest NEC inflections are neutral for mood and tense. They consist of a prefix-suffix combination of position 5 (Speech Act Participant [SAP]), or a suffix of position 8 or 9 (non-SAP). More complex inflections may be made of seven suffixes (out of ten), a prefix, and some preforms or preverbs, if needed. In order to exemplify what has been said, let us look at the internal structure of a pair of independent verbs as in example (1) (subscripted numbers represent position class):[2]

(1) a. Ni-ki-mîy-â$_2$-nân$_5$-ich$_9$.
1-PROS-give.it.to.him/her.TA-DIR→3-13-PL
'We (13) will give it to them.' (FN 2011, woman, 64)

b. Ni-ki-mîy-iku$_2$-nân$_5$-ich$_9$.
1-PROS-give.it.to.him/her.TA-INV←3-13-PL
'They will give it to us (13).' (FN 2011, woman, 64)

One can see that in this pair of verbs, the affixes forming the inflections—that is, the whole word minus the stem *-mîy-*—exhibit simple exponence: one form is associated with one meaning. However, as we will see in the next section, NEC grammatical morphology also functions with cumulative exponence (one form for many meanings) and multiple exponence (many discontinuous forms for one meaning).

Multiple Exponence and Suffix Optionality

As mentioned earlier, multiple exponence (or discontinuous morphology) and optionality are two identificational criteria associated with templatic morphology. Multiple exponence means that one grammatical meaning is indicated throughout the word with two or more forms that appear scattered in the word. As Spencer (1991:208) puts it, in languages exhibiting templatic morphology:

> we find that the verb consists of a stem together with a set of obligatory affixes and a variety of optional ones. What is striking about such languages is that it is difficult or impossible to analyze the formation of such complex words as the addition of affixes one by one to a stem. Rather, we seem to find that each affix has its position in the string and optional affixes are slotted into the string, at the appropriate point in the sequence, as required.

A straightforward example of multiple exponence can be observed in the simple exclusive inflection of the AI and TI verb (which share a paradigm). For example, in the verb *ni-mîchisu-nân* 'we (exclusive 13) are eating', the grammatical meaning 'first person' is expressed discontinuously by the SAP prefix *ni-* and the plural suffix *-nân*$_5$. The latter also refers to a third person and can be used by itself in the TA imperative order *asim-i*$_2$*-nân*$_5$ 'Feed us (exclusive)!'.

Let us turn now to another set of examples, taken this time from the obviative morphology of the independent order. One can see from examples (2b) and (2d) that the obviative suffixes of positions 1 *-im*$_1$*-* 'obviative NA object', 3 *-yi*$_3$*-* 'obviative', and 9 *-h*$_9$*-* 'obviative' appear discontinuously in the string, forming some sort of transfixation within the simple inflection *ni-. . . -â*$_2$*-w*$_5$:

(2) a. Ni-chî-mîy-â$_2$-w$_5$ ni-kâwî-Ø.
1-perf-give.it.to.him/her.TA-DIR-3 1-mother.NAD-3
'I gave it to my mother.' (FN 2011, woman, 64)

b. Ni-chî-mîy-**im**$_1$-â$_2$-**yi**$_3$-u$_5$-**h**$_9$ u-kâwî-h.
1-perf-give.it.to.him/her.TA-OBV-DIR-3′-3-3′ 3-mother.nad-3'
'I gave it to his (3) mother (3′).' (FN 2011, woman, 64)

c. Chi-chî-mîy-â$_2$-w$_5$ ni-kâwî-Ø.
2-perf-give.it.to.him/her.TA-DIR-3 1-mother.NAD-3
'You gave it to my mother.' (FN 2011, woman, 64)

d. Chi-chî-mîy-**im**$_1$-â$_2$-**yi**$_3$-u$_5$-**h**$_9$ u-kâwî-h.
2-perf-give.it.to.him/her.ta- OBV-DIR-3′-3-3′ 3-mother.NAD-3′
'You gave it to his (3) mother (3′).' (FN 2011, woman, 64)

This co-occurrence of *-im*$_1$- and *-yi*$_3$- with singular SAP inflections is an innovation proper to East Cree that is probably based on a perceived lack of distinct grammatical function in synchrony. However, when a stem ends in a nasal consonant like /m/, the suffix *-im*$_1$- 'obviative NA object' is often deleted by two phonological rules: deletion of a short vowel between two homorganic consonants, and degemination. This is common in the speech of some younger speakers and especially in rapid delivery. Surprisingly, in the exclusive inflection (us but not you) of the same paradigm, *-yi*$_3$- is prohibited, as can be seen from the following examples.

e. Ni-chî-mîy-**im**$_1$-â$_2$-nân$_5$-**h**$_9$ u-kâwî-h.
1-PERF-give.it.to.him/her.TA-OBV-DIR-3′ 3-mother.NAD-3′
'We (13) gave it to his (3) mother (3′).' (FN 2011, woman, 64)

f. *Ni-chî-mîy-im$_1$-â$_2$-yi$_3$-nân$_5$-h$_9$ u-kâwî-h.
1-PERF-give.it.to.him/her.TA-OBV-DIR-3′-13-3′ 3-mother.NAD-3′
'We (13) gave it to his (3) mother (3′).' (FN 2011, woman, 64)

The inclusive 21 and 2PL inflections (2g–h) show the same suffix patterning as that of (2e).

g. Chi-chî-mîy-**im**$_1$-â$_2$-niu$_5$-**h**$_9$ u-kâwî-h.
2-PERF-give.it.to.him/her.TA-OBV-DIR-21-3′ 3-mother.NAD-3′
'We (21) gave it to his (3) mother (3′).' (FN 2011, woman, 64)

h. Chi-chî-mîy-**im**$_1$-â$_2$-wâu$_5$-**h**$_9$ u-kâwî-h.
2-PERF-give.it.to.him/her.TA-OBV-DIR-PL-3′ 3-mother.NAD-3′
'You (2PL) gave it to his (3) mother (3′).' (FN 2011, woman, 64)

However, while the absence of *-im*$_1$- is fully accountable with phonological rules, some speakers do not use it even in contexts where it would be expected to appear (for example, after a vowel or a semivowel), as shown in example (3). Thus, this means that the use of *-im*$_1$- 'obviative NA object' is optional (for some speakers) and is not essential for the semantics of the inflection, since the obviative animate object is also marked by *-yi*$_3$- and *-h*$_9$-.

(3) Ni-chî-wiyâshtutiw-â$_2$-**yi**$_3$-u$_5$-**h**$_9$ u-nâukâtâ-m-h.
1-perf-repair.it.TA-DIR-3′-3-3′ 3-four.wheeler.NAP-POS-3′
'I repaired his (3) four-wheeler (3′).' (FN 2011, man, 22)

The optionality of *-im*$_1$- (3), as well as the particular arrangement of suffixes as in (2e)—which indicates that the presence of *-yi-*$_3$ 'third obviative' is prohibited for one part of the paradigm, but strictly required in another part of the same paradigm—is strong evidence of the templatic nature of verbal morphology since the features ± *-im-*$_1$ and ±*-yi-*$_3$ that characterize this particular paradigm are unpredictable. They have to be learned as such by the language learner.

Suffix Permutation and Variable Suffix Order

One of the main features of templatic morphology is that the ordering of affixes is rigid and not motivated by linguistic factors such as semantic scope, syntax, or phonology. However, strict rigidity is only a tendency since in some languages we find that two affixes may freely change their position in the same word but with no change in meaning. This phenomenon is known as morphological metathesis or affix permutation. For instance, in Mapudungu (Araucanian family) the diminutive *-ka-* and the habituative *-ke-* suffixes can permutate freely with no semantic difference.

TABLE 2. II Verbs of the Conjunct Order (indicative and dubitative)

	INDICATIVE (SIMPLE FORM)	DUBITATIVE NEUTRAL
0	â- . . . -ch_8	. . . -$kwâ_6$
0PL	â- . . . -ch_8-h_9	. . . -$wâ_5$-$kwâ_6$
0′	â- . . . -yi_3-ch_8	. . . -yi_3-$kwâ_6$
0′PL	â- . . . -yi_3-ch_8-h_9	. . . -**yi_3-$wâ_5$**-$kwâ_6$

TABLE 3. II Verbs of the Independent Order (indicative and dubitative)

	INDICATIVE (SIMPLE FORM)	DUBITATIVE NEUTRAL
0	. . . -w_5	. . . -u_5-$kupin_6$
0PL	. . . -u_5-h_9	. . . -$wâ_5$-$kupin_6$-h_9
0′	. . . -yi_3-w_5	. . . -yi_3-$kupin_6$
0′PL	. . . -yi_3-u_5-h_9	. . . -**$wâ_5$-yi_3**-$kupin_6$-h_9

(4) kɨðaw-**ke**-**ka**-n~ kɨðaw-**ka**-**ke**-n
work-HAB-DIM-1SG work-DIM-HAB-1SG
'Usually I work a little bit.' (Grimes 1983:5)

Suffix permutation without scopal relationship as illustrated by the Mapudungu example does not seem to occur in the same word in NEC. However, the same suffixes can change their respective position in minimal pairs in verbal paradigms other than the indicative neutral, also called the simple form. As one can see from the paradigms presented in Tables 2 and 3, suffix permutation happens in the II inflections expressing obviative inanimate plural of the dubitative preterit modality, used in the following examples to express uncertainty (5a) or inference (5b).

Examples:

(5) a. Châ-wînâ-**yi_3**-**$wâ_5$**-$kwâ_6$ u-wâu-h.
CJ.PROS-be.rotten.II-OBV-0PL-DUB 3-egg.NI-0(′)PL
'We will see if her eggs are rotten (or not).' (unpredictability)
(FN 2011, man, 22)

b. Chî-wâpâhutâ-**wâ**$_5$-**yi**$_3$-kupin$_6$-h$_9$ u-chîmân-iwâu-h.
PERF-be.carried.away.II-0PL-OBV-DUB.PRET-0(′)PL 3-boat.NI-PL-0(′)PL
'It appears that their boats (0′PL) got carried away.'
(inference from seashore debris) (FN 2011, man, 68)

Akin to suffix permutation is the phenomenon known as variability in affix ordering (see Nordlinger 2010:335 for examples in Murrinh-Patha). It concerns cases where two affixes expressing meanings belonging to the same grammatical category occur in alternative ordering in the presence of other affixes. An example of this phenomenon can be found in the inflections of the AI/TI dubitative preterit of the conjunct order, as can be observed from Table 4.

Examples:

(6) a. Âkut kâ-yî-y-**ân**$_5$.
that.is.it CJ.REL-say.IA-/y/-1SG
'That is what I said.' (GWR 2011, woman, 64)

b. Châ-ayihti-**w**$_4$-**ân**$_5$-**â**$_6$.
CJ.PROS-do.IA-DUB*-1SG-*DUB
'We'll see what I'll do!' (GWR 2011, man, 68)

c. Âkut kâ-pimuhtâ-**w**$_4$-**âp**$_7$-**ân**$_5$-**â**$_6$.
right.there CJ.REL-walk.IA-DUB*-PRET-1SG-*DUB
'That is where I must have walked.'
(speaker seeing his own tracks in the sand, inference) (FN 2011, man, 64)

TABLE 4. IA/TI Verbs of the Conjunct Order (indicative, dubitative neutral, and preterit)

	INDICATIVE	DUBITATIVE NEUTRAL	DUBITATIVE PRETERIT (SIMPLE FORM)
1SG	â- . . . -ân$_5$	. . . -w$_4$-ân$_5$-â$_6$	kâ- . . . -w$_4$-**âp**$_7$-**ân**$_5$-â$_6$
2SG	â- . . . -in$_5$	. . . -w$_4$-in$_5$-â$_6$	kâ- . . . -w$_4$-**ip**$_7$-**in**$_5$-â$_6$
13	â- . . . -âhch$_5$	. . . -w$_4$-âhch$_5$-â$_6$	kâ- . . . -w$_4$-âhch$_5$-ipin$_7$-â$_6$
21	â- . . . -ihk$^w{}_5$	. . . -w$_4$-ihkw$_5$-â$_6$	kâ- . . . -w$_4$-ihku$_5$-pin$_7$-â$_6$
2PL	â- . . . -âk$^w{}_5$	. . . -w$_4$-âkw$_5$-â$_6$	kâ- . . . -w$_4$-âku$_5$-pin$_7$-â$_6$

Note: While my data do not account for age, dialectal, or idiolectal differences, it should be said that these inflections have very low textual frequency and were not known by younger speakers (twenty-five-years old and younger). This could play an important role in explaining both suffix permutation and the variable suffix order exposed here.

TABLE 5. TA Verbs of the Conjunct Order (indicative and dubitative preterit)

	INDICATIVE (SIMPLE FORM)	DUBITATIVE PRETERIT
2SG←1SG	â- . . . -it$_2$-ân$_5$	kâ- . . . -iti$_2$-w$_4$-**âp$_7$-ân$_5$**-â$_6$
2SG←13	â- . . . -it$_2$-âhch$_5$	kâ- . . . -iti$_2$-w$_4$-âhch$_5$-ipin$_7$-â$_6$
2SG→1SG	â- . . . -i$_2$-/y/-in$_5$	kâ- . . . -Ø$_2$-u$_4$-**ip$_7$-in$_5$**-â$_6$
2SG→13	â- . . . -i$_2$-/y/-âhch$_5$	kâ- . . . -Ø$_2$-w$_4$-âhch$_5$-ipin$_7$-â$_6$

The dubitative (neutral and preterit) inflections are quite complicated, and their internal structure has to be briefly explained. First and foremost, it should be noted that the dubitative modality is indicated in some verbal paradigms (in TA inverse, for instance) by a full suffix *-uwâ*$_6$- while in other paradigms the circumfixal allomorph *-w*$_4$- . . . *-â*$_6$- is used.

In Algonquian languages, the preterit is expressed by one or more modern reflexes of the following suffixes of Proto-Algonquian **-htay-*, **-h*, or **-epan*. Moose Factory Cree has retained the HT preterit for non-third, and P preterit for third person, while Sheshashiu Innu retains all three forms (MacKenzie and Clarke 1981). In Chisasibi HT, H, and P preterit forms are used, while in Whapmagoostui the H forms are absent. Since these suffixes form a grammatical paradigm, they seem to belong to the same position, that is, to position 4. However, this is a purely theoretical requirement stemming from the structuralist foundation of the templatic technique, namely the assumption that a grammatical opposition can only be obtained with morphemes belonging to the same position classes. However, the language facts are not so homogeneous, and there are good reasons to reject this assumption. First, we have seen that templatic morphology is characterized by the lack of functional unity (criterion G: the affixes expressing the terms of a grammatical opposition can belong to different positions). For instance, the singular inflections for the simple AI/TI conjunct inflections (*-ân*$_5$ '1 singular', *-in*$_5$ '2 singular', and *-t*$_8$ ~ *-k*$_8$ '3 singular') do not belong to the same position but yet form a coherent grammatical paradigm. Second, a brief glance at Cree-Innu-Naskapi-Atikamekw dialectology (see MacKenzie and Clarke 1981, for instance) reveals that the P preterit is systematically slotted after position 5 suffixes (indicating person/number and direction in some paradigms). Given these facts, it is clear that the short P preterit allomorphs (*-âp-* ~ *-ip-*) are not in their original position in the conjunct dubitative preterit paradigm listed in Table 4. Moreover, the P preterit allomorph *-(i)pin*, which retains the morphology of its Proto-Algonquian reflex **-epan*, is used only in the plural inflections, and all plural inflections are or may be used to talk about a group of persons including one or more third persons, while the short *P* preterit forms are used exclusively with speech-act-participants. This is concomitant with the fact that SAP and non-SAP are very different functionally and are placed in different positions in some of the Cree verbal paradigms. However, in other inflections the singular suffixes appear, irrespective of the ordinal person ranking, in the same position. Thus, since East Cree does not maintain the SAP versus non-SAP distinction everywhere, it seems plausible to say that the number distinction is more important functionally than the SAP versus non-SAP distinction. This would explain the appearance of *-w-* 'third singular' in position 5.

The variable suffix ordering involving short *P* preterit allomorphs and cumulative person/number suffixes of position 5 can also be observed in the TA conjunct dubitative preterit paradigm of the SAP persons, as can be seen in Table 5.

Examples:

(7) a. Val d'Or, âkut kâ-wâpim-**it**$_2$-**ân**$_5$.
Val d'Or right.there CJ.REL-see.him/her.TA-2←1-1SG
'Val d'Or, that is where I saw you.' (FN 2011, woman, 80)

b. Val d'Or, âkut kâ-wâpim-**iti**$_2$-**w**$_4$-**âp**$_7$-**ân**$_5$-**â**$_6$.
Val d'Or right.there CJ.REL-see.him/her.TA-2←1-DUB*-PRET-1SG-*DUB
'Val d'Or, that is where I must have seen you.' (FN 2011, woman, 80)

The conjunct dubitative preterit inflections are probably the most complex components of grammatical morphology one can encounter in NEC. Hopefully, my analysis of the internal structure of the aforementioned inflections has shed light on the relative prominence of syntagmatic axis in the internal structure of verbal paradigms in NEC. As we have seen, the ordering of suffixes for some complex inflections is unpredictable and cannot be deduced from canonical suffix ordering observed in the rest of the paradigms. Purely syntagmatic phenomena like these indicate the prominence, for some cells of the concerned paradigms, of syntagmatic axis over the paradigmatic axis (see Van Marle 2000 for a discussion of purely syntagmatic phenomena in Turkish morphology).

Iconicity in Person/Number Marking

We have seen in the introduction of this paper that one of the founding blocks of templatic morphology relates to the assumption that in that type of morphology, the relation between positions is purely formal and not semantically driven. Since my hypothesis is that nothing prevents the relative ordering of affixes in a given language to be both motivated and unmotivated, one should not be surprised to discover, after careful examination, that in some particular zone of the template the ordering of suffixes is motivated iconically. The concept of iconicity has its origin in the philosophy of Charles S. Peirce (1839–1914), but was imported into linguistics by Roman Jakobson (1965). While in the Peircian philosophy the icon indicates a factual similitude between a signifier (let us say the sign ✉) and a significate ('letter' or by metonymy 'post office'), in linguistics, iconicity is linked to the fact that the structure of language reflects something of the world we live in as speakers. Concerning the order of meaningful elements, Greenberg (1966:103) stated that "the order of elements in language parallels that in physical experience or the order of knowledge." In what follows, I show that in NEC, the order of the suffixes expressing person and number is often motivated iconically, meaning that the syntagmatic ordering reflects how plurality is obtained physically.

In order to introduce the problem, let us take a look at the marking of plurality for the simple AI/TI inflections in the conjunct order. In the following paradigm, one can see that the suffixes are cumulative in nature (since they express both person and number) and stand in a complete relation of paradigmatic substitution because they are all mutually exclusive.

However, the internal structure of the corresponding inflections for the independent order is much more complex, as can be seen from Table 6. (Note here that the singular SAP suffix -n_5 requires a long epenthetic vowel /a:/ when another suffix is attached.)

We can see from Table 6 that the singular SAP is expressed via a prefix-suffix combination (also called parasynthetic combination).[3] Most important, the plural SAPs are expressed with a prefix-suffix combination and the addition of another suffix of position 5. The ordering pattern for 3 plural is also consistent with the other plural inflections.

The occurrence of two affixes belonging to the same position has seldom been reported in the literature (see Trask 1993:276) and is truly problematic for the structuralist foundation underlying the methodology of templatic morphology

TABLE 6. IA/TI Verbs of the Independent Order (indicative)

	SINGULAR		PLURAL
1SG	ni- . . . -n_5	13	ni- . . . -$nân_5$
2SG	chi- . . . -n_5	21	chi- . . . -($nâ_5$)-niw_5
3SG	t . . . -w_5	2PL	chi- . . . -$nâ_5$-
		3PL	$wâw_5$ . . . -w_5-ich_9

Note: The suffix -nân-$_5$ is obtained by haplology of /na:+na:n/, and thus has the same structure as the other plural inflections (see Goddard 1983:361).

TABLE 7. IA/TI Verbs of the Conjunct Order (indicative)

	SINGULAR		PLURAL
1SG	â- . . . -$ân_5$	13	â- . . . -$âhch_5$
2SG	â- . . . -in_5	21	â- . . . -$ihk^w{}_5$
3SG	â- . . . -t_8 ~ -k_8	2PL	â- . . . -$âk^w{}_5$
		3PL	â- . . . -ch_9

because it runs against the assumption of mutual exclusivity traditionally associated with grammatical systems. More precisely, data like these challenge the view that binarity, such as A versus B (which holds for the conjunct inflections in Table 7), is the unique mechanism underlying the internal structure of grammatical systems, or even of human cognition in general. But let us be clear here: there is a semantic opposition between inflection *chi-. . . -n* '2 singular' (A) and inflection *chi-. . . -nâwâw* '2 plural' (B), for instance; it is just that the internal structure of inflection B rests on a syntagmatic combination or contrast of suffixes of the type *a* versus *ab* and not on a pure paradigmatic substitution of the type *a* versus *b*. Drawing from Greenberg (1966:103) and Haiman (1980, 1983), my point is that the ordering of the suffixes entering in the plural inflections of the independent order reflects, or mimics, the logic existing between the meanings expressed by these same suffixes. For instance, if, in the world we live in, no plurality is conceivable without some prior accumulation of singular entities, I suggest that this is reflected in the internal structure of some independent inflections because what can be observed is that the plural suffixes are added AFTER the singular suffixes -$nâ_5$ or -w_5. Since the ordering for number marking starts invariably with the singular then adds the plural marker for the inflections of the independent order, my claim is that, at least for this part of the morphology, the ordering is iconically motivated because it reflects how a given plurality is obtained in the extralinguistic world—that is, by aggregation of singularities.

Conclusion

The main objective of this paper was to study some identificational criteria related to templatic morphology in light of the grammatical morphology of NEC. I have documented the factuality of at least three of these criteria for the language under study, that is, multiple exponence, optionality, and suffix permutation, including variable affix order (see Collette 2014 for a thorough discussion of the other criteria). These phenomena are symptomatic of a purely formal relation between positions since they involve unpredictability and idiosyncrasy. They also bring light to the fact that verbal paradigms and the ordering of affixes are a product of the human mind and of history, and are thus subject to many accidents and irregularities. The second objective was to explore other ways to account for the observed suffix ordering. My analysis of the simple plural inflections has shown that grammatical meaning can be analyzed in terms of paradigmatic oppositions (A versus B) or syntagmatic contrasts (A versus AB), the latter being closely associated with iconicity. It would be interesting to try to extend this inquiry on a comparative level and to gather more data on dialectal differences regarding grammatical suffix ordering in the Cree-Innu-Naskapi-Atikamekw dialectal continuum.

NOTES

1. It is important to note that the term "dubitative," even though it is widespread in Algonquian linguistics, does not cover all the semantic functions of these suffixes. As shown here, it can indicate the source of information of the speaker (and relates thus to evidentiality), although in other contexts it expresses the speaker's truth commitment regarding what she or he is saying (dubitative modality). Since the separation (or not) of evidentiality and modality is a complex and hotly debated matter in the linguistic literature, I will keep the term "dubitative" in this article.
2. The abbreviations are: 13 = exclusive plural, me and him but not you; 21 = inclusive plural, me and you and possibly him; 2PL = second-person plural; 0 = inanimate subject; 3 = animate subject; AI = animate intransitive verb; CJ = conjunct order; CJ.REL = relative

conjunct clause; CPL = complementizer; DIM = diminutive; DIR = direct; DUB = dubitative; GWR = Great-Whale River; HAB = habituative; II = inanimate intransitive verb; INV = inverse; NA = animate noun; NAD = dependent animate noun; NAP = animate noun participle; NI = inanimate noun; PERF = perfective aspect; PL = plural; POS = possessive suffix; PROS = prospective aspect; TA = transitive animate verb; TI = transitive inanimate verb.

3. A parasynthetic combination (Malkiel 1978:146) is a case where two functionally independent and nonadjacent affixes (usually a prefix and a suffix) appear obligatorily together in the same inflection or word.

REFERENCES

Bakker, Peter. 2006. Algonquian verb structure. In *What's in a Verb: Studies in the Verbal Morphology of the Languages of the Americas*, edited by Grazyna J. Rowicka and Eithne B. Carlin, 1–26. Utrecht: LOT Publications.

Bloomfield, Leonard. 1958. *Eastern Ojibwa, Grammatical Sketch, Texts and Word List.* Ann Arbor: University of Michigan Press.

———. 1962. *The Menomini Language.* Edited by Charles F. Hockett. New Haven, CT: Yale University Press.

Collette, Vincent. 2014. Description de la morphologie grammaticale du cri de l'Est (dialecte du Nord, Whapmagoostui). PhD thesis, Université Laval.

Goddard, Ives. 1983. The eastern Algonquian subordinate mode and the importance of morphology. *International Journal of American Linguistics* 49:351–387.

Greenberg, Joseph. 1966. Some universals of grammar with particular reference to the order of meaningful elements. In *Universals of Language*, edited by Joseph Greenberg, 73–113. Cambridge, MA: MIT Press.

Grimes, Joseph. 1983. *Affix Positions and Co-occurrence: The PARADIGM Program.* Dallas: Summer Institute of Linguistics.

Haiman, John. 1980. The iconicity of grammar: Isomorphism and motivation. *Language* 56:515–540.

———. 1983. Iconic and economic motivation. *Language* 59:781–819.

Jakobson, Roman. 1965. Quest for the essence of language. *Diogenes* 13:21–37.

Kari, James. 1989. Affix positions and zones in the Athabaskan verb complex: Ahtna and Navajo. *International Journal of American Linguistics* 55:424–455.

MacKenzie, Marguerite, and Sandra Clarke. 1981. Dialect relations in Cree/Montagnais/Naskapi: Verb paradigms. *Montreal Working Papers in Linguistics, Linguistique*

Amérindienne II Études Algonquiennes 16:135–191.

Malkiel, Yakov. 1978. Derivational categories. In *Universals of Human Language*. Vol. 3, *Word Structure*, edited by Joseph Greenberg, 125–149. Stanford, CA: Stanford University Press.

Manova, Stela, and Mark Aronoff. 2010. Modeling affix order. *Morphology* 20:109–131.

Mel'čuk, Igor. 1997. *Cours de morphologie générale*, Vol. 4. Montreal: Presses de l'Université de Montréal, CNRS.

Nida, Eugene. 1949. *Morphology: The Descriptive Analysis of Words*. Ann Arbor: University of Michigan Press.

Nordlinger, Rachel. 2010. Verbal morphology in Murrinh-Patha: Evidence for templates. *Morphology* 20:321–341.

Rice, Karen. 2000. *Morpheme Order and Semantic Scope*. Cambridge: Cambridge University Press.

Sherwood, David F. 1986. *Maliseet-Passamaquoddy Verb Morphology*. *Mercury Series: Paper (Canadian Ethnology Service)* 105. Ottawa: National Museums of Canada, Canadian Ethnology Service.

Simpson, Jane, and Marta Withgott. 1986. Pronominal clitic clusters and templates. In *The Syntax of Pronominal Clitics: Syntax and Semantics* 19, edited by Hagit Borer, 149–174. New York: Academic Press.

Spencer, Andrew. 1991. *Morphological Theory: An Introduction to Word Structure in Generative Theory*. Cambridge: Blackwell.

Stump, Gregory. 2006. Template morphology. In *Encyclopedia of Language and Linguistics*, edited by K. Brown, 559–562. Oxford: Elsevier.

Trask, Robert Lawrence. 1993. *A Dictionary of Grammatical Terms in Linguistics*. London: Routlegde.

Van Marle, Jaap. 2000. Paradigmatic and syntagmatic relations. In *Morphologie/Morphology: An International Handbook of Inflection and Word-Formation*, edited by Geert E. Booij, Christian Lehmann, Joachim Mugdan, and Stavros Skopeteas, 225–233. Berlin: Walter de Gruyter.

Wolfart, H. C. 1973. *Plains Cree: A Grammatical Study*. Transactions of the American Philosophical Society, n.s., Vol. 63, part 5, Philadelphia.

Seeking Consensus on the Fundamentals of Algonquian Word Order

Amy Dahlstrom

Leonard Bloomfield, speaking of Eastern Ojibwa, declared, "Word order is decidedly flexible."[1] Surely everyone who has investigated Algonquian syntax would agree with that statement! Likewise, most Algonquianists would agree that at a macro-level—that is, considering the relative ordering of a verb and its arguments—similar patterns seem to obtain across the family.[2] Consider, for example, clauses from Ojibwa, Miami-Illinois, Menominee, and Meskwaki, all illustrating the tendency for an indefinite pronoun 'someone' (in boldface) to precede the verb:[3]

(1) **waaya** ngii-waabmaa
someone I-saw-him
'I saw someone.' (Ojibwa; Tomlin and Rhodes 1979:309, (5bi))

(2) Ancaamaci **aweeya** pyaaci . . .
desiderative, hopefully someone he.comes
'I wish someone would come.' (Miami-Illinois; Costa 2012:36)

(3) Eneq-peh taeh **weyak** ke:s-pes-pi:htikaet
'And then someone came in.' (Menominee; Shields 2004:385, (8))

(4) me·kwe·h=ča·h=meko **owiye·ha** nekahkita·kona·na
I.believe=SO=EMPH someone hide.O2.from.3>1P/IND
'So probably someone hid it from us.' (Meskwaki; Kiyana 1913:102)

Less agreement, however, can be found in the various accounts proposed for the observed word order patterns. The examples in (1)–(4) could be categorized simply as instances of OV (Object-Verb) or SV (Subject-Verb) order, using notation familiar from Greenberg 1963 and later works on word order typology, or pragmatic or information structure notions may be appealed to. For example, Tomlin and Rhodes (1979) analyze (1) as exhibiting RHEME before THEME order; Costa (2012) counts (2) as an instance of the tendency for INDEFINITES to precede the verb; Shields (2004) classifies (3) as SV and additionally notes that NEW INFORMATION precedes the verb; Dahlstrom (1993 and later articles) analyzes indefinite pronouns in similar Meskwaki examples as a variety of FOCUS, which precedes the verb.[4]

In other words, even though a great deal of work has been done on Algonquian word order in the thirty-five years since Tomlin and Rhodes 1979, there is little agreement in the explanations proposed. With this paper I hope that we can begin to reach a consensus regarding the mix of syntactic and discourse-pragmatic factors influencing the observed word order patterns, in order to discover the areas of agreement across the languages of the family and where individual languages diverge. Though the discussion here is necessarily incomplete given limitations of space, four specific points are emphasized: first, a Greenbergian-style classification of an Algonquian language must resolve issues such as the syntactic status of inverse verbs; second, information structure notions such as topic and focus should be recognized as playing a significant role; third, Algonquian word order investigations should include not only subjects and (first) objects but also the syntactic relations of secondary object and oblique; and fourth, word order investigations must attend to hierarchical structure as well as linear order.

Greenbergian Approaches

Work on Algonquian word order often begins by trying to discover which of Greenberg's (1963) six basic word order types fits the language best, or by using the Greenbergian types as an initial sorting of the data (e.g., Shields 2004, Sullivan 2016).[5] Algonquianists typically find attestations of nearly all possible permutations.

For example, Thomason (2004), working with a large corpus from 153 Meskwaki texts, found 1,279 clauses containing a verb and two NPs, where the NPs represented subject, object, or second object. Twenty distinct word order patterns were displayed within this set.[6]

Some methodological questions arise in trying to apply the classic Greenbergian approach to Algonquian data. For example, the labels S and O presuppose the existence of subject and object constituents. Some Algonquianists, however, analyze the NPs (or DPs) in construction with the verb as being adjuncts coreferential to the real subject and object, which are instantiated by the inflectional morphology on the verb (following Jelinek 1984, inter alia). Junker's (2004) work on East Cree is in this tradition. Wolvengrey (2011) goes further, questioning whether a notion of syntactic grammatical relations is needed at all for Plains Cree: that is, whether semantic and pragmatic notions on their own can provide complete explanations for the observed word order variation, without reference to syntax. In other words, Junker and Wolvengrey are indeed investigating the relative order of constituents, but they are not using the vocabulary of grammatical relations to describe or explain the observed patterns.

For those scholars who do analyze NPs in construction with the verb as subjects and objects, it is necessary to establish the syntactic status of inverse verbs, the morphologically marked form of verbs inflected for a third-person agent and a non-third-person patient, or for a third-person obviative agent and a third-person proximate patient. There seems to be genuine variation across the family in the syntax of inverse verbs. For example, Dahlstrom (1991) argues for Plains Cree that inverse verbs have the same syntax as direct verbs, with the more agentlike argument as subject and the more patientlike argument as object, but Rhodes (1994), using some of the same tests for grammatical relations as Dahlstrom uses for Plains Cree, argues that Ojibwa inverse verbs involve a reversal of grammatical relations. The syntactic analysis of inverse verbs in a given language naturally has consequences for coding the word order pattern of a specific token. Consider the following Cree and Ojibwa clauses (the inverse suffix is in boldface):

(5)	ki·htahtawe·	ki·mo·c	ki·h–kakwe·cimi**k**	iskwe·wa	kistim . . .
	presently	secretly	PERF–ask.3′>3/IND	woman.OBV	your.d-in-law

'Then some women (obv) secretly asked your daughter-in-law (prox).'
(Plains Cree; Dahlstrom 1991:63)

(6) wgii-zaaghigoon nmishoomsan nookmis
o-gii-zaagih-**igo**-an ni-mishoomis-an n-ookomis
3ERG-PAST-love-INV-OBV 1-grandfather-OBV 1-grandmother
'My grandfather (obv) loved my grandmother (prox).' (Ojibwa; Rhodes 1994:435)

Dahlstrom would count the Cree sentence in (5) as VSO, with the obviative agent as S and the proximate addressee as O; Rhodes would count the Ojibwa sentence in (6) as an example of VOS, with the obviative experiencer as O and the proximate theme as S. Given this variation, it is incumbent upon any Algonquianist asserting that there is an underlying order such as VOS (e.g., Tomlin and Rhodes 1979; Sullivan 2016, both on Ojibwa) to explicitly identify the syntactic status of inverse verbs in the language under investigation.[7]

Another construction frequently encountered in the family, though not unique to Algonquian, is discontinuous constituents: a demonstrative or quantifier appears to the left of the verb with the remainder of the NP to the right, as in (7), with the discontinuous object in boldface:

(7) še·ški **mani** ki·hawato·pena **či·ma·ni**
only this FUT.take.21>0/IND canoe
'We'll take just this canoe.' (Meskwaki; Dahlstrom 2015:13N.)

Such constructions are challenging for a strict application of a Greenbergian classification. Would (7) be coded as OV or VO, or as an ad hoc category of OVO? Analyses appealing to information structure (e.g., Dahlstrom 1995; Junker 2004; Wolvengrey 2011) argue that the left-hand portion of such split NPs may occupy a focus position to the left of the verb, as in (7), where the demonstrative appears with *še·ški* 'only', or a topic position at the left edge of the clause. Without recognizing the discourse functions associated with specific positions at or near the beginning of the clause, it is difficult to accommodate Algonquian data using the classic Greenbergian approach.

Information Structure

Let us now leave the complications of the classic Greenbergian approach and look at some recent work appealing to information structure. A number of researchers have found that the preverbal instances of subject and object NPs (or DPs) can be explained as overt topics or focused elements. Some examples of this approach are Dahlstrom (1993) and later papers on Meskwaki, Junker (2004) on East Cree, Wolvengrey (2011) on Plains Cree, Costa (2012) on Miami-Illinois, Johnson et al. (2015) on Menominee, among others. A template for Meskwaki word order is given below (Dahlstrom 1993, 1995, 2003), which explicitly includes the information structure relations of topic and focus along with the semantic operator NEGATION and a syntactic relation, OBLIQUE.

(8) [$_{S'}$ TOPIC [$_{S}$ NEG FOCUS OBLIQUE V XP*]]
{SUBJ, OBJ, OBJ2, COMP}

As can be seen in (8), there is a position available for topics at the left edge of the clause. The topic position precedes a negative element, if present. Following the negative position there is a separate position available for focused constituents. Constituents bearing the syntactic relation of oblique (discussed further below) typically appear immediately before the verb. To the right of the verb is the unmarked position for subject, object, second object, and complement clauses that are neither topic nor focus. This word order preference is represented by the notation of XP* (any number of constituents, including zero); those constituent(s) may be associated with any of the set of grammatical functions listed in the curly brackets.[8]

The textual Meskwaki example shown in (9) illustrates the ordering of (8):

(9) i·noki=wi·na a·kwi ke·ko·hi kehke·netakini
today=CONTRAST not anything know.3>0/NEG
TOPIC NEG FOCUS V

[mana mehtose·neniwa]
this person
SUBJ
'But today the people don't know anything.' (Meskwaki; Michelson 1927:18.9–10)

The example in (9) has an overt topic *i·noki* 'today', followed by the negative word *a·kwi* 'not'; the indefinite pronoun *ke·ko·hi* 'anything' appears in focus position immediately after the negative, and the overt subject *mana mehtose·neniwa* 'this person' appears after the verb, since it is neither the topic nor the focus of the sentence.[9]

The utility of referring to information structure notions can be clearly seen by comparing two recent papers on Menominee. Shields (2004) is a very thorough report using a Greenbergian-style analysis, with numerous charts and figures considering the effects of a number of factors on the various permutations of S, V, and O. As thorough as it is, one is left at the end with a sense of bewildering chaos because there is no clear explanation of what governs the various patterns. Johnson et al. (2015), on the other hand, improve upon the Shields study in two ways: first, by greatly expanding the database of textual examples, and second, by showing that information structure notions of topic and focus explain the distribution of the NPs appearing to the left of the verb in Menominee.

Although there seems to be a growing consensus regarding the utility of topic and focus, here too there are meta-issues to be aware of. First of all, it is notoriously difficult to get linguists to agree on the definition of topic and focus. I follow work by Lambrecht (1994) and others that takes topic to be a pragmatic relation of aboutness; that means that topic cannot be reduced to simply being old or given information. Likewise, focus is not equivalent to new information; rather, it is information asserted against the backdrop of a presupposed proposition.

The relations of topic and focus are quite different in nature from the discourse statuses of ACTIVATION (givenness) and IDENTIFIABILITY (definiteness), as Lambrecht (1994) argues at length. Topic and focus reflect articulations of an utterance into components of information structure: an utterance may contain a topic, which is what the following comment is about. Similarly, one element of an utterance may function as focus, with the remainder of the utterance representing the presupposed open proposition. Givenness and definiteness, on the other hand, reflect the speaker's assessment of the addressee's mental state: whether a particular discourse entity is active in the addressee's consciousness (given versus new) or whether it is identifiable by the addressee (definiteness). Although topics may often be given and definite, neither feature is a necessary or sufficient criterion for establishing topichood, nor is there any requirement that a focused element be new or indefinite.

In my view, it is at this point an open question whether Algonquian word order analyses need to make reference to the notions of givenness or definiteness or both in addition to appealing to topic and focus. What is clear, however, is that using definiteness or given versus new information alone will not account for the full range of observed data. See, for example, Shields (2004:380) on Menominee, who found that 64 percent of new NPs occurred to the left of the verb and 36 percent after the verb. Likewise, Tomlin and Rhodes (1979) found that many indefinite NPs occur to the left of the verb, but that indefinite NPs may also occur after the verb in presentational constructions or if they are "thematically irrelevant" (Tomlin and Rhodes 1979:316).[10]

A further issue arising in Algonquian studies is the relationship between obviation and notions of topic and focus. In a context where a distinction is made between proximate and obviative third persons, is the proximate third person equivalent to topic? For Meskwaki, at least, the answer is no: obviative NPs can appear in topic position (cf. Dahlstrom 1993:14). A separate question is whether the word order patterns of a given language can be explained entirely in terms of proximate versus obviative, as Junker (2004) reports for East Cree.

Grammatical Relations Beyond Subject and (First) Object

The Greenbergian tradition of classifying word order data in terms of subject, verb, and object has the unfortunate consequence of neglecting other grammatical relations that may be significant for word order studies. For Algonquian languages, it is important to distinguish between first and second objects of ditransitive verbs such as 'give', where the recipient is first object and the thing given is second object. Furthermore, Rhodes (1991) and Dahlstrom (2009) argue for Ojibwa and Meskwaki, respectively, that the nonsubject argument of the AI+O class of verbs is a "second object," not an ordinary first object.[11] In the Meskwaki clause in (10), for example, the second object of the verb 'depend on' is an independent pronoun *ki·ya·wa·wi* 'you plural' (Dahlstrom 1988).

(10) ahpe·nemowaki ki·ya·wa·wi
depend.on.3P/IND you.PL
'They depend on you (pl).' (Meskwaki; Kiyana 1913:249)

AI+O verbs are relatively common in Algonquian languages, in part resulting from syntactic operations on ditransitive stems that suppress the first object (for example, reflexivization, reciprocalization, antipassivization) as discussed in Dahlstrom 2009.

In an important study on Southwestern Ojibwe, Sullivan (2016) elicited sentences by showing pictures to a speaker and asking for a description. He found a preference for VOS order, with some unexplained cases of VSO. However, an example he provides of VSO order appears to be in fact VSO2—second object instead of first object—pointing up the need for a more fine-grained classification of arguments:

(11)	Zhakamoonindizo	a'aw	chi-ogimaa	iniw	gwekiwebinigan-an.
	spoon.feed.self	DET	president	DET	pancake-OBV

'The president is feeding himself pancakes.' (Southwestern Ojibwa; Sullivan 2016, (17))

As mentioned above, deriving a reflexive form of a ditransitive such as 'feed' results in the AI+O pattern; *gwekiwebinigan-an* 'pancakes' would therefore be a second object in (11). It is worth investigating whether AI+O clauses exhibit idiosyncratic word order.

Another grammatical relation that plays a prominent role in Algonquian syntax is OBLIQUE, a term that I use to denote what is called in traditional Algonquianist terminology an antecedent of a relative root (e.g., Bloomfield 1958:130).[12] In the Meskwaki example in (12), the oblique argument expresses source and is associated with the relative root preverb *oči–* 'from', both in boldface.

(12)	**wa·wi·tawiškwa·te**	e·**hoči**–nowi·wa·či	neswi	neniwaki
	doors.on.both.ends	from–go.out.3P/AOR	three	men

'Three men went out from the doors on both ends.' (Meskwaki; Kiyana 1913:163)

In Meskwaki, obliques are subject to much less variation in word order than objects or subjects are: they are nearly always found immediately to the left of the verb. It is important, therefore, in classifying data on word order to distinguish obliques from other grammatical relations. This is not always the case in the literature: for example, Branigan and Mackenzie (2002b:116) analyze quotes as direct objects rather than as the oblique argument of the quoting verb.

Word Order and Subordinate Clauses

A further set of issues for classifying word order data arises when considering sentences in which a single third-person referent is a syntactic argument in more than one clause. In such contexts it is likely that there will be at most one NP expressing the third-person referent; the referent's role in the other clause(s) will be expressed only by the inflectional morphology on the verb, in this instance functioning pronominally. The question for a linguist collecting data on word order patterns is to which clause does the NP belong? It is important to keep in mind that constituents appearing to the right of the main verb of a sentence display a great deal of flexibility in their word order. As a consequence, a linear order of V-V-NP does not necessarily entail that the NP must belong to the lower clause. Rather, the NP may function as an argument of the higher verb, preceded by a complement clause, as in the Meskwaki example in (13):

(13)	nahi,	ano·hka·na·ta·we	[wi·hni·mihenakwe]	**kesese·hena·na**
	well	give.O.job.of.21<3/IMP	FUT.cause.to.dance.3<21/AOR	our.elder.brother
		V	COMP	OBJ

'Well, let's get our elder brother to give us a dance!' (Meskwaki; Kiyana 1913:983)

In (13) *kesese·hena·na* 'our elder brother' is the object of the main verb *ano·h-ka·n-* 'give [object] the job of', and is coreferential with the pronominal inflection for the third-person subject of the lower verb *ni·mih-* 'cause to dance'.

Sequences of V-NP-V, where the referent of the NP plays a syntactic role in both clauses, may also present challenges for word order classification. Dahlstrom (2006) discusses Meskwaki examples like the one in (14), arguing that the NP *o·sani* 'his father' belongs to the first clause and not to the second. Consequently, (14) is an example of VS order. (If *o·sani* 'his father' belonged to the second clause, we would instead have an example of OV order.)

(14)	pye·ya·niči	**o·sani,**
	come.3'/CH.CONJ	his.father.OBV
	e·ha·čimoha·či	e·na·hpawa·či.
	tell.3>3'/AOR	dream.thus.3/PART/OBLIQUE.HEAD

'When his father (obv) came, he told him (obv) what he had dreamed.' (Meskwaki; Dahlstrom 2006:135)

Note further that an NP in such a sequence should not be counted twice, once as an argument of the first clause and again as part of the second clause: syntactically, the lexical NP can belong only to a single clause. The verb of the other clause bears inflection that is anaphoric to the coreferential NP.

A final pan-Algonquian construction to consider is that known variously as copying to object, or raising to object, or long-distance agreement (Frantz 1978; Dahlstrom 1991; Rhodes 1994; Branigan and MacKenzie 2002a; Fry and Hamilton 2016; among others). In this construction, the matrix verb (often a verb of mental action) is inflected for an object agreeing with one of the arguments of the complement clause. For example, in the Meskwaki example in (15), the matrix verb *ke·hke·nem-* 'know' is inflected for an obviative third-person object, agreeing with *owiye·hani* 'someone-obv', which is the subject of the lower verb *nep-* 'die'.

(15)	ke·hke·nema·ta	**owiye·hani**	na·hina·hi	wi·hnepeniči
	know.3>3′/PART/3	someone.OBV	when	FUT.die.3′/AOR
	'the one who knew when someone would die.' (Meskwaki; Dahlstrom 2015:12E)			

For the purposes of collecting data on word order, it is important to determine the syntactic position of NPs like *owiye·hani* in (15). Does the copying to object construction entail a movement of the NP out of the lower clause, putting *owiye·hani* in the higher clause? If so, it is an example of VO order. Alternatively, the copying to object construction could be analyzed as simply involving a peculiar agreement rule in the morphology, with no change in the syntactic position of the 'copied' NP. In that case, we would count (15) as an instance of SV order in the lower clause.[13]

Conclusion

This discussion, necessarily incomplete, has argued for the necessity of recognizing both syntax and information structure in explaining Algonquian word order: in syntax, we need to establish the status of inverse verbs if Greenbergian classification is undertaken; the relations of second object and oblique must be given as much attention as subjects and first objects; and hierarchical clause structure must be recognized as well. For information structure, the relations of topic and focus play a key role and cannot be reduced to the discourse statuses of given/new or definiteness. I hope this review of issues can initiate fruitful conversations among Algonquianists investigating word order patterns.

NOTES

1. Bloomfield (1958:131), cited in Tomlin and Rhodes 1979. Thanks to the audience in Ottawa and the PAC reviewers for many useful suggestions. All remaining omissions and inadequacies are my own responsibility.
2. At a more local level, differences among the languages may be observed—for example, in the ordering of elements in copular constructions. Plains Cree seems to prefer ordering the predicate first (cf. Wolvengrey 2011:293), while Meskwaki equational sentences tend to have the predicate last (cf. Dahlstrom 1988:176).
3. Abbreviations in Meskwaki and Cree examples: 0 = inanimate, 1P = first-person exclusive plural; 21 = first-person inclusive plural; 3P = third-person plural; 3′ = obviative; AOR = aorist conjunct; CH.CONJ = changed conjunct; CONTRAST = contrastive; EMPH = emphatic; FUT = future; IMP = imperative; IND = independent indicative; NEG = negative; O = (first) object; O2 = second object; OBV = obviative; PART = conjunct participle; PERF = perfective. ">" separates subject and object in the gloss of transitive verbs. In other examples, the glosses (or lack thereof) have been reproduced from the source.
4. Not discussed here due to space limitations are several recent formal analyses of Algonquian word order, for example, Brittain (2001) on Cree-Innu-Naskapi, Bruening (2001) on Passamaquoddy, Bliss (2013) on Blackfoot, among others.
5. For critiques of the classic Greenbergian approach, see Dryer (1997), as well as Dryer (1995), which includes a discussion of Tomlin and Rhodes (1979) on Ojibwa. See also Mithun (1987), which questions the relevance of the notion of basic word order in languages that display a wide variety of surface orders. Indeed, Dryer (2013) marks all Algonquian representatives in the WALS online atlas as lacking a dominant basic order.
6. Thomason's (2004) survey of 1,279 Meskwaki clauses reveals interesting patterns, which Thomason describes in terms of higher- and lower-ranked NPs (animate > inanimate, proximate > obviative, nearer obviative > further obviative). Lower-ranked NPs tend to occur after the verb; higher-ranked NPs tend to occur at the edge of clauses, where they are "strongly focused" if clause-initial, or "strongly defocused" if clause-final. In the terms of Dahlstrom (1995), Thomason's "strongly focused" corresponds to overt topics and focus and "strongly defocused" to ANTI-TOPIC (cf. Lambrecht 1994).
7. A similar issue arises with transitive verb stems inflected for an INDEFINITE ACTOR (cf. Bloomfield 1957:vi). Dahlstrom (1991) and Rhodes (1994) argue for Plains Cree and Ojibwa, respectively, that the indefinite actor construction is an agentless passive. The nonagent argument in the Cree and Ojibwa constructions should therefore be counted as a subject. The passive analysis is, however, not necessarily correct for indefinite actor verbs elsewhere in the Algonquian family.

8. Tomlin and Rhodes's (1979) analysis of Ojibwa can also align with the template in (8) if we take their T-fronted elements to be overt topics, rheme to correspond to the focus position, and theme to correspond to the unmarked postverbal position(s).
9. Note that the contrastive enclitic *=wi·na* may occur with overt topics, as in (9), marking a shift from the topic of the previous utterances. In the translation of (9), the force of the contrastive enclitic is rendered by 'But . . . '. It is clear that *i·noki* 'today' is not playing the role of focus in (9). If it were focus, there would be a presupposition that 'the people don't know anything at x time' and the missing time element would be identified as 'today'. Note further that *mana mehtose·neniwa* 'this person' is grammatically singular but here used in a collective sense of 'the people'.
10. See Dahlstrom (2003) for Meskwaki word order in presentational constructions.
11. AI+O verbs are inflected as if they are intransitive but require two arguments.
12. Rhodes (2005, 2010) uses the term "oblique" differently: to denote adjuncts (temporal, locative, instrumental) that are NOT complements of a relative root.
13. The appearance of *owiye·hani* to the left of *na·hina·hi* 'when' in (15) may indicate that *owiye·hani* is either in the matrix clause or in topic position in the lower clause.

REFERENCES

Bliss, Heather. 2013. The Blackfoot configurationality conspiracy: Parallels and differences in clausal and nominal structures. PhD thesis, University of British Columbia.

Bloomfield, Leonard. 1957. *Eastern Ojibwa: Grammatical Sketch, Texts and Word List*. Edited by Charles F. Hockett. Ann Arbor: University of Michigan Press.

Branigan, Phil, and Marguerite MacKenzie. 2002a. Altruism, Ā-movement, and object agreement in Innu-aimûn. *Linguistic Inquiry* 33:385–407.

———. 2002b. Word order variation at the left periphery in Innu-aimûn. In *Papers of the Thirty-Third Algonquian Conference*, edited by H. C. Wolfart, 110–119. Winnipeg: University of Manitoba.

Brittain, Julie. 2001. *The Morphosyntax of the Algonquian Conjunct Verb: A Minimalist Approach*. New York: Garland.

Bruening, Benjamin. 2001. Syntax at the edge: Cross-clausal phenomena and the syntax of Passamaquoddy. PhD thesis, MIT.

Costa, David J. 2012. Word order in Miami-Illinois. Paper read at the Forty-Fourth Algonquian Conference, Chicago.

Dahlstrom, Amy. 1988. Independent pronouns in Fox. In *In Honor of Mary Haas*, edited by William Shipley, 165–194. Berlin: Mouton de Gruyter.

———. 1991. *Plains Cree Morphosyntax*. New York: Garland.

———. 1993. The syntax of discourse functions in Fox. In *Proceedings of BLS 19* (*Special session on syntactic issues in Native American languages*), edited by David A. Peterson, 11–21. Berkeley, CA: Berkeley Linguistics Society.

———. 1995. *Topic, Focus, and Other Word Order Problems in Algonquian.* The Belcourt Lecture. Winnipeg: Voices of Rupert's Land.

———. 2003. Focus constructions in Meskwaki (Fox). In *Proceedings of the LFG03 Conference*, edited by Miriam Butt and Tracy Holloway King, 144–163. Stanford, CA: CSLI Publications.

———. 2006. The syntax of Algonquian ethnopoetics. In *Actes du Trente-Septième Congrès des Algonquinistes*, sous la dir. de H. C. Wolfart, 131–147. Winnipeg: University of Manitoba.

———. 2009. OBJ_{θ} without OBJ: A typology of Meskwaki objects. In *Proceedings of the LFG09 Conference*, edited by Miriam Butt and Tracy Holloway King, 222–239. Stanford, CA: CSLI Publications.

———. 2015. Highlighting rhetorical structure through syntactic analysis: An illustrated Meskwaki text by Alfred Kiyana. In *New Voices for Old Words: Editing Algonquian Texts*, edited by David J. Costa, 118–197. Lincoln: University of Nebraska Press.

Dryer, Matthew S. 1995. Frequency and pragmatically unmarked word order. In *Word Order in Discourse*, edited by Pamela Downing and Michael Noonan, 105–135. Amsterdam: Benjamins.

———. 1997. On the six-way word order typology. *Studies in Language* 21:69–103.

———. 2013. Order of subject, object, and verb. In *The World Atlas of Language Structures Online*, edited by Matthew S. Dryer and Martin Haspelmath. Leipzig: Max Planck Institute for Evolutionary Anthropology. http://wals.info/chapter/81.

Frantz, Donald G. 1978. Copying from complements in Blackfoot. In *Linguistic Studies of Native Canada*, edited by Eung-Do Cook and Jonathan Kaye, 89–109. Vancouver: University of British Columbia Press.

Fry, Brandon J. and Michael David Hamilton. 2016. Long-distance agreement in Algonquian: Accounting for syntactic variation. In *Proceedings of CLS 50*, edited by Ross Burkholder et al. Chicago: Chicago Linguistic Society.

Greenberg, Joseph H. 1963. Some universals of grammar with particular reference to the order of meaningful elements. In *Universals of Language*, edited by Joseph H. Greenberg, 73–113. Cambridge, MA: MIT Press.

Jelinek, Eloise. 1984. Empty categories, case, and configurationality. *Natural Language & Linguistic Theory* 2:39–76.

Johnson, Meredith, Monica Macaulay, Bryan Rosen, and Rachel Wang. 2015. A survey of word order in Menominee. In *Papers of the Forty-Third Algonquian Conference*, edited by Monica Macaulay and J. Randolph Valentine, 154–178. Albany, NY: SUNY Press.

Junker, Marie-Odile. 2004. Focus, obviation and word order in East Cree. *Lingua* 114:345–365.

Kiyana, Alfred. 1913. *Wisakea osani okyeni osimeani okomeseani.* [Wisahkeha, his father, his mother, his younger brother, his grandmother.] Manuscript 2958-a in National Anthropological Archives, Smithsonian Institution, Washington, DC.

Lambrecht, Knud. 1994. *Information Structure and Sentence Form.* Cambridge: Cambridge University Press.

Michelson, Truman. 1927. *Contributions to Fox Ethnology.* Smithsonian Institution Bureau of American Ethnology Bulletin 85. Washington, DC: Government Printing Office.

Mithun, Marianne. 1987. Is basic word order universal? In *Coherence and Grounding in Discourse,* edited by Russell S. Tomlin, 281–328. Amsterdam: Benjamins.

Rhodes, Richard A. 1991. Secondary objects in Ojibwe. In *Grammatical Relations: A Cross-Theoretical Perspective*, edited by Katarzyna Dziwirek, Patrick Farrell, and Errapel Mejías-Bikandi, 401–414. Stanford, CA: CSLI Pubications.

———. 1994. Agency, inversion, and thematic alignment in Ojibwe. In *Proceedings of BLS 20*, edited by Susanna Gahl et al., 431–446. Berkeley, CA: Berkeley Linguistics Society.

———. 2005. *Clause Structure, Core Arguments, and the Algonquian Relative Root Construction.* The 1998 Belcourt Lecture. Winnipeg: Voices of Rupert's Land.

———. 2010. Relative root complement: A unique grammatical relation in Algonquian syntax. In *Rara & Rarissima: Documenting the Fringes of Linguistic Diversity*, edited by Jan Wohlgemuth and Michael Cysouw, 305–324. Berlin: De Gruyter Mouton.

Shields, Rebecca. 2004. Word order and discourse in Menominee. In *Papers of the Thirty-Fifth Algonquian Conference*, edited by H. C. Wolfart, 373–388. Winnipeg: University of Manitoba.

Sullivan, Michael. 2016. Making statements in Ojibwe: A survey of word order in spontaneous sentences. In *Papers of the Forty-Fourth Algonquian Conference*, edited by Monica Macaulay, Margaret Noodin, and J. Randolph Valentine, 329-347. Albany, NY: SUNY Press.

Thomason, Lucy. 2004. Two, three and four noun phrases per clause in Meskwaki. In *Papers of the Thirty-Fifth Algonquian Conference*, edited by H. C. Wolfart, 407–430. Winnipeg: University of Manitoba.

Tomlin, Russell, and Richard Rhodes. 1979. An introduction to information distribution in Ojibwa. In *Proceedings of CLS 15*, edited by Paul Clyne et al., 307–321. Chicago: Chicago Linguistic Society.

Wolvengrey, Arok Elessar. 2011. *Semantic and Pragmatic Functions in Plains Cree Syntax.*

Multiple Instances of Agreement in Mi'gmaq Verbs

Michael David Hamilton

Like many Algonquian languages, Mi'gmaq has multiple verbal affixes, which index the phi(ϕ)-features (person, number, gender) of arguments, shown in bold in (1).[1]

(1)	mu	ges-	-al	**-ugsi**	-'w	**-eg**	-pn	**-ig**
	NEG	love	-VTA	**-3>SAP.PL**	-NEG	**-1PL**	-PST.DK	**-3PL**

'They didn't love us (me and another)'

One possible analysis is that verbal affixes are instances of agreement, a relationship (Agree) between a functional head (probe) and a DP argument (goal) resulting in the functional head displaying the ϕ-features of the goal (Chomsky 2000). Another possibility is that verbal affixes are clitics, a D-like pronoun, which is a copy of the ϕ-features of a DP argument and attaches to a functional projection (Preminger 2009). In this paper I show that Mi'gmaq has both agreement affixes (theme signs and inner suffixes) and clitics (outer suffixes).

The presence of multiple agreement affixes is important as it supports the presence of ϕ-feature agreement in the thematic domain (Oxford 2013), as opposed to agreement being solely limited to the inflectional domain (Woolford 2010; Nevins

2011). I conclude that theme signs and inner suffixes are instances of ϕ-agreement on Voice^0 and T^0 respectively. However, these cannot simply be classified as object and subject agreement, as multiple arguments can, and often must, be probed in order to account for the conditioning of agreement affixes. I find evidence to support two different notions of multiple argument probing, Cyclic Agree (Béjar and Rezac 2009) and Multiple Agree (Nevins 2011), which are not mutually exclusive but represent the specific nature of Agree on Voice^0 and T^0 respectively.

Background

A recent line of research hypothesizes that what appears to be object agreement on verbs is actually clitic doubling (e.g., Preminger 2009; Woolford 2010; Nevins 2011). In its strongest form, this hypothesis only recognizes subject agreement as a true instance of ϕ-feature agreement within the clause (Woolford 2010). This has sparked interest in the distinction between agreement affixes and clitics.

The appearance of an agreement affix is the result of an Agree relation between a functional head and a DP (Chomsky 2000). A functional head with unvalued ϕ-features (uvϕ) probes downward in its search space (the domain it c-commands) for a DP with valued ϕ-features (vϕ), and enters into an Agree relation with an appropriate goal DP; as a result, the ϕ-features on the functional head are valued correspondingly. In (2), v^0 has uvϕ and probes its search space finding the object DP in Spec-VP with vϕ. Then v^0 enters into an Agree relation with the object DP, and the D's ϕ-features value the ϕ-features of v^0.

It is also possible to have a more complex pattern of agreement where more than one goal is probed—for example, Cyclic Agree (Béjar and Rezac 2009) and Multiple Agree (Nevins 2011). In the Cyclic Agree model, the probe is in between two goals, and the functional head can probe upward and enter into an Agree relation with the subject DP if the probe is not satisfied with the ϕ-features of the object DP on the first probe downward, as in (3a). In the Multiple Agree pattern, the probe is situated above both goals, and the functional head probes down for two arguments simultaneously, and can chose either, or both, to enter into an Agree relation with, as in (3b).[2]

When multiple arguments are probed, it is possible for an agreement affix to index both arguments, resulting in a portmanteau, or to select one, depending on the conditioning of the probe. Given a probe-goal account, locality restrictions

(2)

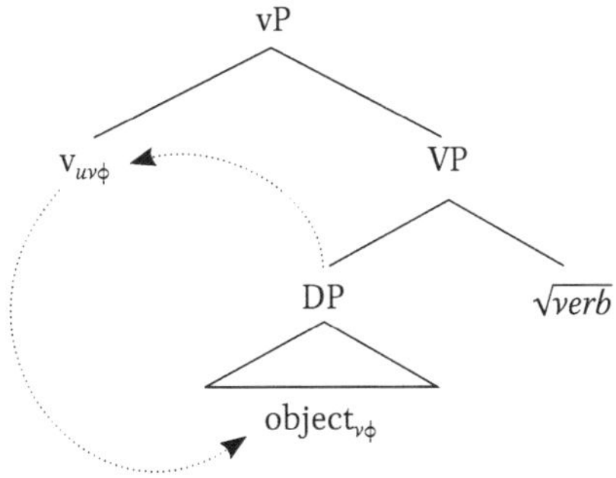

(3) a.

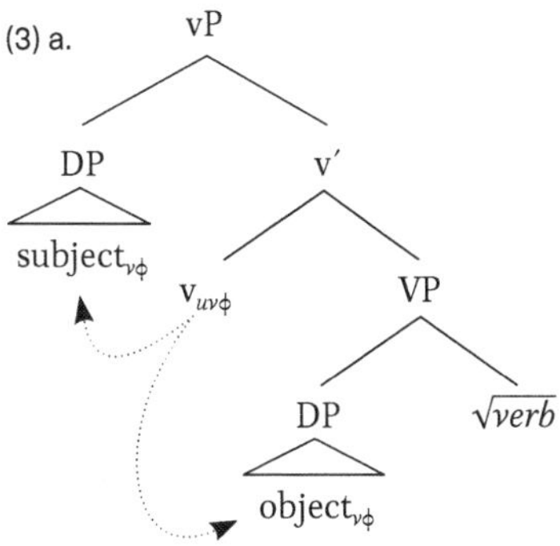

(3) b.

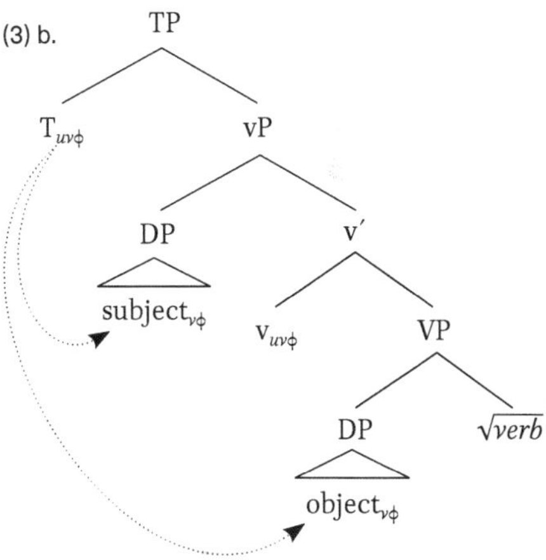

are predicted on Agree, since structural proximity to the probe will determine accessibility of a goal to a probe (Preminger 2009). In addition, since agreement affixes are mandatory, default forms should appear if an Agree relation cannot be entered, that is, a probe cannot find a suitable goal (Preminger 2009).

Clitics, on the other hand, have been argued to be determiner (D) pronounlike elements that are base generated as adjuncts in a "big-DP structure," as in (4) (Roberts 2010; Nevins 2011). The clitic then moves to Spec-*v*P, as in (4a), and attaches via morphological merger (Matushansky 2006) to the verbal stem at PF (Nevins 2011), as in (4b). Given their proclitic or enclitic status, clitics undergo a form of postsyntactic linearization at PF (Kramer 2016); this places them either verb initially or finally depending on how clitics are linearized in specific languages.

(4) a.

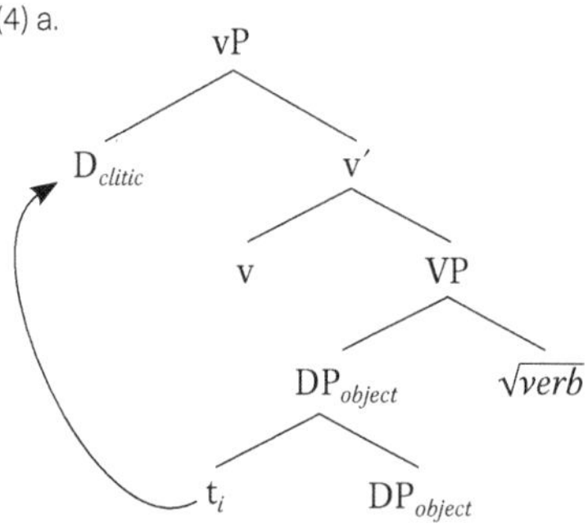

(4) b.

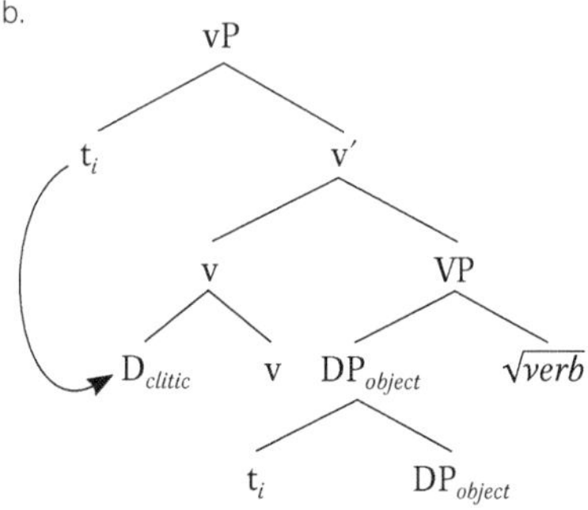

Unlike agreement morphemes, clitics are optional, thus default forms, and locality restrictions in general are not predicted. Given that clitics are linearized postsyntactically, clitics are only expected at the edge of words or inside other clitics, and specifically outside of material linearized syntactically, for example, functional heads and agreement affixes (Zwicky and Pullum 1983). As such, we do not expect the form of clitics to be conditioned by other morphemes—for example, functional heads, agreement affixes, or other clitics (Nevins 2011)—or to index the ϕ-features of multiple arguments (Woolford 2014). A summary comparison between the properties of agreement affixes and clitics is shown in Table 1.

Couched within this debate, Oxford (2013) argues that Proto-Algonquian provides evidence of both subject (inner suffixes) and object (theme signs) agreement. I support this analysis by showing that there are two separate instances of ϕ-feature agreement in Mi'gmaq: one in the thematic domain on Voice^0 (theme signs) and another in the inflectional domain on T^0 (inner suffixes). However, I show that neither is exclusively subject or object indexing. Depending on the ϕ-features of the object, agreement on Voice^0 is either solely object or both subject and object indexing. The agreement on T^0 indexes either the subject or object depending on the ϕ-features of the subject. I show that the agreement on Voice^0 fits a Cyclic Agree model, while agreement on T^0 fits with a Multiple Agree model.

In the following sections, I present five diagnostics in turn to determine whether each verbal ϕ-indexing suffix in Mi'gmaq is an agreement affix or clitic: linear order within the verbal complex, ϕ-feature realization, locality, default agreement, and tense-variance. Based on these diagnostics, I conclude that theme signs and inner suffixes are instances of agreement, while outer suffixes are clitics.

TABLE 1. Agreement versus Clitics

PROPERTIES	AGREEMENT	CLITIC
Form	affix	morphophonological clitic
Appearance	obligatory	optional
Realization on functional head	valued ϕ	adjoined D
Linearization	syntactic	post-syntactic
Ordering	any	edges of words
Portmanteau	possible	not possible
Multiple-goal conditioning	possible	not possible
Locality restrictions	yes	no
Default form	yes	no
Tense-variant	yes (on T^0)	no

Ordering

The ordering of verbal affixes within the verb is an important diagnostic for the agreement-clitic distinction given their contrast in syntactic or postsyntactic linearization. Based on the assumption that no syntactic operations, such as Agree, can follow clitic placement (Zwicky and Pullum 1983), clitics are expected to be able to appear outside of agreement morphemes (or other clitics), but agreement morphemes are not expected to be able to appear outside of clitics. Since agreement surfaces on functional heads, clitics are expected to appear outside of functional heads but not inside them, that is, not between functional heads or between functional heads and the verb root. In Mi'gmaq, theme signs and inner suffixes appear inside or between functional heads, which supports an agreement analysis, while the position of outer suffixes on the periphery is inconclusive.

Based on Oxford's (2013) template for Proto-Algonquian, I propose a template for the verbal suffixes in realis mood, shown and exemplified in (5) (see also Coon and Bale 2013).[3] It is important to note that Mi'gmaq does not have person prefixes in these, or most, environments.

(5) Template

	Root	*Final*	*Theme sign*	NEG	*Inner suffix*	*T*	*Outer suffix*
mu	ges-	-al	**-ugsi**	-'w	**-eg**	-pn	**-ig**
NEG	love	VTA	**3>SAP.PL**	NEG	**1PL**	PST.DK	**3PL**

'They didn't love us (me and another).'

Theme signs appear between the verb final and negation—for example, *ges-* 'love' and *-'w* in (5)—and inner suffixes appear between negation and tense—for example, *-'w* and *-pn* in (5). This suggests that both are agreement morphemes. The outer suffix, on the other hand, always appears verb final, for example, outside of tense *-pn*. This could be consistent with either an agreement or a clitic analysis.

Based on linear order, the assumption that the verb root raises via head movement, and the Mirror Principle (Baker 1985), I assume the clause structure in (6) throughout. Following ordering evidence supporting theme signs and inner suffixes as agreement, I place the theme sign in Voice^0 (Lochbihler 2009; Coon and Bale 2013; Oxford 2013) and the inner suffix on T^0 (Coon and Bale 2013; Oxford 2013). While Voice^0 and T^0 are canonical object and subject agreement positions respectively, I show in the next section that the argument(s) marked in these positions are conditioned in a more complex manner. Given the inconclusive evidence from order, I leave the outer suffix aside.

Conditioning

The second diagnostic is the conditioning of affixes. Given a probe-goal analysis of Agree, agreement morphemes can be conditioned by multiple arguments (Béjar and Rezac 2009; Nevins 2011). While agreement morphemes can be portmanteau (mark two arguments), clitics cannot by definition, given that they are pronouns (Woolford 2014). So if we find a portmanteau ϕ-indexing affix, this is evidence that it is an agreement morpheme. I show below that there are portmanteau theme signs, further supporting an agreement analysis.

In addition, probing multiple arguments can lead to complex patterns of conditioning depending on the ϕ-features of the argument and the nature of the probe. This can give rise to an alternation between arguments, that is, subject or object, conditioning an agreement affix based upon the specific nature of the probe. This is different from the kind of factors that cause deletion between

(6) MI'GMAQ VTA CLAUSE, *adapted from Oxford (2013); Hamilton (2013)*

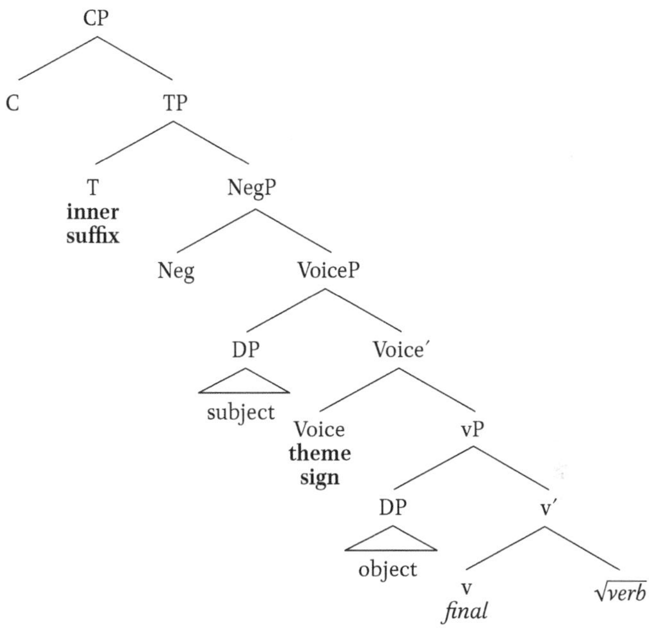

multiple clitics—for example, Person Case Constraint effects—which prohibit the co-occurrence of certain combinations of arguments, such as unmarked>marked (for example, 3>Speech Act Participant [SAP]), and bans on adjacent identity, which is a postsyntactic operation that bans the co-occurrence of two identical clitics, such as [+SAP] (Nevins 2011). Clitic deletion is related to person features, thus not predicted to occur with number (Nevins 2011). I show that agreement on T^0 is conditioned by number, and this supports an agreement analysis of inner suffixes.

Conditioning, on the other hand, is an inconclusive diagnostic for outer suffixes. I discuss each affix in turn below.

Theme Signs

The Mi'gmaq theme signs are shown in Table 2. It is important to note that theme signs are obligatory on transitive verbs with an animate subject and object (VTA), although they may not appear on some forms due to the application of phonological processes. Note that first and second persons are referred to jointly as *SAP* below.

TABLE 2. Theme Signs

FORM	GLOSS	ENVIRONMENT
-(il)i	1.OBJ	2(PL)>1(PL); 3(PL)>1
-ul(n)	2.OBJ	1(PL)>2(PL); 3(PL)>2
-(a)	3.OBJ	2(PL)>3(PL); 1(PL)>3(PL); 3(PL)>**3.OBV**(PL)
-ugsi	3>SAP.PL	3(PL)>2PL; 3(PL)>1PL
-(gwi)	INV	3.OBV(PL)>3(PL)

As well, in Mi'gmaq, the inverse refers to forms in which the subject is third-person animate obviative and the object is third-person animate proximate.[4] There can only be one proximate third person per clause, and typically it is the topic of the sentence or discourse, while all other third persons are marked obviative.

A variety of previous analyses (e.g., McGinnis 1999; Brittain 1999) propose that theme signs exclusively index the ϕ-features of the object. However, this kind of analysis is not possible for Mi'gmaq, since the 3> SAP and inverse theme signs are portmanteau affixes, which index the person features of both the subject and the object. That is, whenever the object is first- or second-person plural, the ϕ-features of the subject must be taken into consideration in order to determine the theme sign. If the subject is third person, then the theme sign will be *-ugsi*, but if the subject is the other SAP, then *-(i'l)i* 'first person' or *-ul(n)* 'second person' will appear. Similarly, whenever the object is third person, the ϕ-features of the subject must also be considered. If the subject is third-person obviative, then the theme sign will be *-(gwi)*, but if the subject is an SAP, then *-(a)* will appear. In fact, it is only when the object is first-person singular, second-person singular, or third-person obviative that the ϕ-features of the subject are irrelevant, since *-(i'l)i*, *-ul(n)* or *-(a)*, respectively will appear regardless of the ϕ-feature specification of the subject. Since some theme signs are portmanteau affixes and often the ϕ-features of both must be considered in determining which one conditions the theme sign, it is clear that both the subject and object can, and often must, be probed. This makes an agreement analysis the most appropriate, supporting Voice^0 as the most appropriate location given that it is in a local configuration with both the subject and object DPs.

As such, a Cyclic Agree (Béjar and Rezac 2009) account is the most appropriate given that the first goal (object DP) is lower than the probe and the second goal (subject DP) is higher than the probe. When Voice^0 Merges, it probes the object DP

TABLE 3. Inner Suffixes

FORM	GLOSS	FORM	GLOSS	FORM	GLOSS
-eg	1PL	*-'gw*	21PL	*-(n)*	2
-oq	2PL	*-(an)*	1	*-t/g*	3

in Spec-*v*P and, if necessary, probes the subject DP when it Merges in Spec-VoiceP. The primacy of probing object DPs allows this relation to bleed subject-probing, which fits the pattern in Mi'gmaq when the object is first- or second-person singular or third-person obviative. In all other cases, the probe on Voice^0 will probe the subject DP, which accounts for portmanteau affixes and conditioning patterns described above.

Inner Suffixes

The inner suffixes and what they index are shown in Table 3. Inner suffixes also appear to be obligatory, but may be deleted due to phonological processes.

Inner suffixes can index the subject or the object. SAP plural will be indexed on the probe regardless of whether it is the subject or object. In forms with both a first-person plural and second-person plural, the second-person plural form will appear as the inner suffix regardless of which is the subject or object. In all other environments with no SAP plural, the subject is marked. Descriptively, it looks like number, particularly SAP plural, conditions the inner suffix, and subject is marked as a default. This supports an agreement analysis of inner suffixes. It is unclear why a preference for overt marking of plural arguments would apply in cliticization.

Inner suffixes are also most appropriately accounted for under an analysis in which multiple arguments are probed, particularly a Multiple Agree account (Nevins 2011), in which omnivorous number arises. Under this account, the functional head is higher than both goal arguments and probes both downward. As such, after T^0 Merges, it probes the subject DP in Spec-VoiceP and then the object DP in Spec-*v*P if necessary. If probing occurs one argument at a time, then an SAP plural in subject position agrees with T^0 and bleeds object-probing. However, in all other cases, the object DP would be probed in a second step, and if it is SAP plural it will agree with T^0. However, if neither is SAP plural, the ϕ-features of the subject will

TABLE 4. Outer Suffixes

FORM	GLOSS	FORM	GLOSS	FORM	GLOSS
-i('g)	3.AN.PL	*-l/n*	3.OBV	*-l/n*	3.IN.PL

value the T^0. If the probing of both the subject and object is done in one step, as Nevins (2011) suggests, then both are probed simultaneously and Agree occurs with the SAP plural argument if present, or the subject otherwise. Either formulation of probing is possible.

Outer Suffixes

A list of outer suffixes and what they index is given in Table 4. Outer suffixes seem to be optional, since they only appear when third-person arguments are present.

Outer suffixes only mark non-SAP arguments and can index the subject or object. Third-person plural, third-person obviative, and third-person inanimate plural arguments are overtly indexed regardless of whether they are subject or object. However, in forms with both a third-person plural animate and third-person obviative, the third-person plural form will appear as the outer suffix.

An argument in favor of an agreement analysis is that only one outer suffix can ever appear, even if there is more than one third-person argument present. If these were clitics, we might expect that two outer suffixes would be possible, for example, a third-person plural subject and a third-person obviative object. However given that only one can appear, and the plural marker is preferred, a Multiple Agree omnivorous number account is plausible, following the one proposed for the inner suffix. Both arguments could be probed from above (possibly from C^0 given linear order[5]) in search of third-person plural, which enters into an Agree relation if present; otherwise any other third-person argument would be indexed.

An alternate hypothesis is that the outer suffix is a clitic (Oxford 2013). This analysis receives superficial, although inconclusive, support from the identical distribution of outer suffixes in the verbal and nominal domain, as in (7).

(7) a. atlai **-'g**
shirt **-3PL**
'shirts (animate)'

b. wi'gatign -**n**
book -**3.IN.PL**
'books (inanimate)'

c. atlai -**l**
shirt -**3.OBV**
'shirt (animate)'

In sum, while a Multiple Agree analysis is possible for outer suffixes, a clitic analysis is equally plausible. While conditioning supports the agreement status of the theme sign and inner suffix, the status of the outer suffix is still consistent with either an agreement or clitic analysis. The conditioning of theme signs and inner suffixes is best accounted for under an Agree relation in which both arguments can be probed, although they will not always be. Interestingly, a Cyclic Agree account seems more appropriate for theme signs, while a Multiple Agree account is more appropriate for inner suffixes. Portmanteau theme signs and conditioning of both theme signs and inner suffixes are unexpected if these are clitics and not agreement affixes.

Locality

The third diagnostic comes from locality restrictions (Preminger 2009). If an Agree relationship holds between a probe and a goal, it will be subject to some form of locality, that is, the available search space of the probe. This is not necessarily the case with clitics. In double object constructions in Mi'gmaq, both the theme sign and the inner suffix can only refer to the ϕ-features of the goal, and not the theme. In (8), the theme sign can only index the ϕ-features of the goal (2PL). The ϕ-features of the theme (3.AN or 3.IN) are not marked, and the theme can be animate, *mijua'ji'j* 'baby', or inanimate, *wi'gatign* 'book'.

(8) mu ignm **-uln** -u **-oq** -op mijua'ji'j/wi'gatign
NEG give.VTA **-2OBJ** -NEG **-2PL** -PST baby(an)/book(in)
'I didn't give you-all the baby/book.'

Assuming that goals are structurally higher than the themes (e.g., Branigan and MacKenzie 1999; Lochbihler 2012), this restriction can be attributed to locality, since

(9)

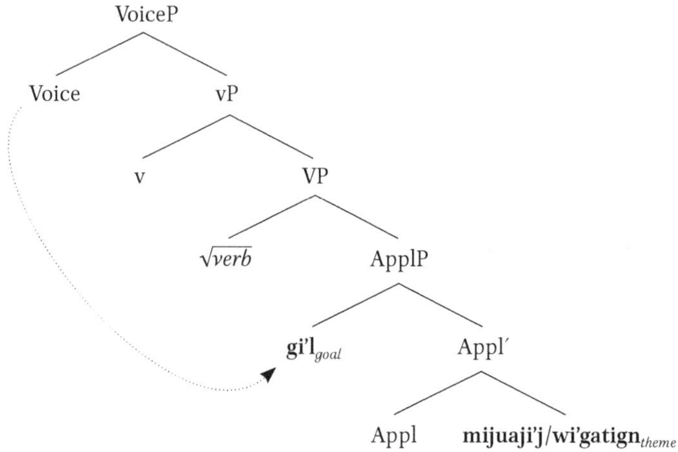

the theme signs can only index the structurally closest DP, the goal. When Voice^0 is merged into the clause, it probes for the closest DP with ϕ-features and finds the goal *gi'l* 'second-person singular' (which will be deleted phonologically) in (9). However, it cannot find a structurally lower DP, the theme *mijua'ji'j/wi'gatign*. Note that this supports the Cyclic Agree analysis for theme signs presented in the last section, as both the goal and theme would be accessible via Multiple Agree from Voice^0. This data also supports a Multiple Agree analysis for inner suffixes, since only the structurally highest arguments (subjects and goals) are accessible from T^0.

In contrast to the theme sign and the inner suffix, the outer suffix can index the theme. The verb forms in (10) crucially differ when animate and inanimate themes are plural. In (10a), the outer suffix indexes third-person animate plural (*-ig*) and is only grammatical with the animate plural theme *atla'ig* 'shirts'. In (10b), however, the outer suffix shows third-person inanimate plural marking (*-n*), which is only grammatical with the inanimate plural theme *wi'gatignn* 'books'. Note again the similarity between the outer suffix on the verb and the plural marker on the respective nominals.

(10) a.

ignm	-uln	-u	-oq	-opn	**-ig**	**atla'i**	**-g**/	*wigatign-n
give.VTA	-2OBJ	-NEG	-2PL	-PST	**-3PL**	**shirt.AN**	**-PL**	book.IN-PL

'I didn't give you-all shirts.'; *'I didn't give you-all books.'

b. ignm -uln -u -oq -opn **-n** **wi'gatign** **-n**/ *atla'i -g
give.VTA -2OBJ -NEG -2PL -PST **-3PL.IN** **book.IN** **-PL** shirt.AN-PL
'I didn't give you-all books.'; *'I didn't give you-all shirts.'

Locality considerations support an agreement analysis of the theme sign and inner suffix, particularly the one developed in the previous section. This contrasts with the outer suffix here, which is not restricted in the same manner and provides evidence in favor of a clitic analysis.

Default Agreement

The fourth diagnostic comes from the appearance of default agreement forms. Preminger (2009) argues that when a probe-goal Agree relationship cannot be established, either a default form appears or the resulting form is ungrammatical. The appearance of a default agreement form is direct evidence in favor of an agreement affix account as agreement is obligatory, whereas clitic doubling is optional. Mi'gmaq, like many Algonquian languages, has Long-Distance Agreement (LDA), which is a construction in which the matrix verb shows agreement with an embedded argument. An example where LDA does not occur is shown in (11a), and an example in which it does is shown in (11b). The matrix verb *ge(j)i-* 'know' in (11a) has the verb final *-tu*, which appears on forms with an animate subject and inanimate object (VTI). In (11b), *ge(j)i-* 'know' lacks the VTI final and appears with the theme sign (*-ugsi* '3>SAP.PL') and inner suffix (*-oq* 'second-person plural') that indexes an embedded argument (*gilew* 'you-all').

(11) a. ge(j)i -tu [(gilew) wigtm -oq plamuei]
know -VTI [(2PL) like.taste.of.VTI -2PL salmon.meat]
'I know you-all like salmon.'

b. gej **-uln** **-oq** [(**gilew**) wigtm -oq plamuei]
know.VTA **-2OBJ** **-2PL** [(**2PL**) like.taste.of.VTI -2PL salmon.meat]
'I know **you-all** like salmon.'

Some analyses of LDA in Algonquian posit that the embedded argument that undergoes LDA is in the left periphery of the embedded clause, for example, Bruening (2001), Branigan and MacKenzie (2002), Mathieu and Lochbihler (2013),

Fry and Hamilton (2013). The goal of LDA is in a local enough configuration for the probe on matrix Voice^0 to check its ϕ-features, and conditions both the theme sign and the inner suffix. But in the cases where LDA does not occur, the potential LDA-triggering argument is not in a local enough configuration, for example, not at the left periphery of the embedded clause. As such, the resulting VTI theme sign inflection on the matrix verb can be analyzed as default agreement (Piggott 1989; Bruening 2001). When the probe on matrix Voice^0 does not find a sufficiently local DP with ϕ-features, a default VTI theme sign appears. This explains why VTI morphology appears with verbs that take a complement clause.

One source of support for this analysis is from conjoined embedded clauses, as the matrix verb will not be marked with a plural inanimate outer suffix. The form in (12a) shows that when the object is third-person inanimate plural, the corresponding outer suffix (*-n*) appears. However, the third-person inanimate plural outer suffix cannot appear with conjoined clauses, as in (12b).

(12) a. gei -tu -n -**n**
know -VTI -2 -**3.IN.PL**
'You know **them** (**IN.PL**), e.g., phone numbers.'

b. gei -tu -n -(***n**) [[Lance pegwatel -g -'p wi'gatign] aq
know -VTI -2 -(**IN.PL**) [[Lance buy -3 -PST book] CONJ

[(ni'n) maqut -m -a -p wenju'su'n]]
[(1) eat -VTI -1 -PST apple]]
'You know [[Lance bought a book] and [I ate an apple]].'

A probe-goal Agree relationship does not exist between the matrix Voice^0 and the complement clause itself, since the CP does not have ϕ-features. Thus, the appearance of the VTI theme sign can be analyzed as default agreement, which occurs when the probe on Voice^0 does not find an internal argument with ϕ-features.

Tense-Variance

The fifth and final diagnostic comes from the ability for affixes to show allomorphy related to the properties of the functional head on which they appear. Nevins (2011) argues that agreement affixes can display allomorphy conditioned by tense,

TABLE 5. VTA Inner Suffix Allomorphy

Φ	REALIS	IRREALIS	Φ	REALIS	IRREALIS
1	-(*an*)	Ø	1PL	*-eg*	*-nen*
2	-(*n*)	-(*g*)	2PL	*-oq*	*-oq*
3	*-t/g*	*-ew*	21PL	*-'gw*	*-nu*

but clitics cannot. However, since Nevins (2011) only considers true agreement as subject agreement on T^0, this should be interpreted as agreement on T^0 potentially showing tense-variance. In fact, if agreement occurs in the verbal complex, as I argue for Mi'gmaq, then we do not expect such agreement to be tense-variant since it occurs on a lower functional head, for example, $Voice^0$. If we find a ϕ-indexing verbal suffix that shows tense-variance, we can conclude both that it is an agreement affix and that it occurs on T^0. This is the prediction for the inner suffix, which I argue is agreement on T^0. However, if we do not find tense variance, then we cannot determine whether the suffix is agreement or a clitic. In fact, this is what we predict for the theme sign, which I argue to be agreement on $voice^0$, as well as for the outer suffix, which appears to be a clitic.

All of these predictions are correct, as in Mi'gmaq only the inner suffix has separate allomorphs, and these appear in irrealis environments (see also Inglis 2002). Table 5 shows the contrast between the realis and irrealis sets, with corresponding examples in (13).

(13) a. 'gs -al -ulsi -tis **-nen**
love.IC -VTA -3>SAP.PL -FUT **-2PL**
'She/he/they will love us (me and another).'

b. ges -al -ugsi **-eg** -pn -ig
love -VTA -3>SAP.PL **-2PL** -PST.DK -3PL
'They loved us (me and another).'

First, it is important to note that although it shows a consonant alternation, *-ulsi*/*-ugsi*, the theme suffix stays constant between irrealis and realis moods. This is consistent with my prediction for the theme sign. Second, the inner suffix shows separate sets of affixes between irrealis mood, for example, *-eg* 'second-person plural' in (13a), and realis mood, for example, *-nen* 'second-person plural' in (13b).

TABLE 6. Summary of the Results

DIAGNOSTIC	THEME SIGNS	INNER SUFFIXES	OUTER SUFFIXES
ordering	**agreement**	**agreement**	agreement/clitic
conditioning	**agreement**	**agreement**	agreement/clitic
locality	**agreement**	**agreement**	**clitic**
default form	**agreement**	agreement/clitic	agreement/clitic
tense-variance	agreement/clitic	**agreement**	agreement/clitic

Although there is still much research to be done regarding the interaction of mood, tense, and evidentiality in Mi'gmaq, this variance is predicted for inner suffixes, given that it is agreement on T^0. Third, the outer suffix does not appear in irrealis contexts, which is not surprising given that optionality is a characteristic of clitics. Thus, this data supports the prediction of tense variance for inner suffixes, but not for theme signs or outer suffixes.

Conclusion

Table 6 summarizes the results from the diagnostics provided. Both theme signs and inner suffixes meet four of the five diagnostics for agreement, with tense variance and default form being inconclusive for each, respectively. I conclude that both are instances of agreement, with the theme sign as agreement on $Voice^0$ and the inner suffix as agreement on T^0. This supports the argument presented in Oxford (2013) in favor of ϕ-agreement in the thematic domain ($Voice^0$) as well as the inflectional domain (T^0). Thus, Mi'gmaq presents further evidence against the hypothesis that there is only one true instance of ϕ-agreement (Woolford 2010). It also provides support for both Cyclic Agree and Multiple Agree, and presents an interesting case for both being possible within a given language.

Although the outer suffix is indeterminate under four of the five diagnostics, the absence of locality effects supports a clitic analysis. This also supports Oxford (2013), and the exact details regarding cliticization and linearization are important topics for further research.

NOTES

1. All data are primary data from the Listuguj dialect. I would like to thank Janine Metallic, Mary Ann Metallic, Janice Vicaire, and Joe Wilmont for sharing their knowledge of Mi'gmaq with me. I would like to thank Jessica Coon, Alan Bale, Michael Wagner, the McGill Mi'gmaq Research group, audiences of the Forty-Fifth Algonquian Conference, and two anonymous reviewers for comments on this paper. Abbreviations: 1 = first person, 2 = second person, 21 = first-person inclusive (including the second person), 3 = animate third-person singular proximate (discourse salient), AN = animate, CONJ = conjunction, DK = direct knowledge, FUT = future, IC = initial change, IN = inanimate, INV = inverse, NEG = negation, OBJ = object, OBV = obviative, PL = plural, PST = past, SAP = speech act participant (first and/or second person), SG = singular, VTA = transitive verb with both animate subject and object, VTI = transitive verb with animate subject and inanimate object; X>Y = X agent, Y patient.
2. Assuming that v^0 is a phase head, the object DP will need to move to Spec,vP in order to be visible to the probe on T^0 given a strict definition of the Phase Impenetrability Constraint (Chomsky 2001). I ignore this motivated movement for ease of exposition.
3. I have collapsed tense and evidentiality into T^0 for convenience and because both certainly occur higher in the syntactic representation, although further research is needed. For more information about the interaction between tense and evidentiality in Mi'gmaq, see Inglis (2002), Loughran (2012), and Little (2013).
4. Thus, the inverse in Mi'gmaq closely resembles the inverse in Proto-Algonquian (Goddard 1974). This is supported by Long-Distance Agreement (LDA) evidence in which 3>SAP.PL forms pattern with the direct, where LDA generally occurs with the subject, rather than the inverse where LDA generally occurs with the object (Fry and Hamilton 2013).
5. Support for the outer suffix as agreement on C^0 comes from the fact that they cannot appear on the verb when it is marked with the subjunctive suffix *-eg*, which is likely on C^0.

REFERENCES

Baker, Mark. 1985. The mirror principle and morphosyntactic explanation. *Linguistic Inquiry* 16:373–415.

Béjar, Susana, and Milan Rezac. 2009. Cyclic agree. *Linguistic Inquiry* 40:35–73.

Branigan, Phil, and Marguerite MacKenzie. 1999. Binding relations and the nature of "pro" in Innu-aimûn. In *Proceedings of NELS 29*, edited by Nancy Hall, Masako Hirotani, and Pius

Tamanji, 475–486. Graduate Linguistic Student Association.

———. 2002. Altruism, A-movement, and object agreement in Innu-aimûn. *Linguistic Inquiry* 33:385–407.

Brittain, Julie. 1999. A reanalysis of transitive animate theme signs as object agreement: Evidence from Western Naskapi. In *Papers of the Thirtieth Algonquian Conference*, edited by David H. Pentland, 34–46. Winnipeg: University of Manitoba.

Bruening, Benjamin. 2001. Syntax at the edge: Cross-clausal phenomenon and the syntax of Passamaquoddy. PhD thesis, MIT.

Chomsky, Noam. 2000. Minimalist inquiries: The framework. In *Step by Step: Essays on Minimalist Syntax in Honor of Howard Lasnik*, edited by Roger Martin, David Michaels, and Juan Uriagereka, 89–15. Cambridge, MA: MIT Press.

———. 2001. Derivation by phase. In *Ken Hale: A Life in Language*, edited by Michael Kenstowicz, 1–52. Cambridge, MA: MIT Press.

Coon, Jessica, and Alan Bale. 2013. The inseparability of person and number in Mi'gmaq. Paper read at Features in Phonology, Morphology, Syntax, and Semantics, University of Tromsø, CASTL, Norway.

Fry, Brandon J., and Michael David Hamilton. 2013. Long-distance agreement in Mi'gmaq and Ojibwe: Towards a comparative study. Paper read at the Forty-Fifth Algonquian Conference, University of Ottawa.

Goddard, Ives. 1974. Remarks on the Algonquian independent indicative. *International Journal of American Linguistics* 40:317–327.

Hamilton, Michael David. 2013. *Wh*-movement in Mi'gmaq. In *Proceedings of the 2013 Annual Conference of the Canadian Linguistics Association*, edited by Shan Luo. University of Victoria.

Inglis, Stephanie Heather. 2002. Speaker's experience: A study of Mi'kmaq modality. PhD thesis, Memorial University of Newfoundland.

Kramer, Ruth. 2016. Clitic doubling or object agreement: The view from Amharic. *Natural Language & Linguistic Theory* 32(2):593–634.

Little, Carol Rose. 2013. Evidentiality in Mi'gmaq. Paper read at the Forty-Fifth Algonquian Conference, University of Ottawa.

Lochbihler, Bethany. 2009. Discontinuous DP constructions. In *Proceedings of the 2009 Annual Conference of the Canadian Linguistics Association*, edited by Frédéric Mailhot, Carleton University.

———. 2012. Aspects of argument licensing. PhD thesis, McGill University.

Loughran, Jenny. 2012. The fusion of tense and evidentiality in Mi'gmaq. MA thesis, McGill University.

Mathieu, Eric, and Bethany Lochbihler. 2013. Clause typing and feature inheritance of discourse features. Unpublished manuscript, University of Ottawa and University of Edinburgh.

Matushansky, Ora. 2006. Head movement in linguistic theory. *Linguistic Inquiry* 37:69–109.

McGinnis, Martha. 1999. Is there syntactic inversion in Ojibwa? In *Workshop on Structure and Constituency in Native American Languages 17*, edited by Leora Bar-El, Rose-Marie Déchaine, and Charlotte Reinholtz, 101–118. University of Calgary.

Nevins, Andrew. 2011. Multiple agree with clitics: Person complementarity vs. omnivorous number. *Natural Language & Linguistic Theory* 29:939–971.

Oxford, William. 2013. Multiple instances of agreement in the clausal spine: Evidence from Algonquian. In *Proceedings of WCCFL 31*, edited by Robert E. Santana–LaBarge, 335–343. Somerville, MA: Cascadilla Proceedings Project.

Piggott, Glyne. 1989. Argument structure and the morphology of the Ojibwa verb. In *Theoretical Perspectives on Native American Languages*, edited by Donna B. Gerdts and Karin Michelson, 35–49. Albany, NY: SUNY Press

Preminger, Omer. 2009. Breaking agreements: Distinguishing agreement and clitic doubling by their failures. *Linguistic Inquiry* 40:619–666.

Roberts, Ian. 2010. *Agreement and Head Movement: Clitics, Incorporation, and Defective Goals.* Cambridge, MA: MIT Press.

Woolford, Ellen. 2010. Active-stative agreement in Lakota. Unpublished manuscript, University of Massachusetts, Amherst.

———. 2014. Two types of portmanteau agreement: Syntactic and morphological. Unpublished manuscript, University of Massachusetts, Amherst.

Zwicky, Arnold M., and Geoffrey K. Pullum. 1983. Cliticization vs. inflection: English *n't*. *Language* 59:502–513.

On Menominee Verb Stems and the Noncomplexity of Verb Finals

Meredith Johnson and Bryan Rosen

The purpose of this paper is to investigate the structure of Menominee verb stems by focusing on the status of the FINAL component. Traditionally, the Algonquian verb stem has been described as having three components: INITIAL, MEDIAL, and FINAL. In addition, these analyses also distinguish between two types of finals: ABSTRACT finals only serve to categorize a verb, while CONCRETE finals both categorize a verb and contribute lexical information. Many authors argue that concrete finals are bipartite, consisting of a prefinal and an abstract final (Bloomfield 1946, 1962; Goddard 1990; Piggott and Newell 2006; Slavin 2012). The schemas in (1) illustrate the analyses of the verb stem from the traditional and theoretical perspectives.

(1) a. TRADITIONAL TEMPLATE: [Initial Abstract final $_{\text{stem}}$] OR
[Initial [Prefinal Abstract final $_{\text{final}}$] $_{\text{stem}}$]
b. SLAVIN (2012): [Root v $_{\text{stem}}$] OR [[XP] Root v] $_{\text{stem}}$]

We would like to thank Sarah Lundquist, Monica Macaulay, and Becky Shields for helpful comments and suggestions on this paper, and the members of the Menominee Language and Culture Commission for their guidance.

(1a) shows the traditional Algonquian verb template, in which the verb may consist of either an initial and abstract final or an initial plus the combination of a prefinal and an abstract final that yields a concrete final. The example in (1b) illustrates Slavin's (2012) analysis, which recasts the traditional Algonquian verb stem template in the Distributed Morphology (DM) framework. She proposes that a verb stem may be the combination of a Root (initial) and "little *v*" (abstract final), or a phrase (initial) and a Root-*v* (prefinal plus abstract final) combination to form a concrete final.

We show that these approaches to Algonquian verb stems cannot be straightforwardly extended to Menominee. We present two arguments in favor of our claim that concrete finals are not synchronically decomposable in the Menominee verb stem. First, we demonstrate that there is an asymmetry in productivity between prefinal+abstract final combinations and initial+abstract final combinations. Second, we show that the placement of medials with respect to abstract and concrete finals is problematic for previous syntactic analyses of Algonquian finals. Instead, we propose that the Menominee data is better explained if all finals are in fact "little *v*."

This paper is organized as follows. The next section reviews the previous traditional and theoretical analyses of Algonquian verb stems. The section that follows examines the productivity of prefinals in comparison to the productivity of initials. Then, we show that the placement of medials is problematic for recent theoretical analyses. Next, we show that the distribution of palatalization cannot be used as evidence for bipartite concrete finals in Menominee. Finally, the last section concludes the paper.

Previous Analyses

This section provides background on the previous analyses of Algonquian verb stems. Finals come in two types. ABSTRACT finals are purely categorizing elements, and they also indicate the transitivity of the verb and the animacy of the absolutive argument (that is, the object of transitive verbs and the subject of intransitive verbs). This yields the familiar four types of verb stems in Algonquian languages: Inanimate Intransitive (II), Animate Intransitive (AI), Transitive Inanimate (TI), and Transitive Animate (TA). CONCRETE finals categorize a verb, while adding some lexical information.[1] Valentine (2001:324), in his description of Odawa (Ojibwe), points out that the lexical information provided by concrete finals is largely verbal or adverbial. For example, the Menominee concrete final *-pahtō* 'run' categorizes a verb as AI and provides the manner-of-motion meaning 'run'. Some traditional analyses (e.g., Bloomfield 1946, 1962; Goddard 1990) propose that concrete finals in Algonquian languages can be broken into two pieces—a prefinal and abstract final—while others refer to finals as "more abstract" or "more concrete" (Wolfart 1973).

On the theoretical side, Piggott and Newell (2006) and Slavin (2012) advance analyses of Ojibwe and Ojicree verb stems in the Distributed Morphology framework (DM; Halle and Marantz 1993).[2] Slavin argues that there are two types of verb stems in Ojicree. A "simple" stem is formed by concatenating a Root and *v*, as in (2a). A "complex" stem is the combination of a Root and *v* to form an intermediate constituent (*v′*), which corresponds to a concrete final. An *a*P merges in the specifier of *v*P to realize an initial; see (2b).

(2) a.

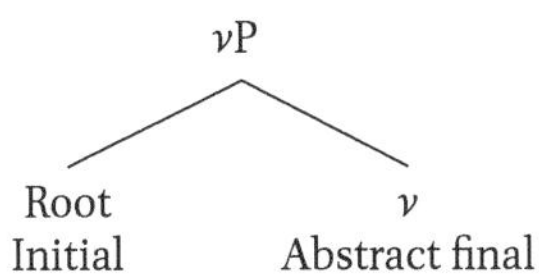

b.

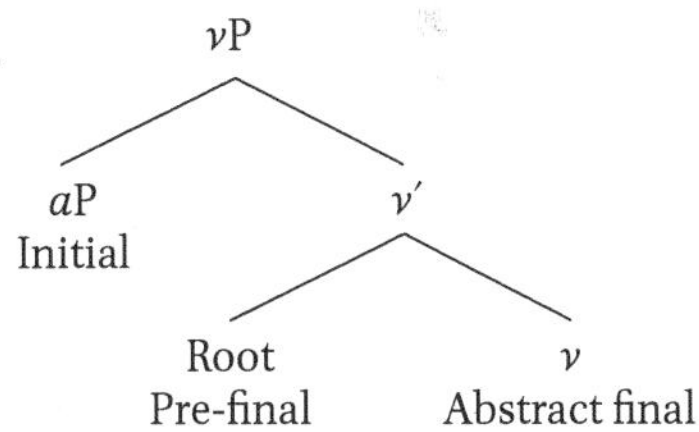

Slavin argues that these structures account for both syntactic and phonological facts in Ojicree. First, this analysis accounts for the fact that verb stems formed with a concrete final are more productive than their abstract final counterparts. This is in line with O'Meara (1990): he notes for Delaware that concrete finals may be added to any initial, whereas sequences of an initial plus an abstract final are more constrained. Slavin follows Arad (2003) and argues that "words" built from Roots (cf. (2a)) are less productive than "words" built from phrases (*x*Ps; cf. (2b)). Second, Slavin's structures also account for the seemingly unpredictable nature of palatalization of [t] to [tʃ] (spelled ⟨c⟩) before an /i/ at a morpheme boundary, as illustrated in (3) below.[3] She argues that the palatalization-triggering vowel *i* has two different structural positions: it is either epenthetic and does not produce palatalization (3a), or it realizes the *a* head of the *a*P in the initial (3b). When *i* is epenthetic, it is inserted late in the derivation for syllabification purposes, and thus cannot cause palatalization. In contrast, when *i* realizes *a*, it is inserted during the derivation, and thus triggers palatalization.

(3) a. piintihse
piint- i -hse
inside EPEN II
'It fell inside.'
b. piincipahtoo
piint-i -pahtoo
inside-*a* run.AI
'He is running inside.' (Slavin 2012:64)

Piggott and Newell (2006) also propose a DM analysis of Ojibwe verbs. Like Slavin (2012), they argue that some verb stems contain just a Root and *v* (4a). Unlike Slavin, however, they claim that verb stems with concrete finals are derived when a prefinal forms a Root-Root compound with an initial (4b).

(4) a.
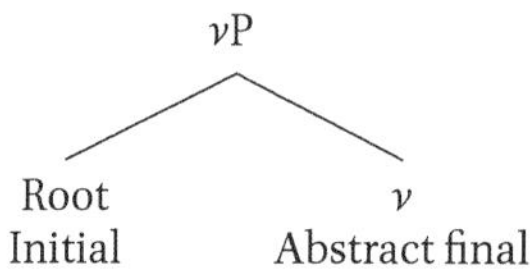

b.
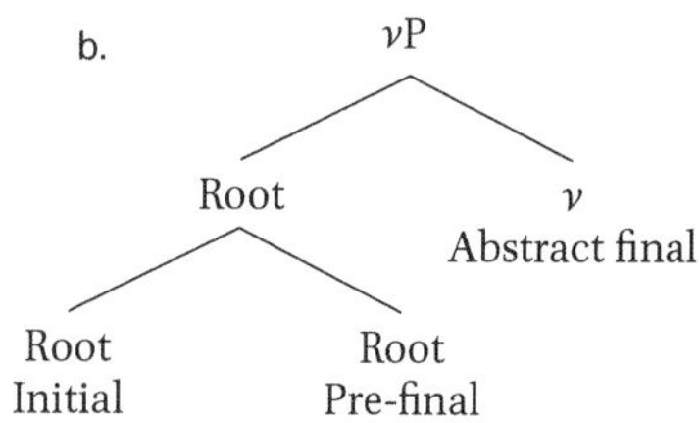

Their proposal is intended to account for the syntactic constraints on hiatus in Ojibwe. They argue that hiatus is only possible at phasal junctures. Since the verb stem corresponds to *v*P—a phase (Chomsky 2001)—hiatus within the verb stem is blocked, but hiatus between the verb stem and external elements (such as a preverb) is tolerated. For example, (5a) and (b) show that a final that begins with a vowel must combine with a consonant-final initial. On the other hand, (5c) illustrates that a vowel-initial verb stem may merge with a preverb that ends in a vowel.

(5) a. bibaamose
bibaa**m**-ose
around-walk.AI
'walk around'
b. *bibaaose
bibaa-ose
around-walk.AI
'walk around'

c. bibaa-aagamose
bibaa-aagam-ose
around-snowshoe-walk.AI
'He walks around in showshoes.' (Piggott and Newell 2006:6–17)

Thus, we see that both Piggott and Newell (2006) and Slavin (2012) argue that prefinals are Roots and that abstract finals are *v*'s.

In what follows, we explore the structure of Menominee verb stems and argue that all finals are *v*. This is in line with Mathieu (2008) and Ritter and Rosen (2010), who claim that both abstract finals and (some) concrete finals in Ojibwe and Blackfoot, respectively, are instantiations of *v*.

Productivity

In the previous section we mentioned that Slavin (2012) analyzes initial+abstract final sequences and concrete finals as having the same structure: as seen in (2) above, they both are formed by combining a Root and *v*. Given this, we would expect a verb stem composed of an initial+abstract final to have similar (if not the same) productivity as a prefinal+abstract final (that is, a concrete final) sequence: both initials and prefinals have the status of Roots. In this section, we show that this prediction is not borne out in Menominee. Instead, verb stems formed from an initial+abstract final are more productive than prefinal+abstract final sequences. That is, initials are able to combine more freely with abstract finals, while prefinals are more limited in which abstract finals they can combine with.

In Menominee, prefinals have a limited distribution: they only combine with (a maximum of) one of each final type (AI/II/TA/TI).[4] This is exemplified with four prefinals in (6)–(9). In (6), the prefinal *p-* 'tie, speed, glide, fly' combines with the AI final *-si* in (a), the II final *-tāē* in (b), the TA final *-N* in (c), and the TI final *-tō* in (d). While it is possible for the prefinal *p-* to combine with each final type, it is restricted to combining with just these abstract finals.

(6) p- *'tie, speed, glide, fly'*

a. kaehpēsow

kaehk-	p-	e	-si	-w
sure/tight	tie/speed/glide/fly	EPEN	AI.REFL	3

'He/she/it is tied.'

b. kaehpetāew

kaehk-	p-	e	-tāe	-w
sure/tight	tie/speed/glide/fly	EPEN	II.REFL	3

'It is tied.'

c. kaehpēnāew

kaehk-	p-	e	-N	-āe	-w
sure/tight	tie/speed/glide/fly	EPEN	TA	TH	3

'He/she/it ties him/her/it.'

d. kaehpētāw

kaehk-	p-	e	-tō	-ā	-w
sure/tight	tie/speed/glide/fly	EPEN	TI	TH	3

'He/she/it ties it.'

A similar pattern also applies to the finals *hN-* 'lie, lay, fall', *t-* 'snag', and *qN-* 'liquid' in (7)–(9). Note that the set of abstract finals used with each prefinal in examples (6)–(9) seems to be lexically determined. In the case of AI finals, *-si* is the one that combines with the prefinal *p-* 'tie, speed, glide, fly' in (6a), *-nāe* is used with *hN-* 'lie, lay, fall' in (7a) and *t-* 'snag' in (8a), and *-e* is the final that joins the prefinal *qN-* 'liquid' in (9a). Thus, while multiple abstract finals are allowed to combine with prefinals, only one of each type of abstract final combines with any one given prefinal.

(7) hN- *'lie, lay, fall'*

a. esēhsen

aeN-	e	hN-	e	-nāe	-w
thither/thus	EPEN	lie/lay/fall	EPEN	AI	3

'He/she falls, lies in that manner.'

b. esēhnen

aeN-	e	hN-	-aen	-w
thither/thus	EPEN	lie/lay/fall	II	3

'It falls, lies in that manner.'

c. esēhsemaew

aeN-	e	hN-	e	-m	-āe	-w
thither/thus	EPEN	lie/lay/fall	EPEN	TA	TH	3

'He/she lays, places him/her/it so.'

d. esēhnetaw

aeN-	e	hN-	-Etō	-ā	-w
thither/thus	EPEN	lie/lay/fall	TI	TH	3

'He/she lays, places it so.'

(8) t- *'snag'*

a. kāskāhkicen

kāsk-	-āhkw-	e	t-	-nāe	-w
scrape	wood/solid	EPEN	snag	AI	3

'He/she/it gets scratched on brambles.'

b. kāskāhkitaew

kāsk-	-āhkw-	e	t-	-āe	-w
scrape	wood/solid	EPEN	snag	AI	3

'It gets scratched on brambles.'

c. kāskāhkicemāew

kāsk-	-āhkw-	e	t-	e	-m	-āe	-w
scrape	wood/solid	EPEN	snag	EPEN	TA	TH	3

'He/she gets him/her/it scratched on brambles.'

d. kāskāhkicēhtaw

kāsk-	-āhkw-	e	t-	e	-htō	-ā	-w
scrape	wood/solid	EPEN	snag	EPEN	TI	TH	3

'He/she gets it scratched on brambles.'

(9) qN- *'liquid'*

a. kesēqsew

kaes-	e	qN-	-e	-w
hot/warm	EPEN	liquid/wet	AI	3

'He/she/it is washed in hot water.'

b. kesēqnen

kaes-	e	qN-	-aen	-w
hot/warm	EPEN	liquid/wet	II	3

'It is washed in hot water.'

c. kesēqnemaew

kaes-	e	qN-	-Em	-āē	-w
hot/warm	EPEN	liquid/wet	TA	TH	3

'It is washed in hot water.'

d. kesēqnetaw

kaes-	e	qN-	-Etō	-ā	-w
hot/warm	EPEN	liquid/wet	TI	TH	3

'It is washed in hot water.'

In contrast, initials can combine with multiple concrete and abstract finals, as exemplified in (10)–(17). The example in (10) shows that *maeyaw-* 'straight' can join with two AI abstract finals: *-ae* and *-aese* 'quality, state', the latter of which Bloomfield (1962:308) describes as "the vaguest and most general abstract AI final in verbs denoting quality or state." In (11), we see that *maeyaw-* 'straight' also combines with several concrete finals. Thus, the examples in (10) and (11) illustrate that initials are more productive than prefinals, as they are able to combine with multiple abstract and concrete finals.

(10) maeyaw- *'straight'*

a. meyāwāēw

maeyaw-	-āē	-w
straight	AI	3

'He/she/it goes in the lead, acts as a leader.'

b. meyāwesew

maeyaw-	-aese	-w
straight	AI	3

'He/she/it is in the proper position, on the right track, in proper command of facts.'

(11) maeyaw- *'straight'*

a. meyāwehsen

maeyaw-	e	hN-	e	-nāē	-w
straight	epen	lie/lay/fall	EPEN	AI	3

'He/she/it falls, lands, lies straight.'

b. meyāwekew

maeyaw-	e	k-	-e	-w
straight	EPEN	grow/shape	AI	3

'He/she/it grows, is straight.'

c. meyāwepāhtaw

maeyaw-	e	pa-	-htō	-w
straight	EPEN	run	AI	3

'He/she/it runs a straight course.'

d. meyāweqtaw

maeyaw-	e	qt-	-ā	-w
straight	EPEN	body.movement/activity	AI	3

'He/she/it runs a straight course.'

As seen in (12), the initial *oN-* 'arrange, put in place' may appear with a few abstract finals, while (13) illustrates that this initial combines with multiple concrete finals as well. Again, we see that an initial may combine with more elements than a prefinal can.

(12) oN- *'arrange, put in place'*

a. osēha̅e̅w

oN-	e	-h	-a̅e̅	-w
arrange/put.in.place	EPEN	TA	TH	3

'He/she makes it, gets him/her/it into shape, ready, fixes it.'

b. onāqnaew

oN-	-aqN	-a̅e̅	-w
arrange/put.in.place	place/have.TA	TH	3

'He/she sets it.'

c. ona̅e̅na̅e̅w

oN-	-aen	-a̅e̅	-w
arrange/put.in.place	by.hand.TA	TH	3

'He/she gets him/her/it ready by hand, places him/her/it in readiness.'

(13) oN- *'arrange, put in place'*

a. ona̅e̅nemaew

oN-	a̅e̅n-	e	-m	-a̅e̅	-w
arrange/put.in.place	think	EPEN	TA	TH	3

'He/she likes, thinks highly of him/her/it.'

b. osēhsemaew

oN-	e	hN-	e	-m	-āē	-w
arrange/put.in.place	EPEN	lie/lay/fall	EPEN	TA	TH	3

'He/she lays him/her/it in place, gets him/her/it ready.'

The examples in (14) and (15) exemplify a similar pattern: *ahkw-* 'so long, so far' may combine with both multiple abstract (14) and concrete (15) finals.

(14) ahkw- *'so long, so far'*

a. ahkōsew

ahkw-	-aese	-w
so.long/so.far	AI	3

'He/she/it is so long, so tall.'

b. ahkōw

ahkw-	-e/-ae	-w
so.long/so.far	AI	3

'He/she/it is so long.'

(15) ahkw- *'so long, so far'*

a. ahkīhsen

ahkw-	e	hN-	e	-nāē	-w
so.long/so.far	EPEN	lie/lay/fall	EPEN	AI	3

'He/she/it lies, extends so far.'

b. ahkuahkasow

ahkw-	āhk-	-asi	-w
so.long/so.far	bury/dry	AI	3

'He/she/it is dried up so far.'

c. ahkīqsew

ahkw-	e	qN-	-e	-w
so.long/so.far	EPEN	liquid/we	AI	3

'He/she/it is wet.'

Finally, consider (16) and (17). In (16), *kēw(ae)-* 'around, back' combines with abstract finals, whereas in (17) this initial may appear with several concrete finals.

(16) kēw(āē)- *'around, back'*

a. kēwāēw

kēw-	-āē	-w
around/back	AI	3

'He/she goes back, goes home, leaves.'

b. kēwesew

kēw-	-aese	-w
around/back	AI	3

'He/she is orphaned.'

(17) kēw(āē)- *'around, back'*

a. kēwaeqsew

kēw-	-aeqN	-e	-w
around/back	wind/blow	AI	3

'He/she/it is blown around.'

b. kēwāēqtaw

kēwāē-	qt-	-ā	-w
around/back	body.movement/activity	AI	3

'He/she/it turns around.'

c. kēwāēpahtaw

kēwāē-	pa-	-htō	-w
around/back	run	AI	3

'He/she/it runs home.'

The traditional analyses cannot easily distinguish the productivity of abstract and concrete finals: if prefinals are an independent unit, they should also be able to merge with a number of abstract finals, contrary to fact. Slavin (2012) would also predict that prefinals would combine with more than just one set of abstract finals. Under her analysis, prefinals have the status of Roots. Thus, it is unclear why initials, which she also classifies as Roots, may combine with a number of abstract finals, but prefinals only combine with one set of abstract finals. Similar problems arise for Piggott and Newell (2006). Since they propose that prefinals form a Root-Root compound with initials, it is not clear why each prefinal can only combine with one given abstract final.

Medials

In this section, we show that the placement of medials and incorporated nouns in Menominee is also problematic for previous generative accounts. Brittain (2003), for example, has analyzed medials (as in (18)) as NP arguments that move between the verb Root and *v*, as shown in (19a). She argues that incorporated nouns right-adjoin to the verb, and that the verb-noun complex then raises to the left edge of the verb stem. Both of these steps are shown in (19b) with an example from Western Naskapi.[5]

(18) nitû -tîhkw -â -w
hunt caribou AI 3
'She/he hunts caribou.'

(19)
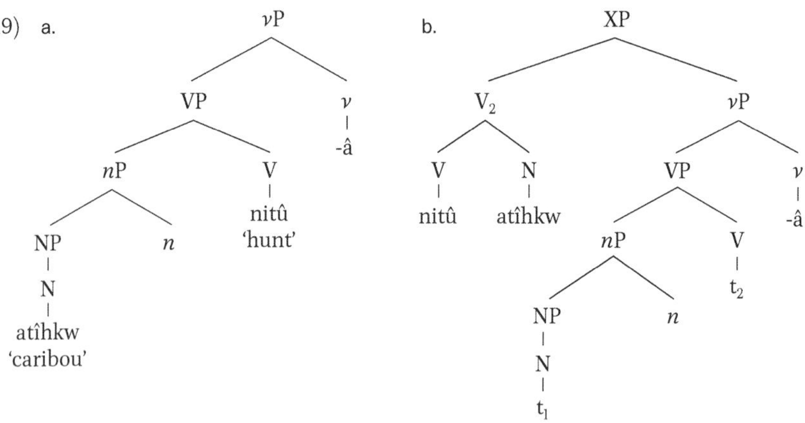

Hirose (2001) has also proposed that incorporated nouns in Plains Cree undergo syntactic noun incorporation. As seen in (20), the noun/medial originates in Spec,vP_1, and then moves into v_2.

(20) a. kisîpêk -in -iyâkan -ê -w
wash by.hand.TI dish AI AGR
'She/he washes a/the dish.'

b. 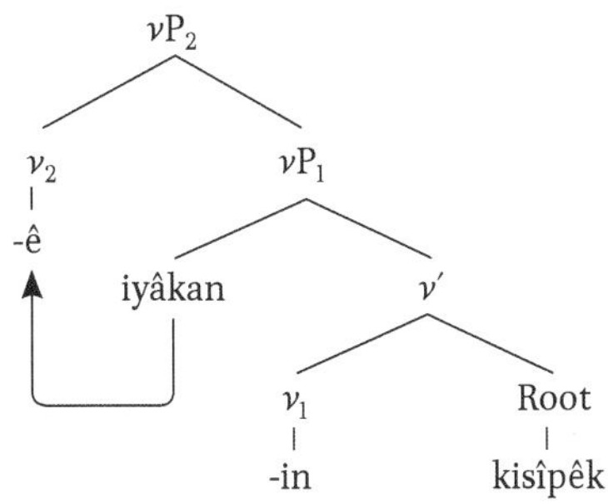

Since Piggott and Newell (2006) and Slavin (2012) argue that both concrete finals and verb stems consisting of an initial plus an abstract final are composed of a Root and *v*, we might expect medials to intervene between these two elements in both cases. That is, medials should occur between initials and abstract finals, and also between prefinals and abstract finals. However, medials in Menominee consistently appear between the initial and final, regardless of whether the final is abstract, as in (21), or concrete, as in (22). In (21a–c), we see that the medials meaning 'face', 'leg', and 'wood' intervene between the initial and the abstract final, and in (22a–c), the same medials also appear between the initial and concrete final.

(21) a. kakīpaehkow

kakīp-	-aehkw-	-e	-w
closed	face/head/hair	AI	3

'He/she/it is blind.'

b. kēskekatāēw

kēsk-	e	-kāt-	-āē	-w
cut.off	EPEN	leg	AI	3

'He/she/it lacks, is missing a leg, has a leg cut off.'

c. wēnosāhkow

wēnos-	-āhkw-	-e	-w
burn.in.blaze	wood/solid	AI	3

'He/she burns brush, trees, wood.'

(22) a. pēhtaehkīqtaw

pēht-	-aehkī-	qt-	-ā	-w
inside.something	face/head/hair	body.movement/activity	AI	3

'He/she/it sticks his/her/its head in.'

b. pūhkikataēhsen

pōhkw-	e	-kātae͞	hN-	e	-nae͞	-w
break	EPENT	leg	lie/lay/fall	EPEN	AI	3

'He/she/it falls and breaks his/her/its leg.'

c. kaeqtāhkwahpesow

kaeqt-	-āhkw-	ahp-	e	-si	-w
near/close.to	wood/solid	tie	EPEN	AI.REFL	3

'He/she/it is tied to a wooden or solid thing.'

It is unclear how either Piggott and Newell or Slavin would account for medial placement, since incorporation would need to target two different positions depending on the type of final present. For examples like (21a) with an abstract final, the medial would need to move between the Root and *v* to derive the correct ordering, as schematized in (23). However, medials would need to move to a different position when a concrete final is present. Under Slavin's approach, the medial in examples like (22a) would need to move between the *a*P and *v*′, rather than between the Root and *v*, as in (24a). Under Piggott and Newell's analysis, the medial would have to break up the Root-Root compound (24b).

(23)

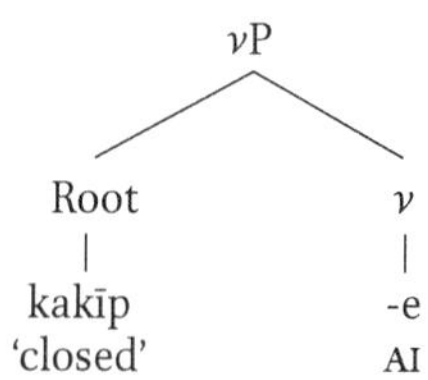

(24)

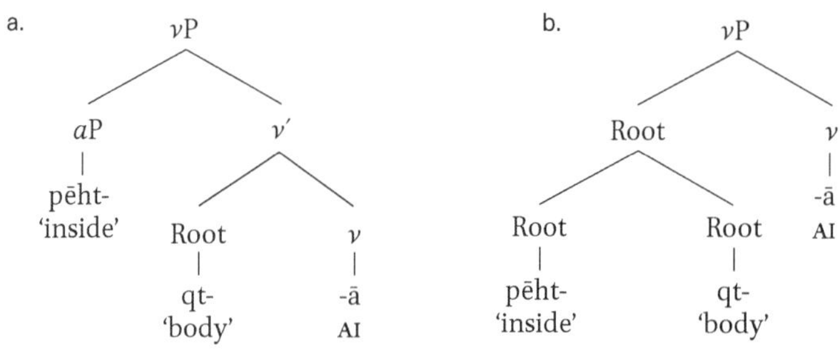

Thus, the data in (21) and (22) indicate that Piggott and Newell's and Slavin's analyses cannot straightforwardly account for the placement of medials in Menominee.

Palatalization

A third diagnostic for testing the structure of Algonquian verb stems concerns the distribution of palatalization. Menominee has palatalization of [t] to [tʃ] (spelled ⟨c⟩) before a word boundary *-e*. However, as we show here, it behaves differently than what Slavin (2012) reports for Ojicree. Recall that Slavin attributes palatalization of [t] to [tʃ] to the fact that *i* in verbs with concrete finals is the realization of "little *a*." Since *i* is present in the syntax, it may affect phonological rules (for example, palatalization). Consider (3) again, repeated in (25) below: the *t* in the initial in (25a) surfaces as [t] since *i* is epenthetic, while the *t* in (25b) surfaces as [tʃ] since *i* is the category-forming head *a*.

(25) a. piintihse

piint-	i	-hse
inside	EPEN	II

'It fell inside.'

b. piincipahtoo

piint-i	-pahtoo
inside-*a*	run.AI

'He is running inside.' (Slavin 2012:64)

Like Ojicree, palatalization is triggered in Menominee when *e* is inserted between an initial and prefinal. As seen in (26), the underlying form of each initial ends in *t*, which surfaces as [tʃ].

(26) a. kāhcekaen

kāht-	e	k-	-aen	-w
push	EPEN	grow/shape	II	3

'It grows pushing through the ground.'

b. pēhcepesow

pēht-	e	p-	e	-si	-w
inside.something	EPEN	tie/speed/glide/fly	EPEN	AI	3

'He/she/it speeds, flies, falls into a place, into a hole, into mud.'

c. acēcekapowew

acēt-	e	kāpw-	-aewe	-w
upside.down	EPEN	stand	AI	3

'He/she/it stands upside down.'

d. anāēcemayakwat

anāēt-	e	myā-	-Ekwat	-w
decayed	EPEN	smell	II	3

'It smells decayed.'

Unlike Ojicree, palatalization also occurs when *e* is inserted between an initial and an abstract final. The examples in (27a) and (b) show that /t/ changes to [tʃ] before *e*.

(27) a. amācehaew

amat-	e	-h	-āē	-w
wake.up	EPEN	TA	TH	3

'She/he wakes up him/her/it.'

b. pemācehtaw

paemāt-	e	-ht	-ā	-w
live	EPEN	TI	TH	3

'He/she makes it live.'

Also unlike Ojicree, epenthesis between a prefinal and final also triggers palatalization of /t/ to [tʃ] in the example in (28).

(28) kāskāhkicen

kāsk-	-āhkw-	e	t-	e	-nāē	-w
scrape	wood/solid	EPEN	snag	EPEN	AI	3

'He/she/it gets scratched on brambles.'

Since palatalization is triggered in more environments in Menominee than in Ojicree, we conclude that the presence of palatalization does not tell us anything about the structure of Menominee verb stems.

An Alternate Analysis: All Finals Are v

Based on the arguments given in the previous three sections, we conclude that concrete finals are not synchronically decomposable. Instead, we develop an analysis where both concrete and abstract finals in Menominee are *v*. We propose that the initial can be either a Root or a phrase (regardless of final type), as in (29).

(29)

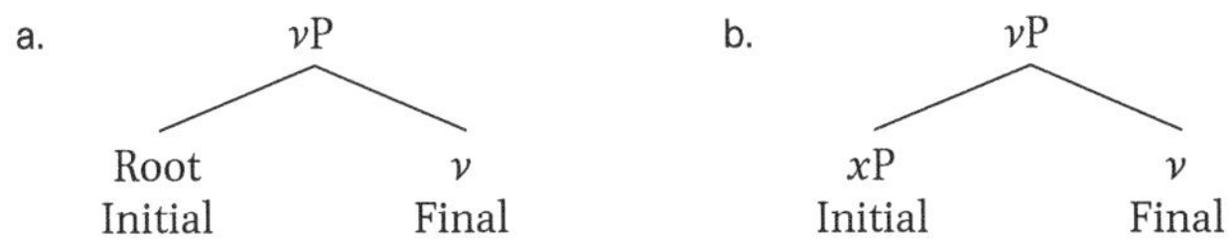

Thus, our analysis of (30a) with an abstract final and (30b) with a concrete final is shown in (31a, b), respectively. We treat the initial *maeyaw-* 'straight' as a Root in both instances.

(30) a. meyāwāēw

maeyaw-	-āē	-w
straight	AI	3

'He/she/it goes in the lead, acts as a leader.'

b. meyāwehsen

maeyaw-	e	hN-	e	-nāē	-w
straight	epen	lie/lay/fall	EPEN	AI	3

'He/she/it falls, lands, lies straight.'

(31)

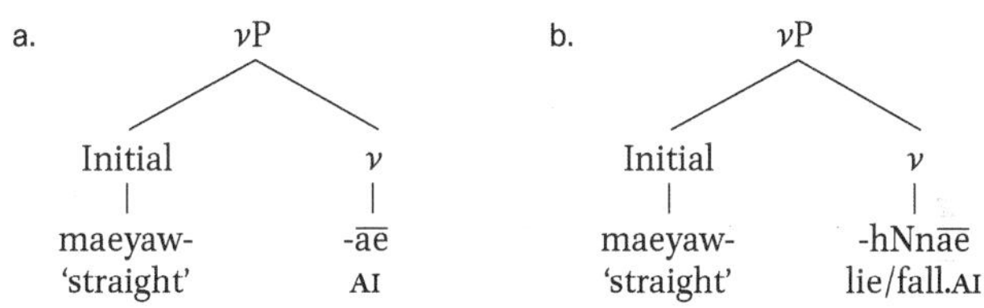

We also suggest that the initial position can be filled by either a Root or a phrasal constituent with concrete finals. For instance, consider the verb stems in (32) and (33) with the concrete final *-pahtō* 'run'.

(32) a. waskēpahtaw

wask-	e	pa-	-htō	-w
go.back	EPEN	run	AI	3

'He/she/it runs back.'

b. menīpahtaw

maenw-	e	pa-	-htō	-w
good/well/pleasureably	EPEN	run	AI	3

'He/she/it runs in good form.'

(33) a. ehkuahtawaepahtaw

[aehkw-	-āhtawāē]	pa-	-htō	-w
upward	climb.AI	run	AI	3

'He/she/it runs up climbing.'

b. mesākāēpahtaw

[maes-	-akāē]	pa-	-htō	-w
cross	AI	run	AI	3

'He/she/it runs across a body of water.'

As shown in (32), *-pahtō* 'run' can combine with Roots, such as *wask-* 'go back' and *maenw-* 'good, well'. The examples in (33) demonstrate that *-pahtō* 'run' can attach to full verb stems, such as *ehkuahtawae-* 'climb (AI)' and *mesākāē-* 'cross (AI)'. We treat the initials of the examples in (33a, b) as full verb stems because they contain the AI finals *-āhtawāē* and *-akāē*, respectively, and they can stand alone as independent verbs; see (34a, b).

(34) a. ehkuahtawaew

aehkw-	-āhtawāē	-w
upward	climb.AI	3

'He/she climbs up, goes up a ladder, stairway.'

b. mesākāēw

maes-	-akāē	-w
cross	AI	3

'He/she/it crosses a body of water; fords, ferries across, crosses on a bridge.'

This account overcomes the issues that the previous generative approaches face with respect to Menominee. First, if finals are *v*, then there is no longer the issue of productivity between the prefinal and the abstract final: they are synchronically frozen forms. Second, our analysis predicts that medials/incorporated nominals will always appear before the final, regardless of whether it is an abstract or concrete final: there is no other available position for it in the verb stem. Finally, since palatalization behaves differently than Slavin (2012) reports for Ojicree, we are not restricted to proposing that palatalization is limited to certain syntactic environments.

While space constraints prevent a full-fledged justification of this analysis, we briefly show that our claim that all Menominee finals instantiate *v* is consistent with other previous work on Algonquian finals and light verbs cross-linguistically. Our analysis for Menominee is in line with Ritter and Rosen's (2010) and Mathieu's (2008) approach to Algonquian finals. Ritter and Rosen in particular follow Butt (2003) and argue that Blackfoot finals are not quite functional and not quite lexical. Under this approach, Mathieu (2008) notes that Algonquian languages have more light verbs than other more commonly studied languages. In fact, there are a handful of languages that have a large inventory of light verbs with lexical meanings.

Folli et al. (2003) have listed a "sample" of twenty-two light verbs in Persian, most of which have strong lexical content. We list a few representative examples here in (35). They also note that constructions using light verbs have "gradually replaced simple verbs in Persian since the thirteenth century."

(35)	kardan	'to do'	dâdan	'to give'
	zadan	'to hit'	gereftan	'to catch, to take'
	bordan	'to carry, to take'	sepordan	'to entrust'
	nemudan	'to show'	keshidan	'to draw, to pull'

Bowern (2004) has also noted that there are a number of light verbs in Bardi that are bleached of some of their meaning, but still contribute some lexical content. Some examples are shown in (36).

(36)	-ar-	'kill/spear (lice)'	-banji-	'share/exchange'
	-gal(a)-	'walk/visit'	-gama-	'laugh'
	-moondoo-	'wet something'	-ni-	'sit'

The fact that Menominee concrete finals appear to contain abstract finals suggests that these forms used to be synchronically decomposable; however, it is common cross-linguistically for light verbs to be historically formed from the reanalysis of lexical verbs (as is the case in Persian; see also Bowern 2008; Butt 2010). Thus, a light verb analysis can also account for the apparent morphological complexity of (some) concrete finals in Menominee. We tentatively suggest that concrete finals are historically derived from the combination of a prefinal and abstract final (as previous analyses argue); however, we contend that the data in the previous three sections support our analysis in which finals are no longer synchronically decomposable and instead instantiate *v*.

Conclusion

To conclude, we have presented data from Menominee verb stems that are not easily handled by previous traditional and theoretical analyses. These previous approaches argue that abstract and concrete finals are structurally distinct; however, we have argued that a heterogeneous analysis of the two final types cannot account for the limited productivity of prefinals, the position of medials with respect to finals, and the distribution of palatalization. We have instead suggested an analysis where all finals are *v*. Furthermore, we have shown that this analysis is in line with other cross-linguistic studies on light verbs. The scope of the current paper is limited to Menominee; we leave it to future research to determine if the proposal that all finals instantiate *v* can be extended to other Algonquian languages.

NOTES

1. Following Valentine (2001) and Slavin (2012), we use the term CONCRETE FINAL for either mono- or bimorphemic finals.
2. There are many other syntactic analyses of verb stems in Algonquian languages; see, for example, Hirose (2001), Brittain (2003), and Mathieu (2008). These analyses all treat at least some abstract finals as instances of *v*; however, they do not take a strong stance on the status of concrete finals, and thus we do not treat them in detail here.
3. Abbreviations: 3 = third person; AI = animate intransitive; EPEN = epenthetic; II = inanimate intransitive; REFL = reflexive; TA = transitive animate; TH = theme sign; TI = transitive inanimate. /E/ represents a morphophoneme that usually surfaces as [e], whereas /N/ is a morpheme that surfaces either as [n] or [s]/[ʃ] (Bloomfield 1962). For more information about the various (morpho)phonological alternations in the Menominee examples, see Bloomfield (1962). All Menominee data cited in this paper come from Bloomfield (1975) via a database created by Monica Macaulay at the University of Wisconsin–Madison.
4. This claim is based on an exhaustive tally of the morphological analyses of concrete

finals given in Bloomfield 1962. See also Bloomfield (1927:395): "Usually it is possible to analyze these [concrete finals] into a simple final preceded by a prefinal element. As, however, this prefinal is always restricted to certain definite finals, the two form a unit."

5. For reasons that need not concern us here, Brittain (2003) argues that the Left Edge in Algonquian verb stems must be filled with phonologically overt material before Spell-Out.

REFERENCES

Arad, Maya. 2003. Locality constraints on the interpretation of roots: The case of Hebrew denominal verbs. *Natural Language & Linguistic Theory* 21:737–778.

Bloomfield, Leonard. 1927. The word-stems of Central Algonquian. In *Festschrift Meinhof*, 393–402. Hamburg: L. Friederichsen.

———. 1946. Algonquian. In *Linguistic Structures of North America*, edited by Harry Hoijer et al., 85–129. New York: Viking Fund.

———. 1962. *The Menomini Language*. Edited by Charles F. Hockett. New Haven, CT: Yale University Press.

———. 1975. *Menominee Lexicon*. Edited by Charles F. Hockett. Milwaukee Public Museum Publications in Anthropology and History 3.

Bowern, Claire. 2004. Bardi verb morphology in the historical perspective. PhD thesis, Harvard University.

———. 2008. The diachrony of complex predicates. *Diachronica* 25:161–185

Brittain, Julie. 2003. A distributed morphology account of the syntax of the Algonquian verb. In *Proceedings of the 2003 Annual Conference of the Canadian Linguistic Association*, 25–39. Université du Québec à Montréal.

Butt, Miriam. 2003. The light verb jungle. *Harvard Working Papers in Linguistics* 9:1–49.

———. 2010. The light verb jungle: Still hacking away. In *Complex Predicates: Cross-Linguisitc Perspectives on Event Structure*, edited by Mengistu Amberber, Brett Baker, and Mark Harvey, 48–78. Cambridge: Cambridge University Press.

Chomsky, Noam. 2001. Derivation by phase. In *Ken Hale: A Life in Language*, edited by Mark Kenstowicz, 1–52. Cambridge, MA: MIT Press.

Folli, Raffaella, Heidi Harley, and Simin Karimi. 2003. Determinants of event structure in Persian complex predicates. *Lingua* 115:1365–1401.

Goddard, Ives. 1990. Primary and secondary stem derivation in Algonquian. *International Journal of American Linguistics* 56:449–483.

Halle, Morris, and Alec Marantz. 1993. Distributed morphology and the pieces of inflection. In *The View from Building 20: Essays in Linguistics in Honor of Sylvain Bromberger*, edited by

Kenneth Hale and Samuel Jay Keyser, 111–176. Cambridge, MA: MIT Press.

Hirose, Tomio. 2001. Origins of predicates: Evidence from Plains Cree. PhD thesis, University of British Columbia.

Mathieu, Éric. 2008. The syntax of abstract and concrete finals in Ojibwe. In *Proceedings of NELS 37*, edited by Emily Elfner, and Martin Walkow, 101–114. BookSurge Publishing.

O'Meara, John. 1990. Delaware stem morphology. PhD thesis, McGill University.

Piggott, Glyne, and Heather Newell. 2006. Syllabification, stress and derivation by phase in Ojibwa. In *McGill Working Papers* 20, edited by E. Dobler and Y. Furukawa.

Ritter, Elizabeth, and Sara Thomas Rosen. 2010. Animacy in Blackfoot: Implications for event structure and clause structure. In *Lexical Semantics, Syntax, and Event Structure*, edited by Malka Rappaport Hovav, Edit Doron, and Ivy Sichel, 124–152. New York: Oxford University Press.

Slavin, Tanya. 2012. The syntax and semantics of stem composition in Ojicree. PhD thesis, University of Toronto.

Valentine, J. Randolph. 2001. *Nishnaabemwin Reference Grammar.* Toronto: University of Toronto Press.

Wolfart, H. C. 1973. *Plains Cree: A Grammatical Study.* Transactions of the American Philosophical Society, n.s., Vol. 63, part 5, Philadelphia

Expressions of Location and Direction in Menominee

Sarah Lundquist and Monica Macaulay

This paper describes the multiple alternative strategies available for expressing location and direction in Menominee. We survey the use of nouns, particles, demonstratives, preverbs, and verbs, and also argue that there exists a category of prepositions in Menominee, contra the standard description (Bloomfield 1962).

We assume without further comment the definitions of FIGURE, GROUND, and PATH established by Talmy (1985):

> The basic motion event consists of one object (the 'Figure') moving or located with respect to another object (the reference-object or 'Ground'). It is analyzed as having four components: besides 'Figure' and 'Ground', there are 'Path' and 'Motion'. The

We are very grateful to the Menominee speakers who have shared their language with us over the years, including: Marie Floring (MF), Margaret King (MK), Bill Penass (BP), Lavina Shawano (LS), Larry Tomow (LT), and Tillie Zhuckkahosee (TZ). We are also grateful to the members of the Menominee Language and Culture Commission for their guidance. Thanks to Meredith Johnson, Bryan Rosen, and Becky Shields for comments on an earlier version of the paper. Our research has been supported in part by the National Science Foundation under Grants No. 0235873 and 0553958, and by several grants from the University of Wisconsin–Madison Graduate School.

> 'Path' . . . is the course followed or site occupied by the Figure object with respect to the Ground object. (Talmy 1985:60–61)

The paper proceeds as follows: We first discuss the many lexical and morphological means of expressing location and direction in Menominee. We then consider the syntax of expressions of location, including arguments for including PREPOSITION as a lexical category.

Types of Expressions

We begin by laying out the many parts of the grammar that can come into play in expressions of location and direction in Menominee.

Zero-Marked Nouns

First, locative nouns can be zero-marked, as in (1):[1]

(1) a. Eneq 's aqtaek **eneh** **mahkāh**.
that.INAN.PRED AOR be.located.3CONJ that.INAN box
'It's in the box.' (MF, LT 1/17/13)

b. Awāētokēhsak eneq 's ayītuaq **eneh** **ohpāēn.**
worm.PL there.PRED AOR be.in.the.place.3PL.IC that.INAN potato
'There are worms in that potato.' (LT 1/17/13)

In all such cases, some other element in the sentence provides a locative feature; for example, in (1a) we see the verb of location *aqtaek*, and in (1b) another verb of location (a form of *īw*) plus a predicative locative demonstrative (*eneq*).

Other examples with zero-marked nouns contain verbs of motion, as in (2):

(2) a. Hāw, **ketāēnenyamenawak** ketāēsiaq!
now our.men go.2PL
'Let's go to where our men are!' (PHK 123)

b. Kēs-akuaqtaw **nepēhsaeh.**
CP-get.out.3 lake
'He got out of the lake.' (MF 2/7/13)

The noun in such a construction generally plays the role of goal, although (2b) shows that it can also be a source.

Many examples with bare nouns also contain locative demonstratives (which we discuss separately below), as illustrated in (3):

(3) a. Anōhkanak aqnawak **enes** **ahkāēh.**
raspberries put.1>3PL there pail
'I put the berries in the pail.' (MF, LT 1/17/13)

b. Eneq kēs-wēkeyah **omas** **Keshena Falls.**
then.PRED CP-live.1PL.CONJ here Keshena Falls
'We lived here by Keshena Falls.' (BLS 003)

Thus, for bare nouns to be interpreted as locative, there must be some other element in the sentence to provide a locative feature.

The Locative Suffix -Eh

Locative nouns can also be marked with the locative suffix *-Eh*,[2] as in (5) (in which the locative phrase is in boldface and the locative suffix is italicized):[3]

(4) a. Nānēpowet **eskuahtem*eh*,**
stand.3CONJ.RED door.LOC
'As he stood for a while by the entry, . . . ' (RS 108)

b. **Ahkāēhko*h*** ohsām eneh kāskāhkwahekan.
kettle.LOC boil.3 that.INAN scraping.RED
'He boils those scrapings in a kettle.' (PA 003)

The meaning of *-Eh* is very general. We have found it translated as 'at, by, from, in, inside, into, on, over', and 'to', with the specific interpretation arising from context.

Like zero-marked nouns, locative nouns can co-occur with a variety of other locative elements:

(5) a. Weyak 's **pes**-pāhpakahekaet **emes** **eskuahtem*eh*.**
someone AOR coming-knock.at.door.3CONJ over.there door.LOC
'Someone knocks at the outside door.' (BLS 032)

b. Nekōtāēs ēh-ayom kehtekāēwenaeniw eneq 's
once this.one.here farmer then.PRED AOR

māēk-īt **pīhtik** **enes** **tanāwikameko*h*.**
DUR-be.in.place.3CONJ inside there barn.LOC
'Once there was a farmer in a barn.' (BP 11/17/00)

In (5a), for example, we find a deictic motion preverb ('coming') and a locative demonstrative adverb ('over there'), and in (5b) the locative noun co-occurs with a verb of location, a preposition, and the locative 'there'. However, unlike bare nouns, locative nouns are not required to occur with some other locative element (as we see in (4b)).

Prepositions

Algonquian languages are traditionally described without mention of prepositions, and Bloomfield's grammar of Menominee is no exception to this rule. Instead, Bloomfield describes a very large category of uninflectable particles. But following Oxford (2007, 2008, 2011, 2014) and LeSourd (2014), we argue that some of these particles are in fact prepositions. We address syntactic arguments for the prepositional status of these elements below; at this point we give the list in (6), containing forms that we have found functioning as prepositions to date—but we stress that there may be others as well.

(6) *Menominee prepositions*

a. *In use as prepositions by current first-language speakers*

anāmiah	'under, underneath, down below'
anāēp	'off to one side, (on) one side, the other side (of)'
āsaw	'on the other side (of), beyond, across'
cēk	'close, close by, close up, next to, near'
espāēmiah	'up above'
kaeqceh	'close by, near'
kekēh	'with, along (with)'
nāweyaw, nānāweyaw, nāweyoh	'in the middle (of), along the center (of)'
otīh	'back, in back, in the rear (of), behind'

pīhtik	'inside, within [usually a building]'
wahkēc	'on, on top (of)'

b. *Attested as prepositions in Bloomfield (1928) but not currently in use as such*

akāmiah	'at the far side (of), over across'
ākaw	'behind, beyond something, across, cut off from vision'
āyētoh	'at both ends, sides (of)'
cīkesitaem	'by the shore, bank (of)'
eskuaqc	'at the end, at one end of the place'
tepāh	'exactly opposite'

A few of the prepositions are exemplified in (7) (and are in boldface in the examples):

(7) a.

Eneq	's	aqtaek	[**anāmiah**	atūhpwan(eh)].
that.INAN.PRED	AOR	be.there.3CONJ	under	table(LOC)

'It's under the table.' (MF, MK, LT 9/13/12, 11/15/12)

b.

Nekēs-nāēwāw	[**kekēh**	nīcianok].
1CP-see.1>3	with	child.PL

'I saw him with the children.' (MK 10/7/13)

c.

Eneq	's	wēket	[enes	**āsaw**	mīhekaneh].
that.INAN.PRED	AOR	live.3CONJ	there	across	road.LOC

'She lives in a house on the other side of the road.' (MF 9/16/13)

These have the typical function of prepositions: they express a relationship between a Figure and a Ground. For example, in (7a), *anāmiah* 'under' tells us how the Figure ('it', in this case a jacket) is positioned with respect to the Ground (the table).

Particles

The large class of locative particles may be subdivided into five primary semantic classes. The first set contains the particle *nakah* 'direction', as well as particles containing the related derivational suffix *-nakah*. These all mark direction, and in some cases add a deictic element to their meaning as well:

(8) *Direction*

nakah	'direction'
enakah	'in that direction, over that way'
omanakah	'in this direction, over here'

Another class, illustrated in (9) below, contains particles that involve an element of direction as well as further specification of the Path:

(9) *Direction/Path*

meyāw	'straight, directly'
yāh	'back'
yōh	'from there'

The class of particles that indicates distance is exemplified in (10):

(10) *Distance*

ehpeh	'at that distance, at the distance that'
sekas	'a ways off'
wāqnaw	'far, distant'

The class that encodes location is shown in (11):

(11) *Location*[4]

kotaeqnas	'somewhere, anywhere'
mesas	'all over, everywhere'
nuakow	'downstream'

The particles of the final class are more complex than those previously described in that they signal a particular spatial relation to some Ground. Such a Ground is frequently encoded by a concrete final in the word. Examples of such particles, along with their derivational components, are provided in (12):

(12) *Spatial relation to specific Ground*

cēkapah	'by the wall'
	(cēk- 'near' + -apah 'reed wall')
pemāēqtihkanaw	'at one side of the road'
	(paemāēqt- 'straight-line movement' + -ihkanaw 'road')
āpaehtawāhtek	'halfway as high as the trees'
	(āpaehtaw- 'half' + -āhtaek 'stick, wood')

Particles from different classes may, not surprisingly, co-occur when semantically compatible. For example, (13) combines a particle expressing distance with a particle that involves a spatial relation to a specific Ground:

(13) **Wāqnaw** **nōqsoh** pepīm-enāhit.
far away.from.shore on.along-paddle.thus.3CONJ
'He paddled far away from shore.' (BM 088)

Locative Demonstrative "Pronouns"

There are four locative demonstrative "pronouns" (and we explain this terminology below) indicating proximal and distal location. Two have the usual meanings ('here', 'there'), and two have what Bloomfield describes as "more strongly pointing reference" (1962:192); that is, 'over here' and 'over there'.[5] The four are listed in (14):

(14) *Locative demonstrative pronouns (Bloomfield 1962:193)*

yōs	'here' (cf. yōm 'this (inanimate)')
enes	'there' (cf. eneh 'that (inanimate)')
omas	'over here'
emes	'over there'

Bloomfield categorizes the demonstratives with the other pronouns in Menominee for two reasons: first, he analyzes *yōs* and *enes* as locative forms of the demonstrative stems for 'this' and 'that' (containing a suffix *-s*), and second, like other pronouns, all four inflect. The examples in (15) provide the inflected forms of *yōs* 'here':

(15) *Inflected forms of* yōs *'here' (Bloomfield 1962:195–197)*

yōq	'it is here' (predicative)
yōwen	'it is said to be here' (quotative)
yōt	'is it here?' (interrogative)
yōpaq	'but it was here!' (preterit)
yōsaq	'so it is here!' (present)

Oxford (2011) argues that the parallel forms in Innu-aimun are demonstratives, however. Among other arguments, he points out that they cannot co-occur with non-locative demonstratives. This is true in Menominee as well, as (16) shows:

(16) a. *Apēnon **enes** **eneh** atūhpwaneh!
sit.2SG.IMP there that.INAN table.LOC
Intended: 'Sit at the table!' (MK 10/7/13)

b. *Nekēs-aqnawak anōhkanak **enes** **enoh** ahkāēh.
1CP-put.1>3PL raspberry.PL there that.AN pail
Intended: 'I put the raspberries in the pail.' (MF, MK 10/7/13)

In (16a) we see that *enes* 'there' and *eneh* 'that (inan.)' cannot co-occur, and in (16b) we see the same for *enes* and *enoh* 'that (an.)'. Thus, we agree that the Menominee forms are demonstratives rather than pronouns.

Finally, we note that the locative demonstratives co-occur with all other types of locative element; we have seen several examples already, and more appear below.

Preverbs

Location can also be signaled by preverbs, although most mark Path rather than pure location, and others just have a locative or Path component to their meaning. Examples of each type are illustrated in (17) and (18):[6]

(17) *Clearly locative/Path meanings*[7]

es-, eses-	'towards there, there' [RR]
papām-	'around, about, moving continuously with varying direction'
pemīm-, pepīm-	'in passing, by, on along' ('linear movement through space')
pes-, pec-	'toward here, coming'
taseh-	'there, in a place' [RR]
yāh-	'back'
yōh-	'from there' [RR]

(18) *Have locative/Path component to meaning*

ap-	'go off to (and return)'
awēh-	'go off to perform action'
enem-	'on the way' ('movement along a course in space') [RR]

A few examples containing some of these preverbs appear in (19):

(19) a. Awāētok kēs-**pec**-āwew 's mesāhkataewāēt.
spirit CP-to.here-be.3 AOR fast.3CONJ
'A spirit always came when he fasted.' (TAT 024–025)

b. Pesāēhkiw **yōh**-pīmakah nōnākanaep.
cow from.there-come.3CONJ milk
'Milk comes from cows.' (MF, LS 1/20/05)

c. Eneq **pes-yōh**-tatākāpamenah.
there.PRED to.here-from.there-stare.at.3>1PL.INCL
'He's watching us from there.' (DOS 010)

In (19a) the preverb *pec-* adds the direction 'toward here' ('here' being the location of the main character in the story); in (19b) we see the preverb *yōh-* combining with the verb 'come' to introduce a source argument; and in (19c) we find a combination of the preverbs in (a) and (b), yielding a reading that the subject 'he' is staring in our direction from another location.

Verbs

Verbs also play a role in expressing location and direction. We begin by discussing the derivational components (roots, medials, and finals) of Menominee verbs.

First, many roots express locative meanings, and of the three component categories, roots have the most core locative meanings. There are also many that express direction; in fact, many incorporate motion into their semantics. The examples in (20) provide a small selection:

(20) *Examples of roots expressing location/direction*

atōt-	'on something' (e.g., atōtapew 'he, she, it (an.) sits on something')
aehkw-	'upward' (e.g., ehkuapew 'he, she, it (animate) sits up straight')
nīm-	'high, up' (e.g., nīmapew 'he, she, it (animate) sits high on something')
sāk-	'out of a place' (e.g., sākapew 'he, she, it (animate) sits sticking out')

Medials do not express locative relationships, but a number of finals do, as illustrated in (21):

(21) *Finals expressing location*

a. *Pure location*

-ape	'be in place, sit' (AI)
-aqtāē	'be in place' (II)

b. *Type of action/locative relationship/Ground*

-īhcenāē, -īhtāē	'be in water' (AI/II)
-nekāt	'carry on one's shoulder' (TI)
-tācem, -tāceht	'transport on a vehicle' (TA/TI)
-ahoN, -ahosi, -ahot, -ahotāē	'act or convey through a medium' (TA/AI/TI/II)

As the examples in (21) show, there is one AI-II final pair that expresses pure location, but most locative finals specify a combination of some aspect of the state or action, the relationship between the Figure and the Ground, and/or the type or category of Ground itself.

Turning from the derivational components to the verb itself, we first find two that express pure location or existence (and these are obviously related to the finals illustrated in (21a)). These are listed in (22) and exemplified in (23):

(22) a. aqtaew 'it (inan.) is in place, is there' (II)
b. apēw 'he, she, it (an.) is in place, is there' (AI)

(23) a. Eneq 's aqtaek atūhpwaneh.
that.INAN.PRED AOR be.located.3CONJ table.LOC
'It's on the table.' (MF, MK, LT 9/13/12)

b. Nahāw, nekot taeh apēw.
well one and be.located.3
'Well, there was one there [a buggy].' (BB 002)

Apēw also functions as the posture verb 'sit', and in fact it is usually impossible to distinguish the two readings:

(24) Apēnon enes atūhpwaneh!
sit.2SG.IMP there table.LOC
'Sit at the table!' (MF 1/17/13)

A third verb, *īw*, is defined by Bloomfield (1975:64) as 'he is in the place, at the point; at home'. Our consultants say that this verb is used only for human subjects, as in (25a), and, indeed, we have only found it used with humans and spirits in Bloomfield's texts, as in (25b). Our corpus does include a few examples from contemporary speakers with nonhuman animals as subjects (as in (25c)); in these, it seems that *īw* is used in the sense of 'lives' (that is, 'is at home').

(25) a. Nīcianōhsaeh eneq 's ayīt anāmiah
baby that.INAN.PRED AOR be.in.the.place.3CONJ.IC under

wāpoweyāneh.
blanket.LOC
'The baby is under the blanket.' (MF, LS 7/13/05)

b. Kan awāētok okātaw-īnan.
NEG spirit 3.going.to-be.in.the.place.3NEG
'There will be no spirit there.' (NRS 036)

c. Eneq 's ītuaq namāēqsak nepīheh.
that.INAN.PRED AOR be.in.the.place.3PL.CONJ fish.PL water.LOC
'There are fish in the water.' (MF 1/17/13)

Finally, we note here a few classes of verbs that explicitly code location and direction, along with various other meanings. One large set involves direction, and these are generally motion verbs, as in (26):

(26) *Direction*

a. Hāw, eneq-peh cew-espāēhkat.
now then.PRED-time EPIS-go.upward.3CONJ
'Now, then he must have risen up.' (RS 166)

b. Mānīh kēs-akuaqtaw eneh māēc-otācekwan.
Marie CP-get.out.3 that.INAN big-vehicle
'Marie climbed out of the bus.' (MF, MK 10/7/13)

c. Nahāw, katāēs akuaqtah;
now.then it's.time get.out.2SG.IMP
'Now then, get out of the water; . . . ' (ODD 013)

With verbs like these, a Ground is implied, although in some cases we find a conventional implicature of a specific Ground. In (26b), for example, the verb means 'get out (of something)' where the source is a bus, but as we see in (26c), when no other Ground is specified, it is generally used to mean 'get out of water'.

A second large set of verbs codes a nonspecified Ground, as in (27):

(27) *Nonspecified Ground*

a. Enewen āhpakesit enoh māēmāēw,
then.QUOT throw.self.there.3CONJ that.AN woodpecker
'Woodpecker threw himself onto it,' (MGV 015)

b. ahkāēhko*h* taeh enewen 's pēhcepetāēk.
kettle.LOC and there.PRED AOR fall.into.3CONJ
'. . . and it fell down into the kettle.' (MGV 104)

In many such cases, the Ground is supplied by context, so, for example, in (27a) we know that Woodpecker threw himself onto a tree because the previous line in the story is "Inside the lodge there stood a tree." However, in (27b) the Ground is made explicit by the addition of a locative noun ('kettle') indicating where the rice in question fell.

Finally, a third set incorporates a specific Ground to which some Figure is related, as in (28):

(28) *Specific Ground*

a. Māciah; awēh-pīhtikaenon!
go.away.2SG.IMP go.to-go.into.house.2SG.IMP
'Go; go enter that place!' (ODD 018)

b. Espāēt taeh wenah yōwen nesek otōneh
in.daytime and she this.INAN.PRED only 3.mouth.LOC

's kew-sākepit enoh metāēmoh.
AOR HAB-stick.out.of.water.3CONJ that.AN woman
'During the day she would lie with just her mouth above water.' (ODD 011)

c. *Eneq enoh wīhkaeh māēnawac 's
then.PRED that.AN sweet.flag a.little AOR

kew-akuanāēhtah otōn.
HAB.take.into.mouth.3CONJ 3.mouth
Intended: 'Then some of the sweet flag is taken into the mouth.' (MF 10/7/13)

In (28a) the verb contains the medial *-ik-* 'house', and in (28b) the verb contains the medial *-aepy-* 'water, liquid'. In both cases these medials function as an explicit Ground. We did not find any textual examples in which the Ground was repeated separately in the sentence, and our consultants indicated that it could not be, as (28c) shows.[8]

Syntax

At this point, we turn to some observations about the syntax of location and direction in Menominee.

Prepositions

As mentioned before, following Oxford (2007, 2008, 2011, 2014) and LeSourd (2014), we argue that a subset of what Bloomfield considered particles are actually prepositions. We begin by providing evidence for this claim, and then go on to compare some of the behavior of Menominee prepositions with those described by Oxford and LeSourd.

As (29) below demonstrates, we find that PPs can be conjoined, indicating that the P and associated NP form a constituent:

(29)

Eneq	's	awēh-kiasituaq	[**pīhtik**	**newēkiam**]	mesek
there.PRED	AOR	go.to-hide.3PL.CONJ	inside	1.house	and

[**anāmiah**	**netūtācekwaneh**].
under	1.car.LOC

'They're hiding inside my house and under my car.' (MF 8/29/13)

This is a standard test for constituency from which we can conclude that each conjunct forms a phrase.

Further evidence that such expressions form a constituent comes from the placement of *taeh* 'and' in (30):

(30)

cēk	**nepēhsaehseh**	taeh	enewen	enem-enāqsew.
near	lake.LOC	and	then.QUOT	on.the.way-carry.load.of.game.thus.3

'... to the edge of the lake he went with his load.' (SED2 015)

Taeh is a second-position clitic that can either be positioned after the first word or after the first constituent. The fact that it occurs after *cēk nepēhsaehseh* 'near the lake' in this example indicates that *cēk nepēhsaehseh* forms a constituent.

We turn next to establishing that the lexical category of words such as *pīhtik*, *anāmiah*, and *cēk* is in fact PREPOSITION. First, we note that these words co-occur with NPs. We have seen this in a number of previous examples, and we see it again in (31):

(31)

Emeq	's	īt	[**akāmiah**	[yōm
over.there.PRED	AOR	be.in.the.place.3CONJ	over.across	this.INAN

māēc-kaeqcekam]],
big-sea

'He's over there, across the great sea,' (BOM 023)

Obviously, mere co-occurrence is not enough to make this case. LeSourd (2014) approaches the question for Maliseet-Passamaquoddy by making a variety of arguments to show that the words in question function as the head of their phrase. These arguments have varying success for the Menominee data.

First, LeSourd notes that these forms govern the case of the associated noun. In Maliseet-Passamaquoddy, different prepositions behave differently: "some are used optionally or regularly with a nonlocative NP" (LeSourd 2014:19–20). He argues that this shows that the preposition governs the case of the associated NP, noting that "government of the form of a dependent is commonly cited as a defining property of heads (Zwicky 1985:7–8)" (LeSourd 2014:20).

The evidence is not as clear in Menominee, unfortunately. All of the prepositions that we have been able to test take the locative suffix optionally.[9] Because bare nouns and locative nouns can function as locatives without a preposition, we cannot argue that the locative function is due to the presence of the preposition in these phrases.

Second, LeSourd points out that plural marking and locative marking do not co-occur on NPs in Maliseet-Passamaquoddy. We see the same incompatibility in Menominee:

(32)

Māwanew	eneq	's	ītuaq	pīhtik	wēkiaman(*eh).
all	there.PRED	AOR	be.in.the.place.3PL.CONJ	inside	house.PL(*LOC)

'They're all inside their houses.' (MF 9/16/13)

Having established that such strings are phrases, LeSourd argues that the preposition is the only candidate for assigning a locative feature to the phrase in the absence of the locative suffix. As he says, "The element in a phrase that characterizes the phrase as a whole is generally taken to be the head (Zwicky 1985:2)" (LeSourd 2014:20).

Additional similarities between the prepositions that Oxford and LeSourd describe and the Menominee prepositions include the following: first, they can appear postpositionally as well as prepositionally, as we see in (33):

(33) a.

enewen	[watūhsiah	**wahkēc**]	's	aqnacen.
then.QUOT	ember.LOC	on	AOR	place.3>3'.CONJ

'. . . then he placed it over the embers.' (SR2 352)

b.

[Omāēqtekwan	**kekēh**]	pōsewen,
bow	with	board.vessel.3QUOT

'With his bow, he got in the basket,' (RS 370)

Second, they have intransitive as well as transitive uses, as shown in (34):

(34) a.

Eneq	**[kaeqceh]**	's	wēket.
there.PRED	near	AOR	live.3CONJ

'He lives close.' (TZ 11/21/03)

b.

[Cēk]	aqtoh.
next.to	put.2SG>0.IMP

'Put it next to it.' (LS 5/31/07)

Finally, they may occur discontinuously, as (35a, b) demonstrate:

(35) a.

[Ākaw]	eneq	's	wēket	[eneh	mīhekaneh].
across	there.PRED	AOR	live.3CONJ	that.INAN	road.LOC

'She lives in a house on the other side of the road.' (LT 9/16/13)

b.

[nāweyaw]	's	āwek	[yōm	nepēw],
in.center.of	AOR	be.3CONJ	this.INAN	water

yōq	's	kēs-kaehtāqtat	naeqnemāw,
here.PRED	AOR	CP-move.into.enclosing.place.3CONJ	tobacco

'. . . and then in the very center of the water the tobacco went under,' (NRS 047)

In all of the cases of discontinuous PPs that we have found, the preposition is moved to a position before the verb (parallel to the position of a demonstrative or quantifier in discontinuous NPs in Menominee and other Algonquian languages; cf. Dahlstrom 1987; Reinholtz 1999; LeSourd 2006; and others).

Position and Co-occurrence of Locative and Directional Elements

Locative and directional elements are found both pre- and postverbally in Menominee. The examples in (36) illustrate several postverbal locatives:

(36) a.

Eneq	's	nīmaqtaek	**eneh**	**masēnahekan(*eh*).**
there.PRED	AOR	sit.on.top.of.something.3CONJ	that.INAN	book(LOC)

'It's sitting on top of the book.' (MK 2/17/13, 8/29/13)

b. Eneq 's wēket **enes** **āsaw** **mīhekan*eh*.**
there.PRED AOR live.3CONJ there across road.LOC
'She lives in a house on the other side of the road.' (MF 9/16/13)

In (36a) the locative NP can be expressed postverbally (either with or without the locative suffix), and in (36b) we find a combination of a locative demonstrative and a prepositional phrase, which in turn contains a noun bearing the locative suffix.

As in other Algonquian languages (e.g., Meskwaki; Dahlstrom 2004), the structure of the Menominee clause provides preverbal positions for topic and focus (see Johnson et al. 2015).[10] Examples of preverbal locatives are provided in (37):

(37) a. **Anāmiah** **nepīh*eh*** aw-esīw.
under water.LOC IRR-go.there.3
'It will go down under the water.' (NRS 034)

b. **Ayētoh** **sīpiahsaeh** **ohtākam** kenaw-nānīsimuaw.
at.both.sides brook close.by.water 2.IRR-be.two.LCL.PL.RED
'You'll go in pairs on both sides of the brook.' (PHK 062)

Both (37a) and (b) contain preverbal prepositional phrases. In (37a) the noun carries the locative suffix, while (37b) contains a bare noun, as well as an added particle.

Locative particles and demonstratives can also appear in the preverb space; that is, between preverbs (as in (38a)) or between a preverb and the verb (as in (38b)):

(38) a. Hāw, netāwac-**omanakah**-eses-waskēm.
now 1.before-over.there-towards.there-go.back.LCL
'Now, I have to go back to the other place.' (RS 067)

b. Māēk-**enes**-wāēpāpīhahkuaq.
DUR-there-swing.on.string.3PL.CONJ
'They're swinging it around on a string there.' (RS 155)

Finally, we note that locative elements other than PPs are sometimes expressed discontinuously, as in (39):

(39) a. Enewen-peh **enes** āēqnacen **cēkapah.**
then.QUOT-time there place.3>3′CONJ.IC by.the.wall
'He laid them down by the wall.' (MGV 53)

b. **Enes** new kenah ap awēh-onāpenon **atūhpwan*eh*!**
there CTR you too go.and-sit.down.2SG.IMP table.LOC
'You go there, too, and sit at the table!' (ODD 020)

In (39a), *enes* 'there' is separated from *cēkapah* 'by the wall', while in (39b) it is separated from *atūhpwaneh* 'at the table'.

Conclusion

This paper has shown the extensive set of strategies for expressing location and direction in Menominee, including the use of nouns (which can be zero-marked or marked with a locative suffix), prepositions, particles, locative demonstratives, preverbs, and verbs. We have argued for the existence of prepositions in Menominee, and, following Oxford and LeSourd, we have shown that the preposition is the head of its phrase and that the sequence P+NP functions as a constituent.

A striking fact about many of the examples found throughout this paper is that often it is not a single element that encodes the location of some Figure with respect to the Ground, but rather that the expression of location is distributed across multiple elements in the sentence, with all of them working together to produce the end result.

Appendix

Abbreviations for stories from Bloomfield (1928)

BB = Buying a Buggy
BLS = Bill's Life Story
BM = Bead Man
BOM = Birth of Maeqnapos
DOS = Death of a Spy
LNX = Lynx Tries to Kill a Stag
MGV = Maeqnapos Goes A-Visiting
NRS = Nehtsiwihtuk Receives a Sign from the Spring God
ODD = Origin of the Dream Dance
PA = The Prickly Ash
PHK = Pehkutsian

RS = Red Swan
SED = The Shut-eye Dancers
SED2 = The Shut-eye Dancers (version 2)
SF = Sweet Flag
SR2 = The Origin of the Spirit Rock (version 2)
SWR = Sweet Root
TAT = Tales of Ancient Times

NOTES

1. Abbreviations: 1, 2, 3 = first, second, third person; 3′ = third-person obviative; 0 = third-person inanimate; AI = animate intransitive; AN = animate; AOR = aorist; CONJ = conjunct order; CP = completive; CTR = contrast; DUR = durative; EPIS = epistemic; HAB = habitual; IC = initial change; II = inanimate intransitive; IMP = imperative; INCL = inclusive; INAN = inanimate; INV = inverse; IRR = irrealis; LCL = local; LOC = locative; NEG = negative; OBV = obviative; PL = plural; PASS = passive; PRED = predicative; QUOT = quotative; RED = reduplicated; SG = singular; TA = transitive animate; TI = transitive inanimate. Menominee examples make use of the practical orthography, in which ⟨q⟩ represents the glottal stop, ⟨c⟩ represents either [ts] or [č], and vowel length is marked by a macron. We also use Bloomfield's morphophoneme /E/, which surfaces as [e] in most cases, but fuses with other vowels in particular ways. Sources of data and their abbreviations are listed in the appendix.
2. Bloomfield (1962:117) calls this the "local form" of the noun.
3. When a word ends in /Cw/, the locative suffix *-Eh* surfaces as [oh].
4. Some of the particles of this class are ambiguous between a location and a direction reading (for example, *nuakow* 'downstream' could be either a place or a direction).
5. Oxford gives parallel translations for forms in Innu-aimun and says that they "denote a more tightly bounded location" (2010:2).
6. In the lists in (17) and (18) only the relevant meanings are noted. "[RR]" indicates that the preverb in question is a relative root preverb.
7. The preverb definitions are compiled from Bloomfield (1962, 1975) and our fieldwork.
8. These sentences were difficult to elicit, and we note in passing that the sentence that was produced and then rejected (28c) contains an animacy mismatch.
9. As was indicated in (6), modern-day speakers are not familiar with a number of the forms that we have determined to be used as prepositions in Bloomfield's texts, so we are not able to test them all.
10. We leave open the discourse status of the preverbal elements in the examples.

REFERENCES

Bloomfield, Leonard. 1928. *Menomini Texts.* Publications of the American Ethnological Society 12, New York.

———. 1962. *The Menomini Language.* Edited by Charles F. Hockett. New Haven, CT: Yale University Press.

———. 1975. *Menominee Lexicon.* Edited by Charles F. Hockett. Milwaukee Public Museum Publications in Anthropology and History 3.

Dahlstrom, Amy. 1987. Discontinuous constituents in Fox. In *Native American Languages and Grammatical Typology*, edited by Paul D. Kroeber and Robert E. Moore, 53–73. Bloomington: Indiana University Linguistics Club.

———. 2004. External and internal topics in Meskwaki. Paper read at the Thirty-Sixth Algonquian Conference, Madison, WI.

Johnson, Meredith, Monica Macaulay, Bryan Rosen, and Rachel Wang. 2015. A survey of word order in Menominee. In *Papers of the Forty-Third Algonquian Conference*, edited by Monica Macaulay and J. Randolph Valentine, 154–178. Albany, NY: SUNY Press.

LeSourd, Philip S. 2006. Problems for the pronominal argument hypothesis in Maliseet-Passamaquoddy. *Language* 82:486–514.

———. 2014. Prepositional phrases in Maliseet-Passamaquoddy. *International Journal of American Linguistics* 80:209–240.

Oxford, Will. 2007. Towards a grammar of Innu-aimun particles. MA thesis, Memorial University of Newfoundland.

———. 2008. Towards a grammar of Innu-aimun particles. In *Papers of the Fortieth Algonquian Conference*, edited by Karl S. Hele and Regna Darnell, 531–556. London: University of Western Ontario.

———. 2011. The syntax of Innu-aimun locatives. In *University of British Columbia Working Papers in Linguistics 31: The Proceedings of WSCLA* 16:135–50. Vancouver: University of British Columbia. http://www.linguistics.ubc.ca/wscla/16.

———. 2014. A survey of locative expressions in Innu-aimun. In *Papers of the Forty-Second Algonquian Conference*, edited by J. Randolph Valentine and Monica Macaulay, 181–201. Albany, NY: SUNY Press.

Reinholtz, Charlotte. 1999. On the characterization of discontinuous constituents. *International Journal of American Linguistics* 65:201–227.

Talmy, Leonard. 1985. Lexicalization patterns: Semantic structure in lexical forms. In *Language Typology and Syntactic Description*, vol. 3, edited by Timothy Shopen, 57–149. Cambridge: Cambridge University Press.

Zwicky, Arnold. 1985. Heads. *Journal of Linguistics* 21:1–29.

Rethinking Historical Trauma

Gerald P. McKinley

Toward the end of the Truth and Reconciliation Commission on Indian Residential Schools in Canada, Ronald Niezen released his book reviewing the hearings. In it he argues, in part, how the construct of the hearings established the message that the commission was able to put forward (Niezen 2013). In essence, he was responding to the process through which the enunciatory context shapes future understanding of events. Similarly, the construct of historical trauma discourse shapes future understandings of events in the lives of Indigenous people by shaping the narratives of the effect of the event on the community and by circumscribing them within a specific clinical setting. Often, historical trauma discourse crosses generations, determining the response that each generation is able to give. In this paper I reconsider historical trauma discourse from the perspective of narrative healing projects produced by three Indigenous public intellectuals. Each work is a contemporary retelling or reimagining of a windigo narrative used to examine how narrative can be used in relationship with trauma to alter discourse on Indigenous health in a positive way. Each allows a teller to de-pathologize events from the community he or she represents. I do so by defining historical trauma and the concept of the public intellectual. Using a theoretical position derived from

Indigenous and Western scholars, I examine three modern windigo narratives that can be used to reshape historical trauma discourse toward effective healing.

The historical trauma/soul wound discourse is defined by Joseph P. Gone as a construct calling attention to the "complex, collective, cumulate, and intergenerational" effects that past and ongoing colonial policies have on the psychosocial lives of aboriginal peoples (Gone 2013:683). In this construct, past traumatic events affect individuals and communities across generations. The discourse originates from Eduardo Duran, Bonnie Duran, and Maria Yellow Horse Brave Heart-Jordan and their particular clinical readings and writings on Indigenous trauma and social issues. Their individual and collective work and its movement into the field of Indigenous literary scholarship have become well known over the past twenty years.

Originating from Brave Heart-Jordan's dissertation at Smith College School of Social Work in 1995, historical trauma developed out of her research into what she called "historical unresolved grief" among the Lakota (Brave Heart-Jordan 1995:5). It was developed by Brave Heart-Jordan to "indicate that Lakota unsettled bereavement is prominent, significant, and results from generations of devastating losses that have been disenfranchised through the prohibition of indigenous ceremonies as well as through the larger society's denial of the magnitude of genocide against American Indians" (Brave Heart-Jordan 1995:5). A significant aspect of Brave Heart-Jordan's historical unresolved grief is her term "historical trauma," "a term specifically developed . . . [that] is synonymous with cumulative trauma but emphasizes that the trauma is multi-generational and is not limited to life span" (Brave Heart-Jordan 1995:6). Cumulative trauma is defined as "collective and compounding emotional and psychic wounding over time, both over the life span and across generations" (Brave Heart-Jordan 1995:6).

Throughout this paper I explore the role of public intellectuals in the shaping of discourse and thus an enunciatory context that shapes future discourse. I define the public intellectual, using Antonio Gramsci (2003) and Edward Said (1994), as a public figure who has assumed the authority to speak for a community without assuming an elected or official position. The public intellectual voices the silent narratives of the marginalized populations of society. An additional qualification of the public intellectual is that he or she may not be looking to speak for a community, but his or her voice has been adopted as the community's voice. For example, in an interview with Daniel David Moses, he responded to the topic of being a public intellectual with "I don't remember an election" (Daniel David Moses, personal communication, 2011). However, the election to position is irrelevant, as

Said points out. As soon as their work enters public discourse they become public intellectuals (Said 1994), and their works are the representational access point to their community for many non-Indigenous people across Canada.

Narrative Case Studies in Historical Trauma

The first case study reviewed is a comic book that originated with the Healthy Aboriginal Network in British Columbia. The network is using comics such as *Darkness Calls* by Steve Kaweetin Sanderson (2010) from James Smith Cree Nation to create discussion and awareness of social issues facing Indigenous youth. *Darkness Calls* uses the story of the Witigo from Sanderson's Cree narrative traditions to examine youth suicide. In the narrative, Kyle, the young boy facing suicide, is hunted by a Witigo in the woods around his community. The Witigo is using Kyle's sadness, driven by the circumscriptive narratives that tell Kyle of his meaningless future, to isolate and consume him. *Darkness Calls* is similar in structure to the Weasel and Witigo narratives of the Cree (Brightman 2007). In these stories it is Weasel who kills the powerful Witigo when Wīsahkīcāhk is facing certain death. In Sanderson's telling, Kyle takes on the Weasel role, represented by his perceived powerlessness, while his "grandfather" takes Wīsahkīcāhk roles. Kyle's grandfather fulfills two distinct roles in Cree culture: he is Kyle's mother's father's brother and therefore a grandfather in an extended kinship structure; and he is an Other-Than-Human-Being who is alive in the Witigo narrative that Kyle imagines, moving through multiple forms of consciousness with Kyle in an ongoing relationship between the Cree and their Other-Than-Human Being relations.

In *Darkness Calls*, Sanderson uses the Witigo as a means of understanding and coming to terms with the topic of youth suicide. Rather than relying on a clinical report, Sanderson creates a narrative that speaks from his community of James Smith Cree Nation in northern Saskatchewan. The legacy of colonialism facing Kyle and his peers is not pathologized. Instead, it is mediated in terms familiar to Sanderson's own community. Sanderson represents lack of community control of education, internalized community violence, and addiction issues as the hunting tools of the Witigo. Rather than focusing on an abstract concept of a shared history of trauma, *Darkness Calls* brings the causes of Kyle's problems into the community in a very real form. Healing for Kyle and his community takes place when Kyle realizes that there is a Cree way of dealing with the social problems within his community: *nêhiyâwiwin* (Cree-ness), where the knowledge is "held in words and actions" in the face of colonial, acculturating forces (McLeod 2007:13).

The second narrative is a film by Anishinaabek poet and filmmaker Armand Garnet Ruffo. *A Windigo Tale* is an adaptation of Ruffo's play of the same name told as a narrated event of a narrative event (Bauman 1986). A *Windigo Tale* tells an intergenerational story of the long-term effects of residential school on one family and its community. The narrated event is told to Curtis by Uncle Harold as they work through some of Curtis's social problems, including gang membership and criminal activity. Uncle Harold narrates the events of the reunion of Lily with her mother, Doris, after the death of Lily's abusive stepfather. The stepfather, "a good Catholic," is the Windigo in the film. His past includes violence against Doris and sexual and physical abuse of Lily, who was adopted out of the community as a result. Lily was fathered by a priest while Doris was in a residential school. Ruffo's film demonstrates his intention to heal with the adaptation of traditional narratives by situating the narrative of Lily and Doris within the narrative of Curtis and Uncle Harold and basing them all within a Windigo narrative. Doris and Lily battle the power of the Windigo together in an effort to free themselves from their history. In the end they are able to overpower the Windigo using Anishinaabek means, rather than the Catholic values Doris adopted at residential school. The isolation of the two comes to an end with the death of the Windigo.

The third example comes from the novel *As Long as the Rivers Flow* by James Bartleman (2011). Bartleman has created a composite world and history of Cree and Anishinaabek people from northern Ontario in this text. The windigo appears in dreams and stories where Bartleman makes a metaphoric connection to abusive residential school workers and colonial government policy. The story follows Martha and her family in a narrative that traces the effects of residential school and the Sixties Scoop on several generations of her family and their community. Bartleman's work contains a large ethnographic quality derived from his travels into the communities that he writes about. Because of this, he has created a narrative world that is part fictional and part personal testimony. With *As Long as the Rivers Flow*, Bartleman has narrated both the intergenerational damage and the healing potential contained in the history of the community.

The history of treaties, residential school, community realignment in the 1950s, and the Sixties Scoop serves as a metaphor of movement away from an Indigenous Self. This in turn leads to isolation of the individual, dependency on alcohol and drugs, internalized violence, and general community breakdown. Bartleman's narrative parallels the work of A. Irving Hallowell, who identified acculturation stresses with increasing social problems among Anishinaabek people in the 1930s and 1940s (Hallowell 1955). The intergenerational healing in this work starts with Martha and her connection with the Indigenous Self that the residential school removed from her. The final healing for the community begins with a healing circle in which the abusive priest is brought to the community to be confronted by his victims.

In short, these three examples present the following conditions of possibility for social breakdown: isolation of the individual; damaged or circumscribed future prospects; intergenerational, systemic sexual and/or physical violence and abuse; drug and alcohol abuse; residential school experience and colonial interference with the community; and loss of parenting skills as a result of historical experiences in the community. A historical trauma approach in the style of Brave Heart-Jordan would link all of these conditions to the unresolved trauma and grief of the colonial history of Indigenous people (Brave Heart-Jordan 1995:3). However, I argue that by engaging with the narratives it is possible to, and important to, focus on the healing potential of each story and potentially change future versions. Arguably, a community-based narrative allows for a revoicing of community experiences and a reshaping of community expectations of themselves. Given the narrative ontology of Anishinaabek and Cree peoples, community-based narratives do offer a great deal of potential in the healing process.

Drawing on the role of the simulacra, or simulations, in the creation of "Truth," these cultural narratives can provide a clue into the worldview and concepts of social issues held by the community. According to Gilles Deleuze, simulacra can take two forms. The first is the transformative power of the false to create negative representations (Deleuze 1983:48–49). This can be explained as the many negative stereotypes Indigenous youth face each and every day that originate outside of their community. The second form, and the one that is most useful here, is the positive power of transformation. The works of the Indigenous public intellectuals guide the positive simulation of a contemporary Indigenous identity toward a positive representation. The public intellectual often returns complexity to a discourse that has been simplified to fit clinical models such as Brave Heart-Jordan's. The issues public intellectuals deal with in the works mentioned above share the same general themes that exist in historical trauma discourse. However, these works are meant to speak to a community and demonstrate resilience rather than reflect only the pain caused by trauma.

The overall effect is what we might call a cumulative effect where "new objects take shape through a confrontation between individual brains and the world" (Urban 2001:271). Within any collective representation of the community there will almost always be an intergenerational aspect. As the community adopts the narratives of the events into themselves, the trauma of the whole becomes represented in the individual as part of the whole.

Cross-Genre Discourse and the Problematics of Historical Trauma

The preceding case studies represent a small variety of genres that deal with the ongoing effects of colonization on the health of aboriginal people. Each contains the motifs of trauma and healing that can be placed in a theoretical conversation across genres. In his work on the origin of genres, Tzvetan Todorov discusses the active role of perception in the construction of knowledge, warning readers to pay attention to "the view point chosen by the observer [that] reconfigures and redefines his object" (Todorov 1990:16). Todorov argues that because the text has something to say and that saying is contained within an "enunciatory context," it should be considered as discourse articulated by a speaking/writing subject (Todorov 1990:16, 20–21). The enunciatory context is contained by the terms of expression of the "class of text" wherein the codification of discursive properties takes place, which often circumscribes potential meanings and forms of the text (Todorov 1990:17–18). Put another way, the written text can be defined as discourse. That discourse, however, is contained by certain standards of the genre; the constraints of the genre act as a defining measure for the object related by the subject. Therefore, any discussion of the construct of historical trauma discourse must pay attention to the individual genres wherein we contact the construct. Additionally, as the discourse moves from context to context, the meaning contained within the text remains fluid. This process enables the windigo narratives to act as a healing form because they alter the context within which traumatic events are described.

Metis academic Jo-Ann Episkenew has made the concepts of "postcolonial traumatic stress disorder" and "postcolonial traumatic stress response" central to her work in the relationship between literature and healing (Episkenew 2009). Episkenew's starting point is Eduardo Duran and Bonnie Duran and their construct "soul wound," where Duran and Duran's concept is based upon their reflection on Eduardo Duran's work in central California. During his fieldwork, Duran noticed a domination of health discourses by topics of "injustice, the conquest, the dishonored treaties" (Duran and Duran 1995:24). Basing their theory upon Jungian analysis, Duran and Duran isolated the signifiers of injustice, conquest, and dishonored treaties from their discursive setting and converted them into the symbolic form of the soul wound.

Mental images such as the soul wound reflect a psychoanalytic interest in symbolic interpretation over event- or neurological-specific analysis found in other forms of psychiatry and psychology. The image of the soul wound also symbolically reflects a damaged Self, a corruption of the nature of being Indigenous. Their argument is that the soul wound, as historical context rather than construct, needs to be understood by therapeutic services workers working with Indigenous peoples. Episkenew's interest in Duran and Duran leads her to literary sources of analysis: Metis writer and playwright Maria Campbell; postmodernist Anishinaabek Gerald Vizenor; and Kuna/Rappahannock playwright Monique Mojica (Episkenew 2009:9). However, Episkenew moves away from Duran and Duran's Jungian clinical methods toward an effective trope-based understanding of the terms "postcolonial traumatic stress disorder" and "postcolonial traumatic stress response."

The similar concept of "blood memory" has been commonly used by Indigenous authors and academics for some time (Allen 1992; Momaday 1976; Vizenor 1991; Weaver 1997). However, this term is associated with discourse on identity rather than clinical treatments of mental disorders. On this topic, Jace Weaver states that "there are, alas, no stories carried in the blood" (Weaver 1997:7). Citing the example of the Trail of Tears, Weaver notes that its effect on Cherokee people is not "some genetic determinism." Instead, the Trail of Tears is important because "heritage and identity are passed down through story from generation to generation" (Weaver 1997:7). He supports this thesis with a quote from Ngugi wa Thiong'o's *Decolonising the Mind*: "culture does not just reflect the world in images but actually, through those very images, conditions a child to see the world in a certain way" (Ngugi 1986:17). Accordingly, Cree scholar Neal McLeod reflects on cultural narratives as the passing of history. McLeod argues that Cree identity (*nêhiyâwiwin*) is formed from the narratives of the history of the community (McLeod 2007:13).

Despite historical trauma/soul wound discourse's enunciatory context, Episkenew transferred it to a discursive stream that can be used to help define contemporary literary representations of Indigenous social problems and healing projects (Episkenew 2009). For Episkenew, I argue, historical trauma shares similar attributes to blood memory in that they offer tropes for understanding narrative representations of trauma and healing. Historical trauma, as blood memory, is a narrative motif that is present in the works of many Indigenous authors and playwrights (see the works of Alexie 1996; Boyden 2001, 2005, 2008; Highway 1988, 1989, 1998, 2003, 2005; King 1994, 1999, 2003; Maracle 1993; Momaday 1966, 1969, 1976, 1997; Moses 1991, 1998, 2000; Ruffo 2010; and Silko 1977, for example).

Episkenew focuses on post-traumatic stress response (PTSR) as defined by Terry Mitchell and Dawn Maracle (Mitchell and Maracle 2005), rather than post-traumatic stress disorder (PTSD), within the discourse of historical trauma because PTSR reconfirms the historical collective aspects of the discourse. PTSD, by its nature, is an individual responsive condition (DSM-IV) where the symptoms are a response to a trauma. Considering that Mitchell and Maracle were attempting to remove the clinical application of the disorder from Indigenous people and drawing on Joseph P. Gone and Laurence Kirmayer, I suggest that the question of historical trauma and narrative responses must be approached locally, as each Indigenous culture will have its own social and cultural methods for defining and resolving trauma (Gone and Kirmayer 2010). Additionally, the application of a theory of collective, community-based, historical narrative on the causation of social problems as a result of historical trauma should be assumed to be part of a healing process.

Narrative Texts and Trauma

McLeod provides a guide on how to interpret the narratives as an ongoing healing relationship with a community as "echoes" of past events (McLeod 2007). Additionally, Omushkego Elder Louis Bird advises that narratives are a powerful means for healing community from contemporary traumas when their beliefs are "not based simply on personal reaction to fear and pain" (Bird 2007:xxi). In essence, traditional narratives used collectively are being recontextualized as a method for understanding contemporary events and their effect on Indigenous people. If we are to think about the narratives as positive actions, then we should consider Mattingly and Garro's "as narratives are constructed, narratives construct," so that the tone of the narrative can affect the subject either positively with healing or negatively with trauma, which in turn shapes the enunciatory context (Mattingly and Garro 2000). Historical trauma narratives, if left as reports of damage, can produce a negative result. However, healing narratives take the same topics and produce healing.

To this end, the traumatic motifs present in the traditional narratives have been adopted and adapted by contemporary Indigenous public intellectuals in order to deal with the traumatic events discussed in Duran and Duran, Brave Heart-Jordan, and many others in a literary narrative rather than clinical narrative form. When we think about historical traumas in terms of narrative representation, it is useful to consider that we, like the clinical workers, are not discussing the events in and of themselves. What we are discussing is a representation of the event, a symbol in discursive form. My argument is that these symbols are currently being used by Indigenous public intellectuals as part of an identity and cultural healing process that is taking place. For example, in a talk at the University of Western Ontario Bartleman commented that of the approximately 2,000 stories submitted by Indigenous youth for the James Bartleman Aboriginal Creative Writing award, 90 percent made reference to events that could easily be considered traumatic. These references included alienation from the community, drug and alcohol abuse by parents and peers, violence, and poverty (Bartleman 2012).

I believe that there is value in a concept of historical trauma when it is used to define healing. I believe that it is to be found in literary representations rather than in a clinical setting. Ruffo argues that his application of PTSD is combined with traditional oral sources "to tackle contemporary issues and create provocative theatre (as well as other forms of cultural expression)" as a community healing project (Ruffo 2005:178).

The Modern *Wiindigo*

The concept of the Modern *Wiindigo* can be traced to Anishinaabek writer Basil Johnston in his work *The Manitous: The Spiritual World of the Ojibway*. In it, Johnston suggests that the windigo is still active as an Other-Than-Human-Being, still the Being and the action consuming the Anishinaabek (Johnston 1999:235). The Modern *Wiindigo* hunts with the tools of colonialism and capitalism. The new victim of the Modern *Wiindigo* is isolated as before, but this time narratives of historical traumas are central to the isolation. The conversion of windigo into the Modern *Wiindigo* is not without its cross-genre, hermeneutic problems. When discussing the move, we must consider the problem of interpreting a traditional symbol away from its original context.

What is interesting with a narrative approach is how public intellectuals are using their understanding of their own and their community's experiences to define themselves and the community, and how that definition is given voice in their work. In essence, they are attempting to connect the traditional narratives with a contemporary setting, reinscribing a connotational value on the symbols of the narratives as a means of breaking down the metanarratives of "Indian." Drawing a theoretical connection with Gilles Deleuze and Felix Guattari, I adopt the theory of becoming (Deleuze and Guattari 2007). This theory works very well with anthropological approaches to culture that are focused on process rather than fixedness. In short, we are all in a process of becoming something. Deleuze and Guattari argue that we are in a process of becoming minor to a representational major, which establishes a normative mode of seeing the world. To be major is to be the white, male, heterosexual, while, paradoxically, the white male heterosexual is also minor to its major. Using the series and structures of natural science, Deleuze and Guattari argue that we exist in an epistemological world of relations and hierarchies (Deleuze and Guattari 2007:234–235). Under these series and structure the major is to the white male what the white male is to the "Indian," where the "Indian" is a frozen representation of otherness. In Becoming-minoritarian, and I am using Becoming-Anishinaabek to define this process, the public intellectual works to voice an Indigenous epistemology. "Sick Indian" discourse is defined here as a metanarrative that maintains dominant images of aboriginal people as chronically alcoholic, as depressed, or in many other forms of malaise or victimization. This discourse is a tool of the major, while historical trauma can be viewed as a tool in the process of Becoming-healing, where all of the works presenting social issues facing the communities are collective and intergenerational. These issues can be classed either in terms of blood memory or as historical trauma, depending on how we construct the object of our analysis.

Conclusion

Anishinaabek and Cree people connect narratives to the Self and community at an ontological level that is not always present in Western discourse (Bird 2007; Hallowell 1955; McLeod 2007). Where benefits in approaches like historical trauma exist is in preparing the way for intergenre discourse. Medical science, narrative theory, political theory, and Indigenous worldviews, when brought together, provide an opportunity to leave a trace of one on the others. Where the strength lies is in looking for alternative means of approaching the histories of traumas experienced in Indigenous communities via narratives originating from the communities. Narratives provide an opportunity for communities to support resilience programs by providing youth with a narrative representation that positions youth within their own histories and traditions in a positive manner. Narratives used in this way can provide connection points and a process of becoming-healing. We also need to consider the negative outcome of allowing negative narratives to occupy a dominant position. Future research should consider investigating the relationship between Indigenous youth and narratives from the perspective of the youth if we are to be able to fully explore how youth are understanding their own histories.

REFERENCES

Alexie, Sherman. 1996. *Indian Killer*. New York: Atlantic Monthly Press.

Allen, Paula Gunn. 1992. *The Sacred Hoop: Recovering the Feminine in American Indian Traditions*. Boston: Beacon Press.

Bartleman, James. 2011. *As Long as the Rivers Flow*. Toronto: Alfred A. Knopf Canada.

———. 2012. Public lecture. University of Western Ontario.

Bauman, Richard. 1986. *Story, Performance, and Event: Contextual Studies of Oral Narrative*. Cambridge: Cambridge University Press.

Bird, Louis. 2007. *The Spirit Lives in the Mind: Omushkego Stories, Lives and Dreams*. Edited by Susan Elaine Gray. Montreal: McGill-Queen's University Press.

Boyden, Joseph. 2001. *Born with a Tooth*. Toronto: Cormorant Books.

———. 2005. *Three Day Road*. Toronto: Viking Canada.

———. 2008. *Through Black Spruce*. Toronto: Viking Canada.

Brave Heart-Jordan, Maria Yellow Horse. 1995. *The Return to the Sacred Path: Healing from Historical Trauma and Historical Unresolved Grief among the Lakota*. Northampton, MA: Smith College School for Social Work.

Brightman, Robert. 2007. *Ācaðōhkīwina and ācimōwina: Traditional Narratives of the Rock Cree Indians*. Regina, SK: Canadian Plains Research Center.

Deleuze, Gilles. 1983. Plato and the Simulacrum. *October* 27:45–56.

Deleuze, Gilles, and Félix Guattari. 2007 [1987]. *A Thousand Plateaus: Capitalism and Schizophrenia*. Translated by Brian Massumi. Minneapolis: University of Minnesota Press.

Duran, Eduardo, and Bonnie Duran. 1995. *Native American Postcolonial Psychology*. Albany, NY: SUNY Press.

Episkenew, Jo-Ann. 2009. *Taking Back Our Spirit: Indigenous Literature, Public Policy and*

Healing. Winnipeg: University of Manitoba Press.

Gone, Joseph P. 2013. Redressing First Nations historical trauma: Theorizing mechanisms for indigenous culture as mental health treatment. *Transcultural Psychiatry* 50:693–706.

Gone, Joseph P, and Laurence J. Kirmayer. 2010. On the wisdom of considering culture and context in psychopathology. In *Contemporary Directions in Psychopatholog: Scientific Foundations of the DSM-V and ICD-11*, edited by Theodore Millon, Robert F. Krueger, and Erik Simonsen, 72–96. New York: Guilford Press.

Gramsci, Antonio. 2003 [1971]. *Selections from the Prison Notebooks of Antonio Gramsci*. Translated by Quintin Hoare and Geoffrey Nowell Smith. New York: International Publishers.

Hallowell, A. Irving. 1955. *Culture and Experience*. Philadelphia: University of Pennsylvania Press.

Highway, Tomson. 1988. *The Rez Sisters*. Toronto: Fifth House Publishers.

———. 1989. *Dry Lips Oughta Move to Kapuskasing*. Toronto: Fifth House Publishers.

———. 1998. *Kiss of the Fur Queen*. Toronto: Anchor Canada.

———. 2003. *Rose*. Vancouver: Talon Books.

———. 2005. *Ernestine Shuswap Gets Her Trout*. Vancouver: Talon Books.

Johnston, Basil. 1999. *The Manitous: The Spiritual World of the Ojibway*. Toronto: Key Porter.

King, Thomas. 1994. *Green Grass, Running Water*. Toronto: Harper Perennial Canada.

———. 1999. *Truth and Bright Water*. Toronto: Perennial Canada.

———. 2003. *The Truth about Stories: A Native Narrative*. Toronto: House of Anansi Press.

Maracle, Lee. 1993. *Ravensong: A Novel*. Vancouver: Press Gang Publishers.

Mattingly, Cheryl, and Linda C. Garro, eds. 2000. *Narrative and the Cultural Construction of Illness and Healing*. Berkeley: University of California Press.

McLeod, Neal. 2007. *Cree Narrative Memory: From Treaties to Contemporary Times*. Saskatoon: Purich Publishing.

Mitchell, Terry L., and Dawn T. Maracle. 2005. Healing the generations: Post traumatic stress and the health status of aboriginal populations in Canada. *Journal of Aboriginal Health* 2:14–24.

Momaday, N. Scott. 1966. *House Made of Dawn*. New York: Perennial Library.

———. 1969. *The Way to Rainy Mountain*. Albuquerque: University of New Mexico Press.

———. 1976. *The Names: A Memoir*. New York: Harper and Row.

———. 1997. *The Man Made of Words: Essays, Stories, Passages*. New York: St. Martin's Griffin.

Moses, Daniel David. 1991. *Almighty Voice and His Wife: A Play*. Toronto: Playwrights Canada Press.

———. 1998. *Coyote City/City of Shadows: Two Plays*. Toronto: Imago Press.

———. 2000. *Brébeuf's Ghost*. Toronto: Exile Editions.

Ngugi wa Thiong'o. 1986. *Decolonising the Mind: The Politics of Language in African Literature*. London: James Currey.

Niezen, Ronald. 2013. *Truth and Indignation: Canada's Truth and Reconciliation Commission on Indian Residential Schools*. Toronto: University of Toronto Press.

Ruffo, Armand Garnet. 2005. A Windigo tale: Contemporizing and mythologizing the residential school experience. In *Aboriginal Drama and Theatre: Critical Perspectives on Canadian Theatre in English* 1, edited by Rob Appleford, 166–180. Toronto: Playwright Canada Press.

———. 2010. *A Windigo Tale*. Ottawa: Windigo Productions.

Said, Edward W. 1994. *Representations of the Intellectual*. New York: Vintage Books.

Sanderson, Steven Keewatin. 2010. *Darkness Calls*. Vancouver: The Healthy Aboriginal Network.

Silko, Leslie Marmon. 1977. *Ceremony*. New York: Penguin Books.

Todorov, Tzvetan. 1990. *Genres in Discourse*. Cambridge: Cambridge University Press.

Urban, Greg. 2001. *Metaculture: How Culture Moves through the World*. Minneapolis: University of Minnesota Press.

Vizenor, Gerald. 1991. *The Heirs of Columbus*. Hanover, NH: Wesleyan University Press.

Weaver, Jace. 1997. *That the People Might Live: Native American Literatures and Native American Community*. Oxford: Oxford University Press.

Cheyenne Connectives

Sarah E. Murray

Coordinating connectives in English, including *and* (conjunction), *but* (contrastive conjunction), and *or* (disjunction), are monomorphemic. In Cheyenne,[1] the basic form used for conjunction is *naa* (Leman 2011), as illustrated in (1).[2] Other connectives are complex, formed by combining an element with *naa*, such as 'and also' in (2), 'but' in (3), and 'or' in (4) (Fisher et al. 2006; Leman 2011).

(1) Annie é-ho'soo'e **naa** Shelly é-néméne.
Annie 3-dance CONN Shelly 3-sing
'Annie danced and Shelly sang.'

(2) **naa** **máto**
CONN also
'and also'

I would like to thank my Cheyenne consultants, and others I have talked with about Cheyenne, for their collaboration and discussion of Cheyenne data. I would also like to thank Wayne Leman, Monica Macaulay, William Starr, audiences at the Forty-Fifth Algonquian Conference in Ottawa, and two anonymous *PAC 45* reviewers for comments and helpful discussion. Any errors are my own.

(3) **naa** **oha**
conn cntr
'but'

(4) **naa** **mátȯ=héva**
CONN also=maybe
'or'

This paper provides a description of these and other Cheyenne connectives, with attention to both their form and meaning, as well as to whether they should be treated compositionally. The next section describes basic conjunctions with *naa* alone. The section after that looks at other kinds of conjunctions, including additive, as in (2), and contrastive, as in (3). Disjunctions, as in (4), are then described. The final section is a discussion of potential directions for a semantic analysis and the complications for a compositional, truth-functional analysis.

Basic Conjunctions with *naa*

Cheyenne *naa* can be used to conjoin sentences, as in (1) above and (5) below, as well as verbs, which can stand alone as sentences, as in (6) from "Mother's Day" by Elaine Strangeowl.

(5) Xaeh-o é-ohke-mȯšéškanȧhe-o'o méaneva **naa**
weasel-PL 3-HAB-be.brown-PL summer.OBL CONN
é-ohke-vó'omȧhe-o'o aénéva.
3-HAB-be.white-PL winter.OBL
'Weasels are brown in summer and they are white in winter.' (Leman 2011:204)

(6) É-vó'ome-vovó'háse **naa** é-mȯšéškanahe.
3-white-be.spotted CONN 3-be.brown
'It (a pinto) was white-spotted and (it was) brown.' (Leman 1980a:72)

The same connective can be used to conjoin nouns, as in (7) from "The Little Corn Man" by Mrs. Allen Flyingout, and with names, as in (8).[3]

(7) Hē'e **naa** hetane é-h-vée-hoono o'hé'e.
woman CONN man 3-PST-camp-NAR.3PL river.OBL
'A woman and a man were camping by a river.' (Leman 1980a:67)

(8) Annie **naa** Shelly é-ho'sóe-o'o.
Annie CONN Shelly 3-dance-PL
'Annie and Shelly danced.'

When three nouns are combined, *naa* may be repeated between each, as in (9) from "The Trek from Oklahoma" by Ralph Redfox. However, *naa* is not necessary between the first two nouns, as shown by (10) from "My Family Came Back" by Elaine Strangeowl.

(9) Ma'háhkėseh-o naa hetane-o'o naa kȧsováaheh-o
old.man-PL CONN man-PL CONN young.man-PL

mó-'-ȯhke-mé'etanó'tov-ȯ-he-vo-vó-he.
q+3-PST-HAB-REMEMBER-DIR-NEG$_{AN}$-3PL-OBV-INF
'The old men and the men and the young men remembered them, it's said.' (Leman 1980a:9)

(10) Naa oha hoháesto é-nėx-hováneehé-sesto ka'ėškóneh-o mé'ėševot-o
CONN CNTR many 3-CIS-be.gone-RPT.3PL child-PL baby-PL

naa mȧhtamȧháaheh-o.
CONN old.woman-PL
'But many had died, children, babies, and old women, it's said.' (Leman 1980a:10)

Another frequent use of *naa* is at the beginning of sentences, especially in texts, probably to signal discourse continuity. For example, the text "How Birney Got the Name *Oévemanȧhéno*" by Elaine Strangeowl starts off with (11).

(11) **Naa** tséheškéto ná-nȯhtsėstóv-o . . .
CONN mother 1-ask-DIR
'And my mother I asked her . . . ' (Leman 1980a:21)

In "The Whiteman and the Indian" by Leonard Yelloweagle (Leman 2011:206), nearly every sentence starts with *naa*.

Other Conjunctions

Other Cheyenne connectives are formed by combining an element with *naa*. One such connective is *naa máto* 'and also', which I call an additive conjunction. Alone, *máto* means 'also' (Fisher et al. 2006), as in (12) from "The Scalped Father" by Laura Rockroads.

(12)	Måhta'so	**máto**	nėhéstȧhévo	nȧ-htȧ-hósém-o.
	scalped.person	also	that.kind	1-FUT+TRL-tell.about-DIR

'A scalped man, also of that kind (of person), I'm gonna tell about him.' (Leman 1987:295)

Additional examples of *máto* alone are (13) from "Some Cheyenne Beliefs," also by Laura Rockroads, and the question in (14).

(13)	É-ohke-éve-e'h-e-o'o	**máto**	vékėséhe-mėstae-o'o.
	3-HAB-about-fear-PSV-3PL	also	bird-spook-3PL

'Owls are also feared.' (Leman 1987:214)

(14)	**Máto**	hénova'e?
	also	what

'What else?' (Fisher et al. 2006)

Naa can be combined with *máto*, as in (15) from "The Grasshopper and the Ant" by Mrs. Allen Flyingout.

(15)	Ná-to'se-ée-ho'soo'e	**naa**	**máto**	ná-to'se-néméne.
	1-PROS-around-dance	CONN	also	1-PROS-sing

'I'm going to dance around and also I'm going to sing.' (Leman 2011:207)

Like *naa* alone, *naa máto* can conjoin nouns as well as verbs, as in (16) from "The Man Who Turned into Buffalo Bones" by Laura Rockroads.

(16) Mó-'-ée-måhaét-ae-he-vó-he ho'neh-o **naa** **máto**
Q+3-PST-around-eat.all.of-INV-NEG$_{AN}$-OBV-INF wolf-OBV CONN also

ó'kȯhomeh-o.
coyote-OBV
'He must have gotten eaten by wolves and also coyotes.' (Leman 1987:271)

The combination of *naa* and *máto* seems straightforwardly compositional: in (15) and (16), *máto* seems to contribute the same additive semantics as when found alone, as in (12)–(14). Similarly, *naa* can be combined with *nėhe'še*, which alone means 'then', as in (17). Combined, *naa* and *nėhe'še* indicate temporal sequencing, as in (18) from "The Rolling Head" by Albert Hoffman.

(17) **Nėhe'še** nėhéóhe ná-x-hósė-háóéna.
then there 1-PST-again-pray
'Then there I prayed again.' (Leman 1987:157)

(18) É-s-tå-hóse-émȯhónė-hoo'o. **Naa** **nėhe'še**
3-PST-TRL-again-hunt-NAR.3SG CONN then

é-x-hóse-évå-ho'ėhné-hoo'o.
3-PST-again-back-arrive-NAR.3SG
'He again hunted, it's told. And then he again came back, it's told.'(Leman 1980a:3)

However, the contrastive conjunction *naa oha* is less clearly compositional.[4] Used alone, *oha* is similar to English *only* or *except*, as in (19)–(22). Example (21) is from "Turtle Moccasin" by Jeannette Howlingcrane, and (22) is from "The Drumming Owls" by Mrs. Allen Flyingout.

(19) **oha** na'ėstse
CNTR one
'only one' (Fisher et al. 2006)

(20) **Oha** ná-tsėhésenėstsé-táno.
CNTR 1-talk.Cheyenne-want
'I want to speak only Cheyenne.' (Fisher et al. 2006)

(21) **Oha** ma'enóhkevo'eha é-me'-mane.
CNTR Turtle.Moccasin 3-should-drink
'Only Turtle Moccasin should drink.' (Leman 1980a:59)

(22) Hová'éhe ná-ohkė-sáa-'e't-ō-he **oha** méstae-o'o
something 1-HAB-not-fear-IOAM-NEG$_{\text{AN}}$ CNTR owl-PL

tsé-he-onéhavo'é-ehe-se.
IND-have-drum-NOUN.STEM-CNJ.PART.3PL
'I am not afraid of anything except owls who have drums.' (Leman 2011:205)

Combined with *naa*, *oha* creates a contrastive conjunction with a meaning similar to English *but*, as in (23).

(23) Annie é-ho'soo'e **naa** **oha** Shelly é-sáa-ho'sóé-he.
Annie 3-dance CONN CNTR Shelly 3-not-dance-NEG$_{\text{AN}}$
'Annie danced but Shelly didn't dance.'

It is not obvious how the contribution of *oha* in (23) is related to the uses in (19)–(22): it does not mean something parallel to English *and only*, and (23) does not require that only Shelly did not dance. However, they are not completely unrelated—all instances of *oha* contribute some type of contrastive, adversative, or exclusive meaning, similar to English *only*.[5] For example, (21) indicates no one else should drink, and (23) requires that Shelly's not dancing is contrary to expectations. This sentence without *oha*, as in (24), is also grammatical, but does not contribute this contrast with prior expectations.

(24) Annie é-ho'soo'e **naa** Shelly é-sáa-ho'sóé-he.
Annie 3-dance CONN Shelly 3-not-dance-NEG$_{\text{AN}}$
'Annie danced but Shelly didn't dance.'

When the prior expectations are made explicit in the discourse, as in (25), *oha* is required: (26) is infelicitous.

(25)

Mȧhtohto	ka'ėškóneh-o	é-tȧ-hé-ho'sóe-o'o	**naa**	**oha**
ten	child-PL	3-TRL-PURP-dance-PL	CONN	CNTR

Annie	é-no'kė-ho'soo'e.
Annie	3-one-dance

'Ten children went to dance but Annie was the only one who danced.'

(26)

#Mȧhtohto	ka'ėškóneh-o	é-tȧ-hé-ho'sóe-o'o	**naa**
tenchild-PL	3-TRL-PURP-dance-PL	CONN	

Annie	é-no'kė-ho'soo'e.
Annie	3-one-dance

'Ten children went to dance and Annie was the only one who danced.'

In addition, cross-linguistically there are other examples of coordinators combining with contrast marking to form complex, contrastive conjunctions (Malchukov 2004).

Disjunctions

The disjunction *naa mátȯ=héva* combines *naa*, *máto*, and *héva*. As discussed above, *máto* alone is an additive particle, roughly equivalent to English *also*. Alone, *héva* has a wide variety of uses. It can mean 'maybe', 'even', or 'like', depending on the context, as in (27) from "The Cheyenne Sacred Way of Thinking" by Laura Rockroads and (28) from "Straight Teaching" by Elaine Strangeowl.

(27)

Héva	nȧ-htse-vésė-háa'éše-vo'ėstanéhévé-me.
maybe	1-FUT-also-long.time-live-1PL.EXCL

'Perhaps we will live a long time.' (Leman 1987:211)

(28)

Héva	hé'tóhe	é-sáa-pėhéva'é-háne	he'po-htȯtse	tsé-hešévé-se
maybe	this	3-not-be.good-NEG$_{\text{INAN}}$	smoke-NOM	IND-do.that-CNJ.2PL

hétsetseha.
now

'Like this isn't good, smoking, what you're doing now.' (Leman 1987:216)

Héva can also be used in a range of constructions, including the conditional and the inferential evidential (Leman 2011). It may also be combined with various other words and particles, including the question particle *móhe* forming *hévá=móhe* 'apparently' (Fisher et al. 2006).

When *héva* combines with *naa* and *máto*, it forms a disjunction, as in (29) from "Making Chokecherry Patties" by Elva Killsontop.

(29)	É-ohke-péen-ē-nėstse	**naa**	**mátȯ=héva**	é-ohke-pénȯh-é-nėstse.
	3-HAB-grind-PSV-PL.INAN	CONN	also=maybe	3-HAB-pound-PSV-PL.INAN

'They (chokecherries) are ground or they are pounded.' (Leman 1980a:77)

Importantly, in (29) *máto* and *héva* are pronounced together, as *mátȯ=héva*. When pronounced together, *mátȯ=héva* is three syllables: the sequence *tȯ=hé* forms a single, complex syllable (Leman 2011). When pronounced separately, *máto héva* is four syllables. A sequence of *naa máto héva* is also possible, without a change in pronunciation, and with a clearly compositional interpretation. One such example is (30) from "Family Harmony" by Elaine Strangeowl, where the narrator is discussing married couples and how they should discuss and agree on everything.

(30)	**Naa**	**máto**	**héva**	tósa'e	tsé-s-to'sė-ho'ȯhtsē-vȯse.
	CONN	also	maybe	where	IND-CNO-PROS-go-CNJ.3PL

'And also like where they are going to go.' (Leman 1980a:80)

Like *naa* and *naa máto*, *naa mátȯ=héva* can be used to conjoin other categories in addition to verbs. Example (31) from "Flute Playing" by Elaine Strangeowl shows this for nouns, and (32) from "Cooking Chokecherries" by Elva Killsontop shows this for numbers.

(31)	. . . héva	hetane	**naa**	**mátȯ=héva**	kȧsováàhe . . .
	maybe	man	CONN	also=maybe	young.man

'. . . maybe a man or a young man . . . ' (Leman 1980a:11)

(32)

Naa	nėhe'še	é-ohke-ése-énan-ē-nėstse	na'nohto	**naa**	**mátȯ=héva**
CONN	then	3-HAB-in-put-PSV-PL.INAN	eight	CONN	also=maybe

sóohto	tsé-ová'kan-e-e'ėstse.
nine	IND-make.patties-PSV-CNJ.PL.INAN

'And then they are put in, eight or nine patties.' (Leman 1980a:77)

While the disjunction *naa mátȯ=héva* may be related to the morphemes *máto* and *héva*, it no longer seems fully compositional. Indeed, a translation along the lines of (30) would not be appropriate for (32): it does not mean 'And then they are put in, eight and also maybe nine patties'. Yet even if *mátȯ=héva* is analyzed as a unit, it is still combined with *naa*, the conjunction, to form a disjunction, which differs significantly in its truth conditions. For (32), eight or nine patties are added, not both eight and nine patties. Cheyenne (29), (31), and (32) have a true disjunctive interpretation.

Another way of expressing disjunction in Cheyenne is morphologically similar: *naa mó=héá'e*, combining *naa* with the question particle *móhe* and the epistemic particle *hēā'e*.[6] Alone, *hēā'e* is similar to English *maybe* or *perhaps*, as in (33) from the anonymous text "The Brothers-in-law."

(33)

Hēā'e	né-héne'enōv-o	Kėhaéné'e.
maybe	2-know.s.o-DIR	Squint.Eye.Woman

'Maybe you know Squint Eye Woman.' (Leman 1987:174)

The disjunction *naa mó=héá'e* is illustrated in (34) from "The Rolling Head" by Laura Rockroads, (35) from the anonymous text "The Sioux Medicineman,"[7] and (36) from "Some Cheyenne Beliefs" by Laura Rockroads.

(34)

... hēā'e	né=hé'e	**naa**	**mó=héá'e**	né=hetane ...
maybe	that=woman	CONN	Q=maybe	that=man

'... maybe that woman or that man ...' (Leman 1987:251)

(35)

Tótseha	é-ta-voneotse	na'he	éše'he-o'o	**naa**	**mó=heá'ėháma**	hehpeto.
long.ago	3-TRL-be.gone	three	sun-PL	CONN	Q=maybe	later

'She's been gone a long time, three months or maybe more.' (Leman 1987:112)

(36) Naa hétsetseha ná-sáa-héne'enó-he hēā'e
CONN now 1-not-know.s.t-NEG$_{\text{AN}}$ maybe

é-ohke-ée-só'-nė-heše-nė-heso **naa** **mó=héá'e**
3-HAB-around-still-ANA-how-ANA-be.that.way CONN Q=maybe

é-ohkė-sáa-'-éve-éva-nė-hesó-hane.
3-HAB-not-EP-about-back-ANA-be.that.way-NEG$_{\text{INAN}}$
'But now I don't know, maybe that is still so or maybe it isn't so now.'
(Leman 1987:214)

Though there are morphosyntactic similarities between the disjunctions *naa mátȯ=héva* and *naa mó=héá'e*, there are important semantic differences. For example, consider (37), which could be used in a context where the speaker saw Annie drinking something warm, but is not sure if it was coffee or tea.

(37) Annie é-noméne mo'kȯhtávė-hohpe **naa** **mó=héá'e** véhpotsé-hohpe.
Annie 3-drink black-broth CONN Q=maybe leaf-broth
'Annie drank coffee or tea.'

In such a context, replacing the disjunction in (37) with *naa mátȯ=héva* is unacceptable.

Interestingly, *naa* alone can be used as a disjunction in certain contexts, as in (38).

(38) Mó=hé'tóhe **naa** mó=hé'tóhe?
Q=this.one CONN Q=this.one
'Do you mean this one (pointing) or this one (pointing)?'

The question in (38) could be used in a context where the speaker was asked to pass something, say a cup, but is not sure which cup was intended and so asks (38) to clarify. It is an alternative question: possible answers include 'that one (pointing)' but not 'yes' or 'no'. So, in (38) *naa* is interpreted disjunctively. However, this use of *naa* appears to be limited to interrogatives: *naa* does not seem to be a "general use connective" like COORD in American Sign Language (Davidson 2013). An additional example of such a question is (39) from the anonymous text "The Sioux Medicineman."

(39) Mó-'=é-naā'e **naa** mó-'=é-ma'heón-o'eétahe?
Q-EP=3-doctor CONN Q-EP=3-sacred-do.something
'Is he doctoring or is he a magician?' (Leman 1987:112)

Toward an Analysis

In philosophical logic and semantics, it is common to assume a truth functional analysis of connectives: the truth value of a complex sentence is a function of the truth values of its parts. For example, consider English *and* and *or*. A complex sentence *A and B* is true just in case *A* is true and *B* is also true: both sentences have to be true. A complex sentence *A or B* is true just in case *A* is true or *B* is true: at least one of the sentences has to be true (inclusive disjunction). Thus, (inclusive) disjunction is logically weaker than conjunction: if *A and B* is true, *A or B* is also true, but not vice versa. This semantics for connectives is compositional: the meaning of a complex expression is determined by the meaning of the parts and how they are combined.

For Cheyenne, because many connectives are complex, built on *naa* 'and', the issue of a compositional analysis is unavoidable. One option that would maintain compositionality would be to analyze each complex connective as a unit, lexicalized as is. Another analysis would be ambiguity—each lexical item involved in the complex connectives would be (potentially) ambiguous. However, both of these options ignore the morphosyntax of the complex connectives, the semantic similarity between them, and the semantic relation of the parts of the complex connectives to their independent uses. An explanatory analysis should account for these facts.

A truth functional analysis of connectives can be extended to Cheyenne for *naa* alone and clearly compositional combinations such as *naa máto* and *naa nėhe'še*. For example, a complex sentence *A naa B* is true just in case both *A* and *B* are true. However, a simple extension of this analysis is not compatible with the interpretation of *naa* in interrogatives (see, for example, (38)), where neither conjunct has a truth value.

Further complications for a truth functional analysis of Cheyenne connectives come from the contrastive conjunction *naa oha* and the disjunctions *naa mátȯ=héva* and *naa mó=héá'e*. For a complex sentence *A naa oha B*, we do still want to require both *A* and *B* to be true. However, there are two issues: what meaning to assign to *oha* so it can combine with *naa* to form a contrastive conjunction (see (23)) and whether a uniform meaning can be assigned for all occurrences of *oha*.

Difficulties for a truth functional analysis become more acute with the disjunctions: for example, a complex sentence *A naa mátȯ=héva B* requires at least one of *A* or *B* to be true. Even though it includes *naa*, it does not require both *A* and *B* to be true. What kind of meaning could be assigned to *mátȯ=héva* so it could combine with logical conjunction and return disjunction? There is also the issue of what, if any, relation *mátȯ=héva* and *mó=héá'e* have to *máto*, *héva*, *móhe*, and *hēā'e*.

Since all of the complex forms include *naa*, a crucial component of any analysis will be what meaning to assign to *naa*, and whether it can be given a uniform analysis. Davidson (2013) has developed an analysis for a general coordinator in ASL where it has a basic meaning that can take on either conjunctive or disjunctive force, depending on the context. However, Cheyenne *naa* does not seem to take on the same range of interpretations in the same contexts as the general coordinator in ASL, so this type of analysis does not seem directly extendable to *naa*.

One potential avenue of analysis for Cheyenne *naa* is simply as sequential update, a standard way of treating conjunction in dynamic semantics (e.g., Groenendijk and Stokhof 1991).[8] That is, *naa* would sequence together two contributions without adding any additional contribution. This analysis would make sense of its use in texts and interrogatives. It would also allow for a compositional analysis of the complex connectives, up to a point: *mátȯ=héva* may have to be treated as a unit in the analysis of the disjunction *naa mátȯ=héva*. This component of this disjunction may be historically related to its parts (*máto* and *héva*), but it seems to be grammaticized. However, the disjunction *naa mó=héá'e* seems more transparent, allowing variations like *naa mó=heá'ėháma*, which pose similar issues for compositionality. Any uniform analysis of *naa* faces the challenge of reconciling what seems to be a true conjunctive marker with uses in a logically weaker construction, disjunction.

NOTES

1. Cheyenne is a Plains Algonquian language spoken in Montana and Oklahoma. The data presented in this paper were collected by the author during several fieldwork trips to Montana during summers since 2006 and draw on a Cheyenne grammar (Leman 2011), collections of texts (Leman 1980a, 1987), and a dictionary (Fisher et al. 2006). Examples are from fieldwork unless otherwise cited. For all included Cheyenne examples, the morphological analysis, glossing, and translation are my own.

2. Orthography and Abbreviations: V́ = high-pitch vowel; V̄ = mid-pitch vowel; V̇ = voiceless vowel (all final vowels are voiceless; but not marked); 1 = first person; 2 = second person; 3 = third person; AN = animate; ANA = anaphor; CIS = cislocative (toward speaker); CONN = connective; CNJ = conjunct (dependent) clause; CNO = conjunct oblique (past tense, location, or cause in conjunct verbs); CNTR = contrastive; DIR = direct voice; EXCL = exclusive; FUT = future; HAB = habitual; INAN = inanimate; IND = indicative conjunct mode; INF = inferential evidential (mode); INV = inverse voice; IOAM = inanimate object agreement (Rhodes 1976); NAR = narrative (preterit) evidential (mode); NEG = negation agreement suffix; NOM = nominalizer; OBL = oblique; OBV = obviative; PART = participle; PL = plural; PST = past; PROS = prospective; PSV = passive; PURP = purposive; Q = interrogative proclitic; RPT = reportative; TRL = translocative (away from speaker).
3. This is unlike in Menominee, where there are separate coordinators for phrases and clauses (Johnson et al. 2014).
4. This construction could also be called 'adversative coordination', as in Haspelmath 2007.
5. English *only* has adversative uses, as in *Annie went to dance, only she got nervous.* However, in such cases it is not combined with *and*: *#Annie went to dance, and only she got nervous.*
6. Semantically, this disjunction might be analyzed along the lines of Zimmerman (2000), as a conjunction of epistemic possibilities. This seems especially appropriate given the option of having an additional *hēā'e* at the beginning of the disjunction (see (34)), though this can affect the meaning. However, this analysis does not seem appropriate for the disjunction *naa mátȯ=héva*, given the semantic differences (see, for example, (37)).
7. In example (35), the particle *háma* occurs in the disjunction, attached to *hēā'e*: *naa mó=heá'ėháma*, compared to *naa mó=héá'e* in examples (34) and (36). Alone, *heá'ėháma* can be used as 'maybe' and *háma* can occur with other particles, as in *tá'sėháma* 'isn't that right?' (Fisher et al. 2006).
8. See also Winter (1995), where conjunctive morphemes are analyzed as syncategorematic, as not having any denotational contribution to meaning.

REFERENCES

Davidson, Kathryn. 2013. 'And' or 'or': General use coordination in ASL. *Semantics and Pragmatics* 6:1–44.

Fisher, Louise, Wayne Leman, Leroy Pine Sr., and Marie Sanchez. 2006. *Cheyenne Dictionary.* Lame Deer, MT: Chief Dull Knife College. http://www.cdkc.edu/cheyennedictionary/index.html.

Groenendijk, Jeroen, and Martin Stokhof. 1991. Dynamic predicate logic. *Linguistics and Philosophy* 14:39–100.

Haspelmath, Martin. 2007. Coordination. In *Language Typology and Syntactic Description II: Complex Constructions*, edited by Timothy Shopen, 1–51. Cambridge: Cambridge University Press.

Johnson, Meredith, Monica Macaulay, and Bryan Rosen. 2014. *And, and,* and *and and*: Coordination in Menominee. In *Papers of the Forty-Second Algonquian Conference*, edited by J. Randolph Valentine and Monica Macaulay, 159-180. Albany, NY: SUNY Press.

Leman, Wayne, ed. 1980a. *Cheyenne Texts: An Introduction to Cheyenne Literature*. Occasional Publications in Anthropology, Series No. 6. Greeley: Museum of Anthropology, University of Northern Colorado.

———. 1980b. *A Reference Grammar of the Cheyenne Language*. Occasional Publications in Anthropology, Series No. 5. Greely: Museum of Anthropology, University of Northern Colorado.

———, ed. 1987. *Náévàhóó'òhtséme/We are going back home: Cheyenne History and Stories Told by James Shoulderblade and Others*. Algonquian and Iroquoian Linguistics 4, Winnipeg.

———. 2011. *A Reference Grammar of the Cheyenne Language*. Raleigh, NC: Lulu Press.

Malchukov, Andrej L. 2004. Towards a semantic typology of adversative and contrast marking. *Journal of Semantics* 21:177–198.

Rhodes, Richard A. 1976. The morphosyntax of the Central Ojibwa verb. PhD thesis, University of Michigan.

Winter, Yoad. 1995. Syncategorematic conjunction and structured meanings. In *Proceedings from Semantics and Linguistic Theory V*, edited by Mandy Simons and Teresa Galloway, 387–404. Ithaca, NY: CLC Publications.

Zimmerman, Thomas Ede. 2000. Free choice disjunction and epistemic possibility. *Natural Language Semantics* 8:255–290.

Problems and Prospects in the Penobscot Dictionary

Conor McDonough Quinn

Frank T. Siebert (1980) discusses technical issues in developing the *Penobscot Dictionary*, a project unfortunately not completed at the time. We report here on a new effort to complete this work and detail its challenges both old and new. The *Penobscot Dictionary Project* (National Endowment for the Humanities #PD-50027-13; co-PIs Pauleena MacDougall and Conor Quinn) is a collaborative effort of the Penobscot Indian Nation, the University of Maine, and the American Philosophical Society (APS) to revise and publish (both digitally and in print) a manuscript dictionary of Penobscot, an indigenous language of central Maine. The project's three major goals are:

1. Recover, archive, and disseminate versions reflecting the document in its most complete forms from the original 1980s project outcomes.
2. Provide an error-corrected edition linked to those manuscripts, permitting trackback of editing changes.
3. Disseminate the resource in forms maximally accessible both to the Penobscot Nation and outside scholars alike.

Point 3 deserves special note. Our aim is a dictionary usable to more than just a specialist audience, and even carefully detechnicalizing its content and presentation alone does not guarantee wide usability. So our project has a parallel track working with Penobscot Nation educators to help develop plainly framed, pragmatically grounded, and responsive language teaching. With this we hope to maximize accessibility both in the development process—through early and frequent user feedback—and in ultimate outcomes: not just a finished dictionary but also a community of users with sufficient background to get real and meaningful use out of it. Space constraints limit a full discussion of this teaching component, however, so this paper focuses mainly on the first part: how we took a legacy manuscript and structured it into a digital dictionary.

In large part, our target audience is nonlinguist (and/or beginner linguist) heritage language community members who are wrestling with the basics of getting an Algonquian dictionary started and finished, and trying to determine what is most feasible and most worth prioritizing. Many Algonquian language communities struggle with this range of problems, and especially with finding simple, low-overhead solutions to them. A key goal of this project report, then, is to offer some ways for underresourced programs to simplify the basic dictionary-making process.

Our work has been to recover and edit a preexisting digital document, but most of the tools and structures apply equally well to building a dictionary from scratch. What has helped us most is "plaintext minimalism": keeping the dictionary manuscript simple in structure, stored and edited in an open-source, minimal file format (plaintext), and using free but powerful text manipulation tools (REGULAR EXPRESSIONS) in equally simple, minimalist ways. Again, we hope this report can make essential parts of dictionary-making more accessible than they typically have been by modeling how to use digital tools not for their complexity but for their simplicity. In short, anyone who can handle a word processor can—with just some simple, freely available digital tools—quickly and easily create the working outlines of a flexible and powerful digital dictionary.

We first outline the specifics of our recovery process, and then show how plaintext minimalism and its associated tools helped us to create a fully structured digital dictionary document. We then discuss issues and principles that have emerged in editing, archiving, and trackback of stages of the manuscript. Finally, we examine briefly how pedagogical outreach fits into the aim of making a genuinely accessible dictionary.

Recovery

Sources and Their Processing

The manuscript recovery has two components: the digital and print manuscript sources themselves, and the tools for processing them. We have found that some simple but still underutilized digital text manipulation tools, regular expressions, can radically ease recovering and structuring the data into a digital lexicon, and correcting systematic and semisystematic errors. While not new, they have great potential for underfunded dictionary projects, as the set needed for basic lexicography is small and requires no computer skills beyond those needed to use a word processor.

The working manuscript draws from two sources. First is Siebert's personal printout copy from the 1980s project. Containing some handwritten emendations and now archived at the APS, this appears to be the most up-to-date version of the manuscript. Second is a set of 5.25″ disk files, archived at (and in 2011 recovered by) the APS. This is an earlier backup draft: while otherwise quite similar, it noticeably lacks the separate Dependent Nouns section, and also a section from the start of "k" until the "|kati-|" entry, equaling about 4.5 pages, and it has a few smaller omissions more recently discovered.

A full digital version corresponding directly to the Siebert printout therefore requires carefully comparing the two manuscripts and reentering missing material. Before the start of the current project, the original digital files themselves had already undergone two stages of recovery and structuring. First is the APS-commissioned recovery of the original 1980s files (spring 2011). These are plaintext (= ASCII) and include formatting codes (= markup/tags) from the original Gutenberg word-processing application. Second is the Penobscot Nation–commissioned preliminary structuring of that material into machine-ready (= XML-tagged) dictionary fields (fall 2012).

We consider it essential best practice to archive all the intermediate stages in this process, and also document the processing itself, and to make these available as part of the overall digital resource. This makes our workflow transparent to future users, both for back-tracking introduced errors and also to provide a model for similar efforts.

The most noteworthy aspect of this process is how we used simple digital tools to streamline this workflow and create a simple but stable and flexible output; this is examined next.

Basic ASCII to Unicode Replacement

The ASCII character encoding system available in the 1980s lacks certain characters used in the standard Penobscot orthography. To solve this, unused ASCII characters were used to stand in for the missing ones. Examples include:

#	=	ə (schwa)
@	=	α (alpha [= IPA /ɤ/])
$	=	č (c-haček)
*	=	^{w} (superscript w [+ a few isolable real * for historical reconstructions])

This is not an exhaustive list. Accentual diacritics in particular are slightly more complexly coded, but manageable in essentially the same way. Luckily, the replacive ASCII symbols (see (1a)) almost completely correspond one-to-one with the Penobscot characters as the present-day standard (Unicode) encodes them, with a distinct code point for each (as in (1b)). So a simple global replacement (= "Replace All") for each of these correspondences produced a directly legible version of the digital manuscript.

(1) "Replacive" ASCII to unique Unicode replacement

a. Starting form: difficult and non-unique "replacive" ASCII
<P2><BO>**a$ita^w#ssin**<KB> AI <UFI>stat.<UFP> he lies with his head lower than his feet; <BO>**n#ta$ita^w#ssin**<KB> I . . .

b. Ending form: legible and unique Unicode characters
<P2><BO>**ačitáwəssin**<KB> AI <UFI>stat.<UFP> he lies with his head lower than his feet; <BO>**nətačitáwəssin**<KB> I . . .

In this new encoding, the Penobscot data is directly legible, and particularly because it does not depend on dedicated fonts/interpreters for display, it is more readily usable across a wide range of applications—for example, online presentations, smartphone apps, prepress layout, and so on.

Recovering Data Structure from Formatting Markup: The Value of Regular Expressions

Importantly, the Gutenberg-ASCII text also includes—as seen in (1) above—extensive formatting markup/tags, of the following sort:

<P2>	marks paragraphs
<BO> . . . <KB>	marks boldface
<UFI> . . . <UFP>	marks italic font

Originally just layout/design elements, these have provided a way to reestablish a digital data structure for the manuscript. This is because some are used uniquely for distinct parts of the dictionary data structure, that is, entry, headword, part of speech, etc. For example, the paragraph marker is only used at the start of entries, and so becomes an effective tag for the initial edge of an <entry> field. Similarly, boldface is only used for Penobscot-orthography material, and so its tags become an effective marker for the same.

Similarly, each entry's primary part of speech is drawn from a restricted vocabulary, is always formatted in italics, and is consistently positioned after the headword. This unique constellation of features makes it automatically recoverable as well. Thus:

<P2>	marks paragraphs → initial edge of <entry>
<BO> . . . <KB>	marks boldface → anything (and only what is) in Penobscot
<UFI> . . . <UFP>	marks italic font → +restricted set+position = part of speech

In many cases, the precise configuration and/or relative position of these formatting tags unambiguously picks out the start and finish of certain dictionary components. For example, "<P2><BO> . . . <KB>" unambiguously demarcates the (new paragraph) beginning of an entry, followed by its (boldface) headword. We can then relabel this explicitly as "<entry><hw> . . . </hw>."

Most of us are familiar with the find-replace tool in word processors, which can easily make the [# → ə] type of replacement. But to search out and use these positional combinations of formatting tags to recover the dictionary's structure, that is, to do this:

<P2><BO> . . . <KB> → <entry><hw> . . . </hw>

we need something that can do flexible find-replace operations on PATTERNS.

This is exactly what the digital tools known as *regular expressions* do. Freely available and easy to learn, they require no special programming skills or expensive special programs. Most word processors offer some version of them, as do free text editors like TextWrangler and Notepad++, whose design makes using them particularly easy.

So to carry out the above replacement, we do just two things. First, in the search, we replace the "..." above with a special regular expression code .*? (period–asterisk–question mark) that means "this part can be anything" (2a). Then we divide the whole sequence up into three chunks using parentheses (2b).

(2) *Find-replace step 1: setup*

a. <P2><BO>**.*?**<KB> = add in the "anything" part

b. (<P2><BO>)(.*?)(<KB>) = add parentheses

Putting parentheses around a chunk means it can be manipulated separately. Thus, in the replacement, the second of the these three chunks (coded as **\2** in (3) below) can just be passed along unchanged, with the changes we want on either side of it:

(3) *Find-replace step 2: The actual find-replace action*

Find: (<P2><BO>)(**.*?**)(<KB>)

Replace: <entry><hw>**\2**</hw> = use the "\2" to retain the second chunk only

More concretely, if we apply this approach to the relevant part of (1) above, it starts out as (4a) and ends up as (4b).

(4) *Actual implementation*

a. <**P2**><**BO**>ačitáwəssin<**KB**>

b. <**entry**><**hw**>ačitáwəssin</**hw**>

Working from this kind of pattern-based automated search-and-replace (but also with some hand corrections), it was possible to process the Gutenberg-ASCII files into a preliminarily usable form. This is a tag-structured (= XML) file fundamentally composed of <entry> elements, with the following internal structure and components:

(5) *Simple tag-structured dictionary entry*

(hw = headword, (sub)pos = (sub) part of speech)

<entry>

<hw>ačitáwəssin</hw>
<pos>AI</pos>
<subpos>stat.</subpos>
<other> he lies with his head lower than his feet; ⟨BO⟩nətačitáwəssin⟨KB⟩ I . . . </other>
</entry>

In sum, through the use of simple regular expressions first to change original ASCII into modern Unicode orthography, and then to turn old layout and formatting patterns into structure markers, this fully structured dictionary entry was derived from the original Gutenberg-coded form seen in (1), repeated here:

(6) *Original digital manuscript*
<P2><BO>a$ita^w#ssin<KB> AI <UFI>stat.<UFP> he lies with his head lower than his feet; <BO>n#ta$ita^w#ssin<KB> I . . .

(An important detail: at this point we also systematically replaced all remaining original "< . . . >" codes with "⟨ . . . ⟩", so that they would not be confused with those of the new structuring tags. See ⟨*BO*⟩ . . . ⟨*KB*⟩ in (5) for an example.)

With this structure now applied to the entire manuscript, it could already be displayed on a web browser in a familiar dictionary format (separate entries, stand-out headwords, and so on), and its major components could be searched on.

The form reached in (5) was already enough to get a rough working digital dictionary up and running quite early on. Its remaining <other>-tagged material was much messier, however. This consisted of at least the primary gloss of the headword—but it could also include zero to many examples of several kinds of inflection (for example, first-person singular for verbs, plural for nouns, etc.), or of full-sentence usages.

We succeeded in structuring this material relatively quickly and easily, however, simply by not trying to categorize all of these different types of subelements immediately. We noted that after the primary gloss, each subelement typically has up to three parts at most: Penobscot, English, and part of speech. From there, we again used the boldface formatting codes uniquely associated with the Penobscot material, and the italics found only with parts of speech, to locate the edges of subelements, and enclose each in a general tag <x> (for "example"). (Once these <x> elements are established, the different subtypes can later be more specifically tagged based on unique aspects of content; for example, first-person singular forms have "I . . ." in their glosses.) Compared to the previous stage, much more hand correction and realignment were needed to finish this process, but far less than anticipated.

The result was the final fully tag-structured form given in (7).

(7) *Final fully tag-structured dictionary entry*
(xpb, xeg = example-Penobscot, -English)

<entry>
<hw>ačitáwəssin</hw>
<pos>AI</pos>
<subpos>stat.</subpos>
<gloss> he lies with his head lower than his feet; </gloss>
<x>
<xpb>nətačitáwəssin</xpb>
<xeg>I . . . </xeg>
</x>
</entry>

(Not shown here are original editorial notes also found in the <other> section of some entries: these were identified and tagged as <note> through the same process.)

The key point: this requires no computer skills to speak of. Anyone can learn just a few basic codes (such as .*? = "pretty much anything") and immediately start experimenting. As long as we can define the unique pattern we are looking for, regular expressions can find and manipulate it for us.

The time saved is massive. Recovery of the 16,000-entry manuscript into the first Internet- and search-ready form seen in (5) took only about twenty-five hours. This includes developing the search-and-replace patterns themselves and a final visual scan checking for uniformity and errors—which stuck out nicely thanks to the patterns created by regular expressions. Even in the second phase, dealing with the <other> material, the use of regular expressions made it easy to locate inconsistencies and other glitches. One trick we innovated was that we often pinpointed small residual inconsistencies by making a copy of the whole manuscript, and deleting from it everything that fit the "right" pattern. Everything left over in that copy was all that we then had to go back and fix by hand in the original. In short, regular expressions saved us uncountable hours of work, and even helped us speed up key parts of the hand correction of irregular, unpatterned glitches. On top of this, all the resources we used are free: not just the tools themselves, but also extensive online tutorials, reference works, and help forums.

Most strikingly, for our initial purposes—that is, recapitulating a print dictionary—we find that so far we do not need a database application at all. This bare-bones file, made just of plaintext with appropriately structuring tags, is enough to provide us with all core components of the dictionary. And with regular expressions, we can do all kinds of editorially and linguistically relevant "smart" searches like "find all animate nouns that end with /k^w/". The file itself is small (easy to email, quick to back up and archive), and works on anybody's platform: no special fonts, no special applications are needed. Finally, when we as dictionary-makers learn these minimal basics, we reduce costs even further, because our work is now directly legible to and usable by professional programmers. They no longer have to spend long hours (re-)formatting the data, and can instead use their (generally not cheap) time on more advanced manipulations—for example, rich and flexible web presentations and prepress processing.

The main attraction of this approach is that it makes baseline dictionary-making cheaper and more broadly accessible. The key is minimalism: not trying to develop all the specialist skills, but learning and using a small, carefully selected set. With just a few basic tools for handling plaintext and regular expressions, underfunded projects can save greatly in human work-hours and software expenses, and set up a practical and richly usable digital dictionary in a short time at relatively little cost. This in turn makes getting support for further work much easier.

Editing and Archiving

Our key tasks in editing and archiving are to provide an accurate, well-edited, and fully structured final document that can be readily tracked back to its primary sources: that is, the digital and printout manuscripts. As noted above, earlier stages (including the regular expression algorithms used) will be archived with the final digital document with guides on how to search them. One question remains open: Should these be separate files or an integrated component in its own (very large) field, so that they are never separated from the core document?

An archive-quality scan of the Siebert printout manuscript is crucial not only for final content but also as a philological tool for trackback from the final document. Entry-by-entry trackback links would be ideal, but are impracticable both in terms of time cost and inexact correspondence between the two manuscripts. Instead, a field in each entry providing the page number (= scan page number/anchor) can give instant trackback to the printout manuscript scan page. This should suffice for philological purposes and is fairly quick to implement.

We originally considered special version-tracking software (such as that found in TshwanaLex), and at some point may yet go that way. But for now we simply archive date-and-time-stamped drafts on at least a daily basis. There are numerous free applications that can compare any two plaintext documents and list their differences, and with this we have free and simple version-tracking. With a manuscript that has yet to reach 3MB in size, this is quite practicable: daily or even twice-daily backups still will total only a small number of gigabytes of data by the end of the project term. This is another advantage of plaintext minimalism in the working stages of development.

What Kinds of Editing?

A fundamental question when revamping an existing manuscript is, what sort(s) of editing can and/or should we do? Of course we should correct obvious typos and errors—but what should be considered errors is not always clear-cut.

For example, some inflected examples in the manuscript are very likely wrong or artificial. Identifying these and distinguishing them from genuine variation is difficult. This is particularly so for AI stems reflecting Proto–Eastern Algonquian (PEA) **-ā* and **-ē*. On the one hand, they have at least some predictable patterns of distribution: for example, body-part-descriptive AI stems in Penobscot overwhelmingly take reflexes of PEA **-ā* and almost never of **-ē*. But some AI stems in **-ā* also show evidence of historical shifts: for example, Penobscot *-hlα* 'go (quickly), become' superficially reflects PEA **-ā*, but a direct reflex of its Proto-Algonquian source, **-ʔle·* 'fly/go' would reflect PEA **-ē*, that is, as the unattested ***-hle*. For forms of this sort, it is not always easy to distinguish genuine variation and innovation from incorrect or artificially introduced forms. Relatedly, the default format for entries requires complete inflectional forms and part-of-speech information that have not always been documented, and may not be recoverable. This will certainly be the case for supplementary lexical material drawn from texts and other sources. One solution is just to provide whatever forms are attested, plus an abstracted stem form, since that would clearly be a (legitimate) abstraction. It would not be mistakable as a claimed piece of real data, but would still be usable for general lexicographic purposes.

As we cannot recheck usage or translation directly with native speakers, the only way to check questionable data in this area is to search on its textual attestation. Since this is not solid primary data, we remain wary of changing any original sense definitions, even when all such data suggest it.

With these issues in mind, our default protocol is to leave the primary material as unedited as possible and simply annotate it heavily. This will include flags for headword data (etc.) that is likely problematic, and certainly for any cases where we have in fact changed the data, with the rationale and the original manuscript form both provided. One way or another, both need to be available and searchable, since otherwise users may not be able to find information that may actually exist.

Phonological Issues

A full account of phonological issues in the documentation of Penobscot demands a separate treatment (see in particular Siebert 1980 and Quinn 1999). Three points deserve brief note, however.

First, Siebert (1996) noted difficulty in consistently distinguishing vowels from the set /a, ɑ, ə/. This now appears in part to be due to an incomplete picture of their allophonic ranges: in particular, that /a/ often realizes as [ʌ], making it easily confused with /ɑ/ (= [ɤ]) and /ə/. With this known, some uncertain forms may now be recoverable.

Second, schwa before high glides colors strongly toward the corresponding high vowel: /əy/ is nearly indistinguishable from /iy/, and /əw/ from /ow/. Contrastive forms do exist (cf. a partial parallel in Passamaquoddy-Maliseet [LeSourd 1993:48–55]), but these are relatively rare and largely detectable only through related accentual contrasts. For the noncontrastive majority, Siebert's transcriptional variation probably reflects no systematic phonological difference, but nonetheless presents a significant problem for normalization and search optimization.

Finally, comparison with cognates in closely related Passamaquoddy-Maliseet can potentially uncover real transcription errors in the Penobscot documentation, particularly of /a/ versus /ɑ/, as their corresponding Passamaquoddy-Maliseet cognates (/ə/ versus /a/) are less readily confused by documenters. For example, these regular correspondences mean that the attested Penobscot /mánakʷ**a̲**n/ and Passamaquoddy-Maliseet /mə́nə̆kʷ**a̲**n/ 'rainbow' suggest that the Penobscot form may in fact be /mánakʷ**ɑ̲**n/. However, in this and other comparable cases, it is not always possible to exclude the possibility of genuine variation and/or reshaping.

On these three points, we again favor annotational comment over covert correction.

Annotational Design

If annotation over modification is a key principle, how exactly should we design the annotational component? An undifferentiated <note> field is probably unwise, since it can be useful to distinguish editorial-philological notes from purely linguistic notes (usage, cross-reference, and so on). Furthermore, the manuscript itself has occasional notes from Siebert (currently tagged as the only <note> element) that require a distinct categorical treatment. An unrestrained diversity of <note> types is also undesirable, since we aim to keep the data structure maximally simple and transparent. For now, we are restricting <note> categories to no more than the three discussed above, that is, <ednote>, <lingnote>, <siebnote>.

Accessibility

A fundamental principle of this project is that accessibility is not just physical access to the dictionary resource(s) themselves. A barely usable dictionary is little better than no dictionary at all, and can do direct harm to revitalization efforts.

Accessibility of form and content is therefore just as important as physical dissemination. Thoughtful accessibility design applies both to the text's own internal structuring and content as well as to its external presentation to its user communities, in development and final form alike.

As an example of how internal structuring and external presentation relate, we note that with the flexibility of our simple XML-based digital core document, we can offer multiple alternative online presentations: with technical terms minimized, replaced with more transparent alternatives, or simply hidden. For print, we look to the *Passamaquoddy-Maliseet Dictionary*'s (Francis and Leavitt 2008) insightful use of small, lower-case abbreviations to provide technical information (such as parts of speech) to specialists while minimizing its visual impact for lay users.

In particular, while we are interested in using digital tools to address the fundamental problems of lookup in a polysynthetic, head-marking language—that is, a morphological parser and morpheme lexicon (Maxwell and Poser 2013; Poser 2002)—we still think that fuller accessibility comes from solid pedagogical outreach. This approach in turn goes beyond the academic's reflex just to train learners in the difficult metalanguage of Algonquianist linguistic analysis and terminology, and instead rethinks those same linguistic understandings in terms of pragmatic, lay learner–familiar reference points. This reframing, we think, may also open doors to new insights into the phenomena themselves.

Our current teaching materials pursue this detechnicalizing approach, which we find to be particularly well complemented by the visual image-grounded method laid out in Sarkar and Metallic (2009). Here again minimalism is our watchword. Our curriculum design starts from the needs of the busy adult learner: very brief lessons, each one giving a solid, real-life pragmatic/communicative takeaway—but simultaneously also introducing the next in a series of core grammatical patterns (currently kept to a minimal seven) carefully selected as those that lay the direct foundations for the rest. Without this core knowledge, a dictionary is only marginally usable; through these materials and others, we hope to make broadly and readily accessible the opportunity to develop it.

Conclusion

In sum, our project aims for accessibility in every component, both within and without. Hence we highlight how simple, minimalist use of digital tools ("plaintext minimalism") can help underfunded lexicography, and we pursue a conservative, transparent editorial approach, preferring annotation over modification. For us, the success of the dictionary is grounded in the success of the user community's ability to contextualize it fully; that is, to tie it into a working knowledge of the language grounded in real life, rather than decontextualized single-word lookup. To this end, we are working to provide comparably minimalist, low-overhead teaching and learning materials, so that access to the language does not stop simply at the book in hand.

REFERENCES

Francis, David A., and Robert Leavitt. 2008. *A Passamaquoddy-Maliseet Dictionary: Peskotomuhkati Wolastoqewi Latuwewakon.* Orono: University of Maine Press.

LeSourd, Philip. 1993. *Accent and Syllable Structure in Passamaquoddy.* New York: Garland.

Maxwell, Michael, and William Poser. 2013. Morphological interfaces to dictionaries.

Unpublished manuscript, University of Pennsylvania.

Poser, William. 2002. Making Athabaskan dictionaries usable. In *Proceedings of the Athabaskan Languages Conference 2,* edited by Gary Holton, 136–147. Fairbanks: Alaska Native Language Center, University of Alaska.

Quinn, Conor. 1999. Some unresolved issues in the Penobscot materials of Frank T. Siebert, Jr. In *Papers of the Thirtieth Algonquian Conference,* edited by David Pentland, 288–322. Winnipeg: University of Manitoba.

Sarkar, Mela, and Mali A'n Metallic. 2009. Indigenizing the structural syllabus: The challenge of revitalizing Mi'gmaq in Listuguj. *Canadian Modern Language Review* 66:49–71.

Siebert, Frank T., Jr. 1980. The Penobscot dictionary project: Preferences and problems of format, presentation, and entry. In *Papers of the Eleventh Algonquian Conference,* edited by William Cowan, 113–127. Ottawa: Carleton University.

———. 1996. Penobscot dictionary. Unpublished manuscript, American Philosophical Society.

Toward a Semantic Dictionary of Algonquian

Richard A. Rhodes

Since Leonard Bloomfield's first article on the sound system of Proto-Algonquian in 1925 showed that the comparative method worked on all languages, not just European languages, most work on comparative Algonquian has focused on formal similarities between languages, both phonological and syntactic. Relatively little work has been done on historical or comparative semantics. The studies that exist are mostly of two general kinds. On the one hand, studies like Siebert's (1967) attempt to identify the Algonquian homeland in which the semantics are crucial but are not treated in a systematic way. On the other hand, there are systematic studies of semantics based on wider typological studies in which Algonquian languages are incidental examples (e.g., Vejdemo and Lockwood 2015 on temperature).

That said, there are some studies that attempt to provide a systematic approach to historical semantics in Algonquian. One example of such a study focusing systematically on reconstructed forms is found in Rhodes (2000). Inspired by observations in Gamkrelidze and Ivanov (1994) about systematicity in Indo-European semantic shifts as exemplified in tree names (as shown in Table 1), I looked at forms relating to large quadrupeds, most of which are given in Siebert (1967).

I reinterpreted Siebert's reconstructions in terms of our contemporary

TABLE 1. Indo-European Tree Names

PIE	LATIN	GREEK
—	—	μελία 'ash'
*Hos-k^h- 'ash'	ornus 'mountain ash'	ὀξύα 'beech'
*b^{h}aHk'- 'beech'	fagus 'beech'	φηγός 'oak'
*p^{h}er(k^{ho})u-n- 'oak, thundergod'	quercus 'oak'	κεραυνό 'thunderbolt'

Source: Gamkrelidze and Ivanov 1994:538.

understanding of where the Algonquian proto-homeland was (Denny 1992; Goddard 1994). The key terms are given in (1).[1]

(1) PA *mo·swa 'moose' — Me mo·swa, Mi moohswa 'deer', SWO mooz, M moos, Att mo:s, PC mōs, Ch méhe 'female bison', Ar biis 'female bison', Ats byı́íh 'female bison', Mass m8s, Pass mus

Compounds:

*meʔθ-o(·)swa 'big moose' — PC mostos

*ilen-oswa 'ordinary moose' — Me nenoswa 'bison', Mi alenaswa 'bison', Ar hinéni' 'moose'

*(we)mashk-o·swa 'elk' ('grass (?) moose') — SWO omashkooz 'elk', M amaaskos 'elk', Ch mō'e 'elk', Ar hiwóxuu 'elk'

PA *atehkwa 'mule deer' — SWO adik 'caribou', M atεεh 'caribou', PC atihk 'caribou', Pass otuhk '(white-tail) deer', Mic lentug '(white-tail) deer', Mass ahtuhq '(white-tail) deer', Mu atóh '(white-tail) deer'

PA *pešeθkiwa '(large) animal' — SWO bizhiki 'bison' (later 'cow'), M pesεεhkiw 'bison', PC pisiskiw 'animal', Ats keθ'íhiih 'animal' Ar cese'eihii 'animal'

~ *peHšekesiwa — Sh psekzi '(white-tail) deer', Me pešekesiwa '(white-tail) deer'

Other compounds:

PA *ay-a·pe·wa 'male quadruped'	Sh hayaape, SWO ayaabe, M ayaapɛɛw, PC iyāpēw, Ch hotóa'a 'male bison', Ar henéécee 'male bison', Ats hanáákyaa 'male bison', Pass iyap 'buck', Mass aiyump 'buck'

The analysis for the forms in (1) follows from the fact that the fauna in the locations of the various groups at contact was different from the Proto-Algonquian homeland. The speakers of Proto-Algonquian are believed to have lived on the Columbia Plateau, in eastern Washington, Oregon, and Idaho (Goddard 1994), where the large quadrupeds included moose, white-tailed deer, mule deer, elk, and bison. By the time of contact, all Algonquians had moved to places outside of the range of the mule deer, and some had moved into areas where there were caribou. Of particular interest here is that the Miami and Shawnee had moved out of the range of moose. The Shawnee simply lost the 'moose' word, but the Miami replaced the word for 'deer' with the 'moose' word. There are other things to be said about the forms in (1), especially the 'large animal' word, which has an unclear reconstruction because it has been borrowed around (that is, it is a Wanderwort).

A similar argument could be made for the ancestor form in (2), which has a much more limited distribution.

(2)	*wa·ške·Hšiwa '(white-tail) deer' (prob. not PA)	SWO	waawaashkeshi,
		Att	wa·škešiw,
		MoC	waawaashkeshoo,
		PC	wāwāskēsiw 'elk'

The missing piece in the layout of (2) is the systematicity of categories not expressed in a regular way with major morphemes.

What I am proposing is to develop semantically organized layouts that respect the categories that are "natural" in the Algonquian way of thinking. So the data in (1) would be supplemented and presented as in Table 2.

There are a number of missing terms in Table 2, most of which are likely to be simply missing from our sources. Those cells that are in gray indicate that the territory of the group at contact is outside the range of the animal in question. What Table 2 indicates is that formal differences can mask categorial similarities.

TABLE 2. Large Game

	'MALE QUADRUPED'	'FEMALE QUADRUPED'	'WHITE-TAIL DEER'	'MOOSE'	'ELK'	'CARIBOU'	'BISON'
Arapaho	henééce 'bull buffalo'	biis 'buffalo cow'	bih'ih 'mule deer'	hinéni'	hiwóxuu		hiiȝeinóón
Atsina	'anáakyaa' 'bull buffalo'	bʸíih 'buffalo cow'	bih'ih 'mule deer'	'inénhih	'iwɔ́siih		'íítaanɔ́ɔ́ni'
Cheyenne	hotóa'a 'bull buffalo'	méhe 'buffalo cow'	váótséva	mâhpémo'éhe	mō'e		(hotóa'a)
Menominee	ayaapɛɛw		apɛɛhsos	moos	amaaskos	atɛɛh	pesɛɛhkiw
Innu	nàpetikU	nùsetikU		mùsh		atikU	
Naskapi	iyaapaautiihk	nuusaatiihk		muus		atiihkw	
Attikamek	aya:pew		wa:škeššiw	mo:s		atikkw	
Moose Cree	iyaapeo		waawaashkeshoo	moos		atihk	
Plains Cree	iyāpēw	nōse-X	apisimōsos	mōs	wāwāskesiw	atihk	mostos
SW Ojibwe	ayaabe	noozhez	waawaashkeshi	mooz	mishewe/ omashkooz	adik	bizhiki
Algonquin	aiâbe	nonje-X	wawackêci	mônz	micewe/omackos	ininätik	piciki
Ottawa			waawaashkesh	mooz			bgwaji-bzhiki
Potawatomi			seksi	mozo	mshéwé		bgoj-bzheke
Miami			moohswa	**mahkatemihšiwia**	mihšiiwia		alenaswa
Meskwaki/K			pešekesiwa	mo·swa	meše·we·wa		nenoswa
Shawnee	hayaape		psekzi		waapiti		pakwaci-mzoozwa
Passamaquoddy	iyap	sqehkiqs	otuhk	mus			
Massachusett	aiyump	qunnegk	ahtuhq	m8s			
Munsee	lunŭwéexum	oxkwéexum	atóh	móos			

Note: The form in question is a prenoun. The "X" represents the name of the quadruped.

Possibly the most dramatic one is the shift of the 'moose' reflex to refer to 'female bison' in the plains languages. The underlying system includes terms for male and female of the most important game animals, sometimes by hypernym (reflexes of **ayaapewa* in the meaning 'male quadruped'), but sometimes the term is based on the best example, as in Innu (formerly referred to as Montagnais) and Western Naskapi (henceforth Naskapi), so the Cheyenne-Arapaho shift is: first the reflex of **mooswa* gets applied to bison, and then the hypernym male quadruped term supplants the **mooswa* reflex for male bison.

The other thing that is highlighted by a semantic organization like that in Table 2 is the existence of descriptive phrases: PC *apisimōsos* 'deer', M *apεεhsos* (both lit. 'little moose'), and Sh *waapiti* 'elk' (lit. 'white rump').

However, the semantics of flora and fauna are complicated. A more orderly semantic area is the stages of life for humans. Some Indo-European languages have three, like English, where the term(s) are ungendered. One can, of course, quibble over whether *baby* versus *child* should count as one or two, but the gendered part of the system is clear. The fact that we have terms like *infant*, *teenager*, *adolescent*, and *senior* (*citizen*) should not distract us.

The basic terms for stages of life define a small coherent system as shown in (3).

(3)	a.	baby, child	
	b.	boy	girl
	c.	man	woman

But the typical Algonquian system has five stages, as exemplified in Plains Cree in (4).

(4)					
	a.	awāsis	'child'		
	b.	nāpēsis	'boy'	iskwēsis	'girl'
	c.	oskinīkiw	'young man'	oskinīkiskwēw	'young woman'
	d.	nāpēw	'man'	iskwēw	'woman'
	e.	kisēyiniw	'old man'	nōtikwēw	'old woman'

Only the youngest category is not gendered. We want to call the terms in (5) basic in a sense inspired by that used in color term studies (Berlin and Kay 1969; among others), but several of their criteria make little sense applied in any straightforward way to Algonquian (true even in the case of color terms). For

TABLE 3. Stages of Life

	'BABY'	'CHILD'	'BOY'	'GIRL'
Arapaho	teiyoone'he	teiyoone'he	hecéxonóh'oe	hiseihihi'
Cheyenne	mé'ėševȯtse	ka'ėškóne	hetaneka'ėškóne	he'éka'ėškóne
Menominee	pepeehsɛh	oskɛɛcian	apɛɛhniihsɛh	kiiqseehsɛh
Plains Cree	oskawāsis	awāsis	nāpēsis	iskwēsis
SW Ojibwe	abinoojiins	abinoojiinh	gwiiwizens	ikwezens
Miami	apiloohseensa	apiloohsa	kwiiwihsa	ahkwaniswa
Meskwaki	apeno·he·ha	apeno·ha	kwi·yese·ha	ishkwe·se·ha
Shawnee	hapelohza	hapelohza	skilawehziiza	skwehzeeza
Passamaquoddy	pileyahsis		skinuhsis	pilsqehsis
Massachusett	n8nuk	pap8s/ mukki	mukkatchouks	squasese
Munsee	amiimúnzhush	amíimunz	skahúnzuw	oxkwéesus

Berlin and Kay, a basic term must be monomorphemic, be monolexemic, contain no cross-categorial morphology (that is, no term can contain another term), not be referentially restricted, and be salient. Of course applying these notions to Algonquian is challenging. Monomorphemic makes little sense in Algonquian. (One might propose a notion of relevantly monomorphemic, quite useful elsewhere in Algonquian morphosemantics, but even that runs into trouble in this class of data.) Monolexemic does appear to work, but the problem is that since some of the terms are transparently derived, one needs native intuitions to tell what counts as lexical. Not referentially restricted works (but is generally of less relevance in the case of nominals than in the case of modifiers). Salience does, on the other hand, seem to work. Unfortunately, using the combination of lexicalization and salience means that we have to rely heavily on speaker intuitions or inferences regarding speaker intuitions. There is precious little formal help. In the case of terms for stages of life, I am depending heavily on the fact that our often paltry lexicons consistently make these distinctions to infer that the terms in question are both lexicalized and salient, even if some have transparent cross-categorial morphology. This system reaches across the whole family. The deeper implication is that it must also be quite old. The data are shown in Table 3.

An Indo-Europeanist might well recognize by now where I am headed. Discussions highlighting categorizations argued from an Algonquian point of view

'YOUNG MAN'	'YOUNG WOMAN'	'MAN'	'WOMAN'	'OLD MAN'	'OLD WOMAN'
honóh'oe	hiseihiitei'yoo	hinén	hisei	beh'iihehi'	betébi/betebihiisei
kȧsovááhe	kȧse'ééhe	hetane	hē'e	ma'háéso	mȧhtamȧhááhe
oskiineniw	keekaah	enɛɛniw	metɛɛmoh	kɛqc-enɛɛniw	weeyawekɛɛh
oskinīkiw	oskinīkiskwēw	nāpēw	iskwēw	kisēyiniw	nōtikwēw
oshkinawe	oshkiniigikwe	inini	ikwe	akiwenziinh	mindimooyenh
kwiiwa	ahkweehsa	alenia	mitemohsa	kiyošia	mikihkwa
oshkinawe·ha	ihkwe·he·ha	(i)neniwa	ihkwe·wa	pashito·ha	metemo·ha
mayaanileni	mayaaniyhkwe	hileni	yhkweewa	pasitooza	nekipwehza
skinuhs	naksq	skitap	ehpit	ktaqhomuhs	motaqs
wuskenin	nunksq(ua)	ninnu	squáus	kéhchis	kehchisqua
wuskíilŭnuw	wuskóxkweew	lúnuw	óxkweew	mihlóosus	kihtóxkwees

are exactly analogous to what Carl Darling Buck did for Indo-European in his 1949 *Dictionary of Selected Synonyms in the Principal Indo-European Languages*. What I am proposing is that Algonquianists take up a corresponding research program. It will not be enough to simply sit and glean from lexicons the forms for categories that any experienced Algonquianist will recognize as a lexical category in the Algonquian worldview. Assembling those forms into semantic fields will highlight holes in the data. That will drive us back out into the field to access native intuitions about salience and lexicalization, and it will uncover surprises in things we may not have otherwise fully noticed.

For example, take the words for eating and drinking. Everyone has long known that there are interesting morphological and morphosyntactic irregularities in this semantic realm, but put all the forms together and interesting patterns emerge. Consider the forms in Table 4.

Table 4 differs slightly from the other tables in that the languages of the Ojibwe and Cree subfamilies are more fully attested. The system that emerges is one in which the suppletion of the TI and TA forms of 'eat' is continued throughout. While all of the languages retain the irregular TI/TA pairing for the 'eat all/devour' word (as shown in (5)), only two languages (Munsee and SW Ojibwe) retain the full irregularity of the TI in which the end of the stem has a long vowel and acts ambiguously between being an irregular theme sign and having a zero theme sign.

TABLE 4. Eating and Drinking

	'EAT (INTR.)'	'EAT (TI)'	'EAT (TA)'	'FEED (TA)'	'EAT ALL (TI)'	
Arapaho	bii3íhi-	bíí3i-	biin-	hóxob-	hootowkuut-	
Atsina	biicihi-	biici-	biin-	-ooθob-		
Cheyenne	-mésehe	-mese	-mév	-hoxom	-mȧhaéstá	
Menominee	meecehsow	miicwah	miiw	ahsaamɛɛw	ketaam/ mɛɛqtahtam	
Innu	mìtshishu	mìtshu	mueu	shameu	tshitau	
Naskapi	miichisuw	miichuw	muwaaw	aasaahchaaw	maastaahtim	
Attikamek	mi:cisow	mi:ciw	mowe:w	aššame:w		
Moose Cree	mīcisow	mīciw	mowēw	ašamēw	kitāw	
Plains Cree	mīcisow	mīciw	mowēw	asamēw	kitāw	
SW Ojibwe	wiisini	omiijin	odamwaan	odashamaan	ogidaan	
Algonquin	wiisini	mîdjin	amv-	acam-	gitan	
Ottawa	wiisni	wmiijin	wdamwaan	wdashmaad	wgidaan	
Potawatomi	wisnet	mijet	wdemwan	shemat	jagdek	
Miami	wiihsini-	miici-	amw-	ahšam-	ceekantam-	
Meskwaki/K	wi·seniwa	mi·čiwa	amwe·wa	ašame·wa	caakatamwa K	
Shawnee	wihzeniwa	homiici	nitamwa	nitsama	hocaakata	
Passamaquoddy	mitsu-	micin	mah-	ahsom-	nokkahtun	
Massachusett	meetsu	meech	m8wh-	assamaü	mahchip	
Munsee	míitsuw	míichuw	mhwéew	xámeew	ktáam	

(5) a. 'eat all/devour'

	TA	TI
M	ketamw-	ketam-
PC	kitamw-	kitā-
SWO	gidamw-	gidaam-
Ottawa	gdamw-	gdam-
Mu	ktamw-	ktáam

b. TI Mu ktáam, SWO gidaam-.

Looking farther right in the table, we see that most languages retain the AI+O treatment of 'drink' even when the form is restructured and swapped (in one direction or the other) between Ojibwean and Cree after Naskapi-Innu breaks off. In fact, it is exactly the Naskapi-Innu branch that innovates a TI treatment of 'drink'.

This points to an important by-product of organizing our comparative data in these larger semantic charts. Such a layout highlights patterns in the data that potentially bear on questions of classification. The 'eat/drink' table shows two innovations in the controversial Eastern Great Lakes subfamily.[2] The first is the

'EAT ALL (TA)'	'DRINK (AI')'	'DRINK (TI/AIO)'	'GIVE TO DRINK'
hootowkuu3-	bene-	bene-	
	beni'	beni'	benih-
-måhaet	-mane	-mane	
ketaamiiw/ mɛɛqtamiw	menuah	menuah	menaahɛɛw
tshitamueu	minu	minwatim	miniueu
maastimaaw	minuw	minaahtim	minaahaaw
	minikkwe:w		minihe:w
kitamwēw	minihkwēw		
kitamwēw	minikwēw	minikwēw	minahēw
ogidamwaan	minikwe	ominikwen	omina'aan
gidamv-	minikwe	minikwen	minah-
wgidmwaan	mnikwe	wda-mnikwen	wda-mna'aan
jagmat	mnekwét	mnekwét	
ceekam(w)-	men-	men-	menah-
caakamea K	menowa	menowa	menahe·wa
hocaakamaali	menwa	menwa	nimenhha
nokkahl-	tolapuwe	tolapuwe	osihmuw-
mahchipw-	wuttâttum	wuttâttum	(pautous nottattum)
ktámweew	mŭnéew	mŭnéew	mŭnáheew

appropriation of an old root PA **-iHeny-* (cf. Unami *wí:x:ənu* '(he) cooks', Ives Goddard, personal communication) to build an innovative AI for 'eat'. And the second is the innovation of a prothetic *a* on the TA of 'eat'.

Let me conclude with a few remarks about terms referring to the head. Approaching the semantic organization of data in Algonquian can be more daunting than it at first seems because one needs to take into account the fact that the vast majority of Algonquian words are effectively compounds. This means that at least some of the categories relevant to a Buck-type approach will be expressed as initials, medials, or finals, or perhaps as some combination. (I could easily have incorporated columns for AI, TI, and TA finals for eating in Table 4.) When it comes to body parts, the need to deal with the medials directly is pressing. So in Table 5, we see that it is advantageous to treat the three formally distinct medials for 'head' separately.

The biggest problem with the words for head and the parts of the head has to do with metonymic usages. Consider the following Plains Cree forms that demonstrate the problem. Half the terms unambiguously refer to the head, half

TABLE 5. Parts of the Head

	'HEAD'	'MY HEAD'	'HEAD'	'HEAD'
Arapaho	hóókuhu'ee	notókuhu'ee		e'éi-
Cheyenne	me'ko/n/	name'ko		-a'é
Menominee	mees	nees		
Innu	ustikwàn	nistikuàn	-istikuàne-	-iskue-
Naskapi	ustikwaan	nistikwaan	istikwaanaa-	iskwaa-
East Cree	mishtikwaan	ushtikwaan	ishtikwaane	ihkwe, ishkwe
Attikamek	ostikwa:n	nistikwa:n		-iskwe-
Plains	mistikwān	nistikwān	-istikwānē	-iskwē-
NW Ojibwe	mishtikwaan	nishtikwaan, nihtikwaan	ishtikwaane	-ihkwe, ashkwe
SW Ojibwe	oshtigwaanimaa	nishtigwaan	-ishtikwaane	-ikwe-, -aškwe-
Lemoine		nictikwân	ictikwâne-	ikwe
Ottawa	ndib	ndib		-ikwe-
Miami	eephšihkia	nintepikani		-ihkiaa-, -ihkii-
Meskwaki	owi·ši	newi·šemi		-ekwe·-, -eškwe·-
Shawnee	wiisi	niisi		

TABLE 6. Meanings of Plains Cree *-stikwānē-*

UNAMBIGUOUSLY 'HEAD'	UNAMBIGUOUSLY 'HAIR'
ākōstikwānēw 'cover one's head'	kaskitēwistikwānēw 'have dark hair'
mahkistikwānēw 'have a big head'	ohpwēstikwāniwāsiw 'have wind-blown hair'
paskostikwānēw 'be bald-headed'	sakistikwānēcin 'get snagged by the hair'
sākistikwānēw 'have one's head stick out'	sēkwēstikwāniwāsiw 'have wind-blown hair'
tahkistikwānēw 'have a cold head'	tōmistikwānisow 'oil one's own hair'
tēwistikwānēw 'have a headache'	wāpiskistikwānēw 'have white hair'
wēwēkistikwānēnēw 'wrap s.o.'s head'	wīpistikwānēw 'have dirty hair'

AMBIGUOUSLY 'HEAD/HAIR'
sakistikwānēpitēw 'pull s.o. by the head/hair'

the terms unambiguously refer to hair, and a few terms, such as the last one in Table 6, are ambiguous.

While there is much more that could be said in detail, the outline of the argument I am making should be clear. There is significant value in reconstructing the

'HEAD'	'(HEAD) HAIR'	'(HEAD) HAIR'	'MY FACE'	'FACE'
	béi3e'ee		netóóxebió'	e'éi- ?
-ehtséa	me'ko/n/	-ovésé, -ehta'é-	nahtsáne	-éné-
-etɛhpɛɛ-	meenɛqn-	-aaneckwee-, -aanɛhkwee-	neskeehsek	-eqkwe-, -ɛhkwe-
	piskueun	-istikuàne-	nitàstamikU	-ikue-
	piskwaaun	stikwaanaa-	nitaastimikw	-iihkwaa-
	mishtikwaanipiiw	aayihkwe	mitaashtamihkw	ihkwe
	wi:risiss	-a:rikwe-	nihkwiw	-ihkwe-
-itihpē-	mēskatay	-āniskwē-, -istikwānē-	nihkwāhkan	-ihkwē-
-aantipe	wiinisihs	aanikwe	niwiinkwaan	-iinkwe
-indibe-	wiinizis	-aanikwe-	indengway	-iingwe
indipe	ominisis	-anikwe-	nickijik	îngwe
-indibe	wiin'zis	-aanikwe	ndegway	-iinge
-intepikan-	wiilihsi	-ehkwee-		-iinkwee-
-itepe·-	owi·nesi	-a·nehkwe·-		-i·kwe·-
-itepee-	wiilehzi	-aanhkwee-	yeelaapeeya	-iikwee-, -aape-

category systems of the Algonquian family independent of considerations of form. It will even shed light on current concerns about the derivation of complex stems.

Appendix: Sources of Data

Baldwin, Daryl, and David J. Costa. 2005. *Myaamia Neehi Peewaalia Kaloosioni Mahsinaakani: A Miami-Peoria Dictionary.* Miami, OK: Miami Nation.

Baraga, Frederic. 1878–80. *A Dictionary of the Otchipwe Language, Explained in English.* Montreal: Beauchemin & Valois. PDF of 1853 ed., http://home.kpn.nl/cvkolmes/ojibwe/.

Béland, Jean-Pierre. 1978. Atikamekw morphology and lexicon. PhD thesis, University of California, Berkeley.

Bloomfield, Leonard. 1975. *Menomini Lexicon.* Edited by Charles F. Hockett. Milwaukee Public Museum Publications in Anthropology and History 3. Milwaukee.

Buszard-Welcher, Laura. n.d. Potawatomi word list. Unpublished manuscript.

Conathan, Lisa. 2006. English-Arapaho dictionary. http://linguistics.berkeley.edu/~arapaho/arapaho_english.html.

Cowell, Andrew, and Alonzo Moss, Sr., eds. 2005. *Arapaho Historical Traditions Told by Paul Moss.* Winnipeg: University of Manitoba Press.

Drapeau, Lynn. 1994. *Dictionnaire Montagnais-Français*. Quebec: Presses de l'Université du Québec.

Ellis, C. Douglas. 1996. *Spoken Cree: West Coast of James Bay*. Edmonton: University of Alberta Press.

Faries, Richard, ed. 1938. *A Dictionary of the Cree Language as Spoken by the Indians in the Provinces of Quebec, Ontario, Manitoba, Saskatchewan and Alberta*. Toronto: Church of England in Canada.

Fiero, Charles E. 2013. An Ojibwe word list (vocabulary from communities in nothwestern Ontario and eastern Manitoba). Unpublished manuscript.

Fisher, Louise, Wayne Leman, Leroy Pine Sr., and Marie Sanchez. 2007. *Cheyenne Dictionary*. Lame Deer, MT: Chief Dull Knife College. http://cdkc.edu/cheyennedictionary/index.html.

Goddard, Ives. 1994. *Leonard Bloomfield's Fox Lexicon: Critical Edition*. Algonquian and Iroquoian Linguistics Memoir 12. Winnipeg: University of Manitoba Press.

———. 1996. Leonard Bloomfield's Fox lexicon: Critical edition 1994—addenda and corrigenda as of April 1, 1996. *Algonquian and Iroquoian Linguistics* 21:6–7.

Jankiewic, Bill. n.d. Naskapi lexicon. Unpublished manuscript.

Lemoine, Georges. 1912. *Dictionnaire Français-Algonquin*. Quebec: Oblate Fathers.

LeSourd, Philip S.. 1986. *Kolusuwakonol: Philip S. LeSourd's English and Passamaquoddy-Maliseet Dictionary*. Pleasant Pt., Perry, ME: Passamaquoddy-Maliseet Bilingual Program.

MacKenzie, Marguerite, Marie-Odile Junker, Luci Salt, Elsie Duff, Daisy Moar, Ruth Salt, Ella Neeposh, and Bill Jancewicz, eds. 2004–2008. *The Eastern James Bay Cree Dictionary on the Web: English-Cree and Cree-English (Northern and Southern Dialect)*. http://www.eastcree.org/cree/en/dictionary/.

Mailhot, José, and Kateri Lescoop. 1997. Lexique montagnais-français du dialecte de Schefferville, Sept-Iles et Maliotenam. Ministère des affaires culturelles, Direction générale du patrimoine.

Nichols, John D., and Earl Nyholm. 1995. *A Concise Dictionary of Minnesota Ojibwe*. Minneapolis: University of Minnesota Press.

O'Meara, John. 1996. *Delaware-English, English-Delaware Dictionary*. Toronto: University of Toronto Press.

Rhodes, Richard A. 1985. *Eastern Ojibwa–Chippewa–Ottawa Dictionary*. Berlin: Mouton.

Taylor, Allan. 1994. *Gros Ventre Dictionary*. Hays, MT: Gros Ventre Treaty Committee.

Trumbull, James H. 1903. *Natick Dictionary*. Bureau of American Ethnology Bulletin 25. Washington, DC. https://archive.org/details/natickdictionar02trumgoog.

Valentine, J. Randolph. 2012. Cree database (four dialect compendium). Unpublished manuscript, University of Wisconsin–Madison.

Voegelin, Carl F. 1938–1940. *Shawnee Stems and the Jacob P. Dunn Miami Dictionary* (*Prehistory Research Series*). Indianapolis: Indiana Historical Society.

Voorhis, Paul H. 1988. *Kickapoo Vocabulary*. Algonquian and Iroquoian Linguistics Memoir 6. Winnipeg: University of Manitoba Press.

Wolvengrey, Arok, ed. 2001. ᓀᐦᐃᔮᐍᐏᐣ: ᐃᑘᐏᓇ / nēhiýawēwin: itwēwina/Cree: Words. Regina: University of Regina.

NOTES

1. The languages used in this study are: Proto-Algonquian (PA), Arapaho (Ar), Atsina (Ats), Plains Cree (PC), Moose Cree (MoC), East Cree, Attikamek (Att), Innu, Naskapi, Cheyenne (Ch), Menominee (M), Southwestern Ojibwe (SWO), Ottawa, Potawatomi, Meskwaki (formerly known as Fox) (Me), Kickapoo (K), Shawnee (Sh), Miami-Illinois (Mi), Micmaq (Mic), Passamaquoddy (Pass), Massachusett (Mass), Munsee Delaware (Mu), Proto-Indo-European (PIE), Latin, Greek. Sources of data are listed in the Appendix.
2. Almost all points of classification in Algonquian are controversial to some extent. However, since the publication of Goddard (1994), the classification implicit in that work has become widely accepted. The one question is whether there is an Eastern Great Lakes subfamily made up of Sauk-Fox-Kickapoo-Mascouten, Miami-Illinois, Shawnee, and the Ojibwe-Potawatomi subfamily. As pointed out in Rhodes (1988, 1989), these languages share a common treatment of several clusters and, more crucially, a unique leveling of the theme sign in TI2's to *o:*.

REFERENCES

Berlin, Brent, and Paul Kay. 1969. *Basic Color Terms: Their Universality and Evolution*. Berkeley: University of California Press.

Bloomfield, Leonard 1925. On the sound system of Central Algonquian. *Language* 1:130–156.

Buck, Carl Darling. 1949. *A Dictionary of Selected Synonyms in the Principal Indo-European Languages: A Contribution to the History of Ideas*. Chicago: University of Chicago Press.

Denny, J. Peter. 1992. The entry of the Algonquian language into the boreal forest. Paper read at the Canadian Archeological Association, London, ON.

Gamkrelidze, Tomas, and Vačeslav Ivanov. 1994. *Indo-European and the Indo-Europeans*. Translated by John Nichols. Berlin: Mouton de Gruyter.

Goddard, Ives. 1994. The West-to-East cline in Algonquian dialectology. In *Papers of the Twenty-Fifth Algonquian Conference*, edited by William Cowan, 187–211. Ottawa, ON: Carleton University.

Rhodes, Richard A. 1988. The classification of Central Algonquian. Paper read at the Twentieth Algonquian Conference, Hull, QC.

———. 1989. The Cree Connection. Paper read at the Eighty-Eighth Annual Meeting of the American Anthropological Association, Washington, D.C.

———. 2000. (Micro-)categorization, semantic change, and the Sapir-Whorf hypothesis. In *Evidence for Linguistic Relativity*, edited by Susanne Niemeier and René Dirven, 91–103. Amsterdam: John Benjamins.

Siebert, Frank T., Jr. 1967. The original home of the Proto-Algonquian people. In *Contributions to Anthropology: Linguistics I*, edited by A. D. DeBlois, 13–47. National Museum of Canada Bulletin 214. Ottawa, ON.

Vejdemo, Susanne, and Hunter Lockwood. 2015. "There is no thermostat in the forest": The semantics and sociolinguistics of temperature in Ojibwe. In *The Linguistics of Temperature*, edited by Maria Koptjevskaja-Tamm. Amsterdam: John Benjamins.

A Look at Manner-of-Motion Verbs in Ojibwe

Bryan Rosen

This paper provides a preliminary analysis of manner-of-motion verbs in Ojibwe. Manner-of-motion verbs are formed by combining an initial that denotes a direction and a final that expresses a manner-of-motion (1).[1]

(1) a. Ningii-dagobatoo waakaa'iganing.

nin-	gii-	dago-	batoo	waakaa'igan	-ing
1-	PST-	to-	run.AI	house.NI	-LOC

'I ran to the house.'

b. Ningii-izhishim waakaa'iganing.

nin-	gii-	iN-	shimo	waakaa'igan	-ing
1-	PST-	toward-	dance.AI	house.NI	-LOC

'I danced toward the house.'

I am extremely grateful to my Ojibwe consultants (E.O. and S.J.) for teaching me about their language. Thanks to Meredith Johnson, Monica Macaulay, Becky Shields, Tanya Slavin, and Rand Valentine for valuable comments and discussion. I am also grateful to two anonymous *PAC 45* reviewers whose comments and suggestions helped improve this paper.

In (1a), the initial *dago-* 'to' encodes the direction of the predicate, while the final *-batoo* 'run' provides a manner-of-motion. A similar example is shown in (1b) with the initial *izhi-* 'toward' and the final *-shimo* 'dance'.

Previously, Bliss et al. (2013a, b) have argued that PPs in Blackfoot and Plains Cree are always adjuncts to the verb. On the other hand, Oxford (2011) has stated that some PPs can be complements of motion verbs in Innu-aimun. Using evidence from telicity, I argue that the verb in Ojibwe can take a directional PP as a complement, and that the head of this PP incorporates into the verb stem to realize an initial. The structure for (1a) is illustrated in (2).

(2) $[_{vP}$ $[_{v}$ $[_{P}$ dago$]$ batoo$]$ $[_{PP}$ t_{dago} $[_{PP}$ waakaa'iganing$]]]$

Furthermore, in line with cross-linguistic studies such as Koopman (1997), I provide arguments for a multilayered structure of PPs in Ojibwe. Specifically, I argue that directional PPs in Ojibwe contain a locative P embedded under a directional P, as roughly schematized in (3).

(3) $[_{PP}$ P_{dir} $[_{PP}$ P_{loc} NP$]]$

The rest of this paper is organized as follows. The next section provides background on manner-of-motion verbs and locatives in Ojibwe. I then further examine manner-of-motion verbs and provide a structural analysis of Ojibwe manner-of-motion verbs. In the section that follows, I extend the analysis to a cause-motion construction. Finally, the last section concludes the paper.

Some Preliminaries

In this section, I first present background information on manner-of-motion verbs in Ojibwe and provide evidence that they are composed of syntactically independent elements. Finally, I discuss some relevant characteristics of locatives.

TABLE 1. Some Selected Manner-of-Motion Finals in Ojibwe

MANNER-OF-MOTION FINAL	GLOSS	MANNER-OF-MOTION FINAL	GLOSS
-aadage	'swim' (AI)	-batoo	'run' (AI)
-a'atoo	'walk' (AI)	-shimo	'dance' (AI)

TABLE 2. Some Selected Directional Elements in Ojibwe

DIRECTIONAL ELEMENT	GLOSS	DIRECTIONAL ELEMENT	GLOSS
ah-	'toward'	dago-/agw-	'to'
biiji-/biid-, bi-	'hither'	izhi-/in- (underlying: /iN-/)	'toward'

Manner-of-Motion Verbs: Overview

Here I outline the elements that are involved in manner-of-motion verbs in Ojibwe. Recall that these verbs are composed of a directional initial and a manner-of-motion final. The finals discussed in this paper are provided in Table 1.

Ojibwe also has a number of elements (initials and preverbs) that express directionality of path, as outlined in Table 2.[2] The elements *ah-* 'toward', *dago-* 'to', and *izhi-* 'toward' are traditionally referred to as "relative roots": a morpheme that links two semantically related items, where the linked items express a direction, manner, or degree. While the elements *biiji-* and *bi-* 'hither' pattern with the other elements in Table 2 with respect to directionality, they are not considered relative roots in the literature. Thus, for the purposes of this paper, I focus on elements that semantically contribute a directional interpretation, regardless of their traditional classification.

Rhodes (2005:11) states that the element *dago* is neither an initial nor a preverb; rather, it is a "simplex verb stem" that means 'be found/located in a certain place'. However, while both of my consultants can easily form manner-of-motion verbs with *dago-* 'to', one of them did not recognize *dago* as an independent verb. This is evidenced by the ungrammaticality of (4). This suggests that the *dago-* that is the directional initial in manner-of-motion verbs discussed here is different than the one Rhodes refers to.

(4) *Dago besho asin.
be.located.AI near rock.NA
Intended: 'There is a rock nearby.'

Finals in manner-of-motion verbs are syntactically independent

The issue of whether verb stems in Algonquian languages are formed in the syntax or morphology has been controversial.[3] In this section, I present evidence that finals in Ojibwe manner-of-motion verbs are syntactically independent; that is, they do not form a lexical unit with their initial.

The particle *eta* 'only' can appear after the verb stem. In this position, it can scope over just the manner-of-motion final. The examples in (5) and (6) illustrate this fact with the finals *-batoo* 'run' and *-aadage* 'swim', respectively.[4]

(5) a. Ningii-dagobatoo **eta** waakaaiganing.

nin-	gii-	dago-	batoo	eta	waakaa'igan	-ing
1-	PST	to	run.AI	only	house.NI	-LOC

'I went to the house only by running (i.e., not by walking, etc.).'

b. Ningii-izhibatoo **eta** waakaa'iganing.

nin-	gii-	izhi-	batoo	eta	waakaa'igan	-ing
1-	PST-	toward	run.AI	only	house.NI	-LOC

'I went toward the house only by running (i.e., not by walking, etc.).'

(6) Ningii-biidaadage **eta** Thunder Bay.

nin-	gii-	biid-	aadage	eta	Thunder Bay
1-	PST	hither	swim.AI	only	Thunder Bay

'I came to Thunder Bay only by swimming (i.e., not by boat, etc.).'

The preverb *mochi-* 'only' may also modify just the final, as in (7) with *-a'atoo* 'walk'.

(7) Ningii-**mochi**-dagwa'atoo (eta) waakaa'iganing.

nin-	gii-	mochi-	dago-	a'atoo	eta	waakaa'igan	-ing
1-	PST	only	to	walk	only	house.NI	-LOC

'I went to the house only by walking (i.e., not by running, etc.).'

These examples are not readily accounted for under a morphological analysis of verb stems. The fact that *eta* and *mochi-* 'only' may scope just over the final suggests that the initial and final are separately generated and combined in the syntax. This interaction with finals and *eta* 'only' can easily be explained in a non-Lexicalist theory, such as Distributed Morphology (Halle and Marantz 1993) or Ramchand's (2008) first-phase syntax. I therefore follow a theory of the morphology-syntax interface that assumes that words are formed in the syntax.

Some Background on Locatives

Given that manner-of-motion verbs are always accompanied by a locative phrase, I review locatives in Ojibwe, and what a recent proposal has said for other Algonquian languages. Locatives in Ojibwe are licensed by the nominal suffix *-ing*, which sometimes surfaces as *-ong*. Valentine (2001:664) calls *-ing* a "locative case marking." This suffix is required when expressing a location, as evidenced by the ungrammaticality of (8b) and (9b).

(8) a. Brad gii-wiisini wiisiniiwigamig-**ong**.
Brad PST-eat.AI restaurant.NI-LOC
'Brad ate at the restaurant.'
b. *Brad gii-wiisini wiisiniiwigamig.
Brad PST-eat.AI restaurant.NI
'Brad ate at the restaurant.'

(9) a. Meredith niibawi besho mitig-**ong.**
Meredith stand.AI near tree.NA-LOC
'Meredith is standing near the tree.'
b. *Meredith niibawi besho mitig.
Meredith stand.AI near tree.NA
'Meredith is standing near the tree.'

The locative phrases in (8) and (9) (for example, *wiisiniiwigamigong* 'at the restaurant' and *besho mitigong* 'near the tree') are optional. Thus, they appear to be prime examples of adjuncts (as in the Principles and Parameters framework). In fact, Bliss et al. (2013a, b) argue that locative expressions are PP adjuncts that attach at the CP level in Plains Cree and at the IP level in Blackfoot, as illustrated in (10a, b), respectively.

(10) a. Plains Cree *-ihk* b. Blackfoot *it-*

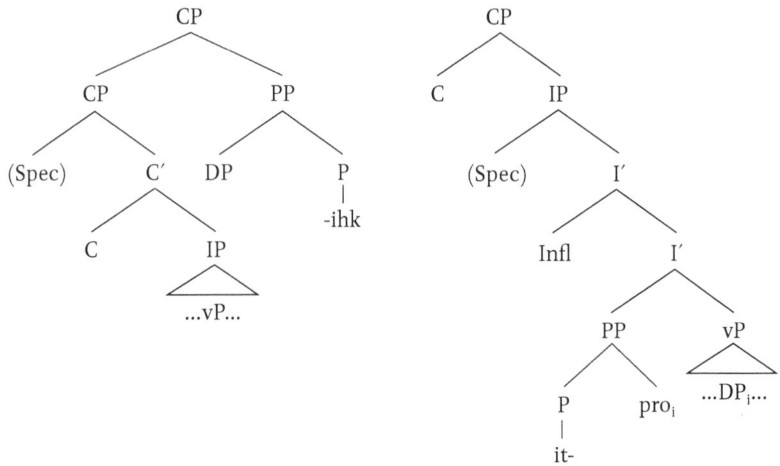

In (10), locatives are licensed by P, which is realized as the nominal suffix *-ihk* in Plains Cree and as the verbal prefix *it-* in Blackfoot. Bliss et al. argue that Blackfoot and Plains Cree lack complement PPs: PPs are not selected for, PPs do not control agreement, and PPs do not participate in the direct/inverse system. First, they show that the verb of 'putting' in Plains Cree has only one form (as in (11)), despite differences in semantic transitivity. Since the verb in (11) remains the same, they suggest that PPs in Plains Cree are not selected by verbs.

(11) a. astâw [Plains Cree]
place.AI.3
'He/she placed (it) there.'

b. Masnêykan **astâw** pîhc-âyih labwêt-ih.
book.NI place.AI.3 inside-STEM box-LOC
'He/she put the book in the box.'

Internal arguments control verb agreement, as shown in (12a) for Plains Cree. (12b) illustrates that locative PPs do not trigger third-person object agreement like NP internal arguments. That is, these PPs do not control verb agreement in Plains Cree.

(12) a. Nisanahamawaw Tomio. [Plains Cree]
ni-sanah-amaw-a-**w** Tomio
1-send-APPL-DIR-3 Tomio
'I sent it to Tomio.'

b. *Nisanahamawaw Calgary.
ni-sanah-amaw-a-**w** Calgary
1-send-APPL-DIR-3 Calgary
'I sent it to Calgary.'

Because the locative in (12b) does not control verb agreement, Bliss et al. conclude that PP locatives are not arguments of the verb, and thus do not have the status of complements.

In contrast, Oxford (2011) observes that locatives in Innu-aimun may appear to the right of goal-selecting verbs, as in (13). He reasons that because locatives are in a postverbal position, they may function as a complement of such a verb.

(13) Nititûte (anite) atâuitshuâpît. [Innu-aimun]
go.past.1s the.LOC store.LOC
'I went to the store.'

In the next section, I use different diagnostics than Bliss et al. to argue that manner-of-motion verbs in Ojibwe may take a directional PP complement.

Manner-of-Motion Verbs in Ojibwe

In this section, I examine the manner-of-motion construction in Ojibwe in more detail. First, I discuss the role of the initial in relation to directional PPs. Next, I argue, based on telicity judgments, that a directional PP is the complement to the final, and that the directional P head undergoes head movement into the verb stem to realize an initial. In the last part of this section, I discuss the structure of complex PPs in Ojibwe.

Manner-of-Motion: Goal of Motion versus Directed Path

As seen above, manner-of-motion verbs consist of an initial that expresses a direction and a final that provides a manner of motion. Consider a few more examples in (14).

(14) a. Ningii-dagobatoo waakaa'iganing.

nin-	gii-	dago-	batoo	waakaa'igan	-ing
1-	PST-	to-	run.AI	house.NI	-LOC

'I ran to the house.'

b. Ningii-izhishim waakaa'iganing.

nin-	gii-	iN-	shimo	waakaa'igan	-ing
1-	PST-	toward-	dance.AI	house.NI	-LOC

'I danced toward the house.'

c. Ningii-biida'atoo waakaa'iganing.

nin-	gii-	biid-	a'atoo	waakaa'igan	-ing
1-	PST-	hither-	walk.AI	house.NI	-LOC

'I came walking toward the house.'

d. Ningii-inaadage Thunder Bay.

nin-	gii-	iN-	aadage	Thunder Bay
1-	PST-	toward-	swim.AI	Thunder Bay

'I swam toward Thunder Bay.'

These verbs must also occur with a locative phrase; otherwise, the sentence results in ungrammaticality. This is illustrated in (15).

(15) *Ningii-dagobatoo

nin-	gii-	dago-	batoo
1-	PST-	to-	run.AI

Intended: 'I ran (to).'

Sentences with manner-of-motion verbs can either have the interpretation that the subject reached the location, or that he or she did not, depending on which element occupies the initial position. If the subject reaches the location, the event is bounded, whereas if the subject does not, then the event is unbounded (Krifka 1989; Jackendoff 1990). Speaker judgments indicate that initials differ with respect to boundedness. We can test the (un)bounded nature of the predicate by using the adverbial *bebangii* 'a bit'.[5] I borrow this test from Zubizarreta and Oh (2007), who argue that only unbounded predicates can be modified by gradable adverbs like 'a bit'.

Verbs with the initials *ah-* 'toward', *biiji-* 'hither', and *in-* 'toward' are unbounded since they can be modified by the adverbial *bebangii* 'a bit'. This is shown by the examples in (16), which do not imply that the subject has reached the house or Thunder Bay.

(16) a. Bebangii ningii-apatoo waakaa'iganing.

bebangii	nin-	gii-	aN-	batoo	waakaa'igan	-ing
a.bit	1-	PST-	toward-	run.AI	house.NI	-LOC

'I ran a bit toward the house.'

b. Bebangii ningii-biijibatoo waakaa'iganing.

bebangii	nin-	gii-	biid-	batoo	waakaa'igan	-ing
a.bit	1-	PST-	hither-	run.AI	house.NI	-LOC

'I came running a bit toward the house.'

c. Bebangii ningii-ina'atoo waakaa'iganing.

bebangii	nin-	gii-	iN-	a'atoo	waakaa'igan	-ing
a.bit	1-	PST-	toward-	walk.AI	house.NI	-LOC

'I walked a bit toward the house.'

d. Bebangii ningii-inaadage Thunder Bay.

bebangii	nin-	gii-	iN-	aadage	Thunder Bay
a.bit	1-	PST-	toward-	swim.AI	Thunder Bay

'I swam a bit toward Thunder Bay.'

By comparison, the bounded nature of a verb stem that contains the initial *dago-* 'to' is shown by the incompatibility with the modifier *bebangii* 'a bit' in (17). These examples contrast with the ones above in (16).

(17) a. *Bebangii ningii-dagobatoo waakaa'iganing.

bebangii	nin-	gii-	dago-	batoo	waakaa'igan	-ing
a.bit	1-	PST-	to-	run.AI	house.NI	-LOC

Intended: 'I ran a bit to the house.'

b. *Bebangii ningii-dagwa'atoo waakaa'iganing.

bebangii	nin-	gii-	dago-	a'atoo	waakaa'igan	-ing
a.bit	1-	PST-	to-	walk.AI	house.NI	-LOC

Intended: 'I walked a bit to the house.'

c. *Bebangii ningii-dagwaadage Thunder Bay.

bebangii	nin-	gii-	dago-	aadage	Thunder Bay
a.bit	1-	PST-	to-	swim.AI	Thunder Bay

Intended: 'I swam a bit to Thunder Bay.'

Thus, (16) shows that *izhi-* 'toward' and *biiji-* 'hither' can only denote a PATH of motion toward an end point in the context of a manner-of-motion final. (17) shows that *dago-* 'to' can denote a GOAL of motion, as an endpoint.

In the previous examples, the directional elements *izhi-* 'toward' and *dago-* 'to' surface in initial position; however, they may also appear as verb stem modifiers (that is, preverbs). The forms in which these directional elements surface all denote unbounded activities; that is, they lack a natural endpoint. Example (18) shows that the event remains unbounded when *izhi-* 'toward' is a preverb. In (19), *dago-* 'to' only denotes a path of motion when it appears as a preverb (cf. (17) above).

(18) Bebangii ningii-**izhi**-gizhiibatoo waakaa'iganing.

bebangii	nin-	gii-	iN-	gizhii-	batoo	waakaa'igan	-ing
a.bit	1-	PST-	toward-	fast-	run.AI	house.NI	-LOC

'I ran quickly a bit toward the house.'

(19) Bebangii ningii-**dago**-gizhiibatoo waakaa'iganing.

bebangii	nin-	gii-	dago-	gizhii-	batoo	waakaa'igan	-ing
a.bit	1-	PST-	to-	fast-	run.AI	house.NI	-LOC

'I ran quickly a bit to the house.'

Example (19) is reminiscent of the English facts in (20). The *to* phrase does not denote a completed action, as the verb can be modified by *for a while* (from Zubizarreta and Oh 2007:129). Since the *for* phrase intervenes between the verb and the *to* phrase, Zubizarreta and Oh suggest that the *to* phrase in (20) has a different structural position than in bounded manner-of-motion predicates: it is an adjunct. In contrast, (21) (also from Zubizarreta and Oh) indicates that the telic *to* phrase must be in a complement position, since it must be immediately adjacent to the verb.

(20) a. John ran for a while to the park.
b. John walked for a while to the park.

(21) a. ??John danced in a minute (in)to the kitchen.
b. ??John walked in an hour to the park.

In sum, Ojibwe has clear examples of manner-of-motion verbs. I have also demonstrated that directional initials control the boundedness of the predicate.

A Structural Analysis of Manner-of-Motion Verbs

In this section, I provide a syntactic analysis for manner-of-motion verbs in Ojibwe. I propose that the final realizes a light verb, "little v," that takes a complex PP complement. The head of the PP then moves into v, realizing an initial.

To illustrate this analysis, consider the derivation of (14), which is repeated below in (22). Following Mathieu (2008), I assume that Ojibwe is head-initial, and that finals are instances of v. Thus, the final *-batoo* 'run' occupies v. As for the complex PP that functions as the complement of v, the initial *dago-* 'to' is first merged as a higher, directional P head and then moves to v. This process strands the lower, locative PP *waakaa'iganing* '(at) the house'.[6] This structure is shown in (23).[7]

(22) Ningii-dagobatoo waakaa'iganing.

nin-	gii-	dago-	batoo	waakaa'igan	-ing
1-	PST-	to-	run.AI	house.ni	-LOC

'I ran to the house.'

(23)

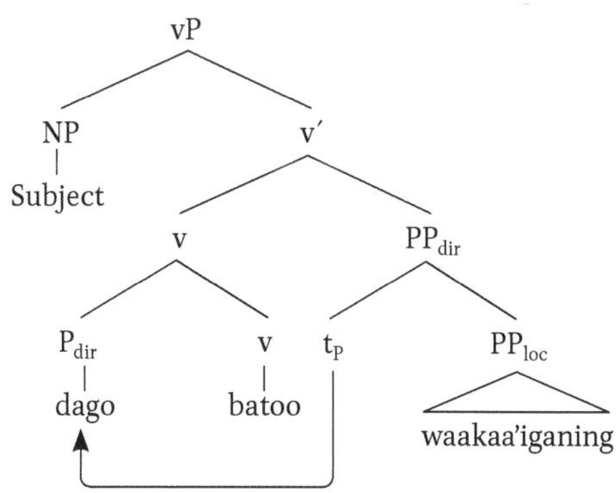

Tenny (1994) and Ramchand (2008), among many others, have argued that the complement position of verbs is the locus of telicity. Since the initial *dago-* gives rise to a culmination point, I argue that the initials under discussion (see Table 2) originate in a complement position of the verb (the final). If this initial were not originally a verbal complement, it would be external to the verb phrase, and thus it could not be part of the core eventuality of the verb phrase (cf. Levin and Rappaport Hovav 1995). Note that nothing prevents an unbounded directional element first merging in the complement position. That is, complements do not have to yield telic predicates, but only complements can produce telic ones. Thus, when the directional elements *dago-* 'to', *izhi-* 'toward', and *biiji-* 'hither' are initials, they merge as the complement of v to realize P_{dir}, regardless of whether they produce a telic or atelic predicate.

The analysis in (23) is consistent with Slavin's (2012) claims that initials merge low in the structure and then move to Spec,vP. Slavin argues that initials in Ojicree verb stems are required to raise to a specifier in order to complete the event composition of the predicate. The exact reason or mechanism, however, is left as "unclear" (Slavin 2012:169). In earlier work, Slavin (2007) proposes that initials move to a higher position in the verb stem for focus reasons. In this paper, I suggest that for manner-of-motion verbs, the directional P raises for morphosyntactic reasons.

Snyder (2001) argues that complex predicate constructions in English are the result of a single parameter, which is based on restrictions in the morphology-syntax interface. He proposes the parameter in (24):

(24) *Compounding Parameter*
The grammar {disallows*, allows} formation of endocentric compounds during the syntactic derivation. [*unmarked value]

According to this parameter, if a language has a marked value of the compounding parameter, the language will have complex predicates, such as adjectival resultative secondary predicates. Beck and Snyder (2001) extend this analysis to directed motion predicates; namely, Goal PPs (for example, *run to the house* in English). In particular, Snyder (2001) claims that complex predicates and N-N compounds are largely the same operation since they are both instances of root compounding. For example, if a language has adjectival resultatives or Goal-PPs, then N-N compounding should also be available in the language. Snyder is not specific as to when complex predicates must form a compound: he only states that they must form a morphological compound at some point of the syntactic derivation (narrow syntax, Logical Form, or Phonological Form) through head movement or head-head Merge. Since the availability of complex predicates in a given language is dependent on the compounding parameter, Snyder's theory predicts that a language that allows N-N compounding will also have complex predicates.

Let us now return to Ojibwe. As seen in (25), Ojibwe exhibits productive N-N compounds.

(25) a. mako-biisimokaan
bear.NA-clock.NA
'a bear clock (a clock shaped like a bear)'

b. bebani-bimisewin
paper.NI-flight.NI
'a paper plane (a plane made of paper)'

Thus, following Beck and Snyder (2001) and Snyder (2001), I suggest that Ojibwe exhibits complex predicates (for example, manner-of-motion verbs) that are also derived through head movement. That is, the directional P raises to v, as shown in (23).[8] A consequence of the present analysis is that a language like Ojibwe allows PPs to be verbal complements in complex predicates because it also has N-N compounding. I maintain a connection between N-N compounding and Goal-PPs (as in Beck and Snyder 2001 and Snyder 2001). Thus, I do not follow the notion that the availability of Goal-PPs depends on whether a language allows *put*-locatives or *to*-datives, as Bliss et al. (2013a, b) do.

Recall that the directional elements that participate in manner-of-motion verbs may also appear as preverbs. Example (19) showed that when *dago-* 'to' is a preverb, the predicate could be modified by *bebangii* 'a bit'. This indicates that a path of motion is implied in (19), but it is not grammatically realized. I therefore suggest that when the directional element appears as a preverb, it is an adjunct that adjoins to vP. This is roughly schematized in (26); its exact position outside of the vP is not crucial to the analysis.

(26)

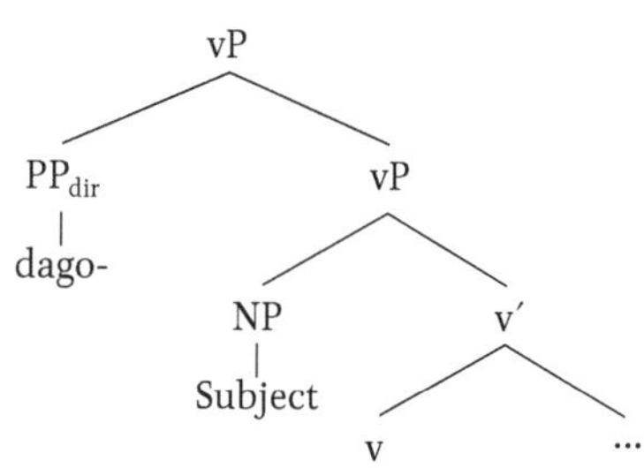

This straightforwardly explains why the predicate is an unbounded activity, as it is no longer part of the core eventuality of the verb phrase. Thus, my analysis also follows Slavin's (2012) account of the Ojicree verb stem: she proposes that the verb stem corresponds to vP. Slavin shows that initials contribute to the event composition, and thus are vP-internal. However, when the same element is a preverb, it takes scope over the entire event from a vP-external position.

Finally, it should be noted that this proposal offers an insight into the observations in Rhodes (2010), in which he shows that "relative-root complements" manifest properties of both arguments and obliques. However, this study suggests that both sets of properties can stem from the nature of the direction-denoting PP and its syntactic position as a complement. The argument characteristics arise because the PP is a complement to the verb. The oblique qualities are due to the fact that the direction has the syntactic status of P.[9]

Complex PPs in Ojibwe

I now turn to the structure of complex PPs. As seen in (23), I analyze the directional element as a type of P head and the locative as a locational preposition. Following Koopman (1997), and Svenonius (2010), among others, I assume that directional PPs consist of a locative P embedded under a directional P. In contrast, locative PPs contain a single P (27). These authors claim, for example, that the English preposition *into* is composed of a locative P *in* that incorporates into a directional P *to*.

(27) a. $[_{PP}\ P_{dir}\ [_{PP}\ P_{loc}\ NP]]$
b. $[_{PP}\ P_{loc}\ NP]$

LeSourd (2012) argues that the locative suffix in Passamaquoddy is licensed by the locative particles (for example, *besho* 'near' in Ojibwe) since the form of the noun is largely dependent on the particle. That is, in the presence of certain locative particles, the associated NP requires the locative suffix (see (8) and (9)). Oxford (2011) instead proposes that the locative suffix is a Kase head (KP) in Innu-aimun. For Ojibwe, the lower P encodes a location, which can either spell out elements like *besho* 'near' (see (9)) or be phonologically null. Following LeSourd (2012), I represent *-ing* as an agreement suffix. In other words, P_{loc} triggers the locative suffix *-ing* on its complement NP. However, my analysis does not hinge on whether *-ing* is an agreement morpheme or is the realization of a Kase-like head.

As mentioned above, initials can give rise to either a telic or an atelic interpretation. Thus, P_{dir} can be either bounded or unbounded, as outlined in (28). This means that the telicity of the predicate depends on whether P_{dir} is bounded or unbounded. Initials, such as *dago-* 'to' and *izhi-* 'toward', realize the higher P head (P_{dir}).

(28) a. dago-/dagw- 'to' is a bounded P_{dir}
b. izhi-/in- 'toward' is an unbounded P_{dir}
c. biiji-/biid- 'hither' is an unbounded P_{dir}

Some evidence for analyzing the directional elements as the head of PP_{dir} that takes a PP_{loc} complement comes from cases where the verb lacks a directional element. In (29), the verb does not contain an initial (or a preverb) that denotes a direction.

(29) Ningii-gizhiibatoo waakaa'iganing.

nin-	gii-	gizhii-	batoo	waakaa'igan	-ing
1-	PST-	fast-	run.AI	house.NI	-LOC

'I ran quickly while at the house.'

The predicate in (29) does not express a direction, but only a location. Since there is no element that encodes a direction, no interpretation of motion along a path or to a goal is possible. In terms of the current analysis, this means that the predicate lacks a PP_{dir} and that *waakaa'iganing* '(at) the house' is a PP_{loc} that is adjoined to vP (cf. (26)).

Finally, Slavin (2012) and others have noted that there does not seem to be any discernible difference in meaning between the stem *niimi* and the final *-shimo* 'dance'. Data from manner-of-motion verbs provides a difference between these two elements. In (14b), we saw that the final *-shimo* may serve as a manner-of-motion verb. However, the examples in (30) show that the stem *niimi* may not. When *niimi* combines with directional preverbs, only a locational interpretation is available. It seems that *-shimo* can license a directional P, whereas *niimi* cannot.[10] This shows that directional Ps are only compatible with certain lexically specified verbs.

(30) a. Nin-gii-izhi-niim waakaa'igan-ing.
1-pst-izhi-dance.AI house.NI-LOC
'I danced inside the house.'
b. Nin-gii-bi-niim waakaa'igan-ing.
1-PST-hither-dance.AI house.NI-LOC
'I came to the house and then danced.'

To summarize, I have argued that P_{dir} realizes an initial that has undergone head movement from a complement position in manner-of-motion verbs. I have also demonstrated that *dago-* 'to' is a bounded P_{dir} that produces a telic interpretation while *izhi-* 'toward' and *biiji-* 'hither' are unbounded realizations of P_{dir} that produce atelic events.

Extending the Analysis: A Cause-Motion Construction

I suggest in this section that the analysis of manner-of-motion verbs in the previous section also accounts for the interpretation of initials in cause-motion verbs. Cause-motion verbs express an event in which the movement toward a goal is predicated on the object, and the verb is attributed to the causing event. An example from English is shown in (31).

(31) I kicked the ball to left field.

Folli and Harley (2006) and Zubizarreta and Oh (2007) argue that the cause-motion construction is structurally similar to the manner-of-motion construction. Zubizarreta and Oh in particular provide the structure of the cause-motion construction that is roughly outlined in (32). Compare (32) with the manner-of-motion construction in (33): the cause-motion construction contains an additional verbal (causative-like; here as "v") layer that hosts an external argument.

(32) [NP [v [NP [V [P_{dir} [P_{loc} . . .]]]]] [cause-motion structure]

(33) [NP [V [P_{dir} [P_{loc} . . .]]] [manner-of-motion structure]

Finals of contact in Ojibwe, such as *-webishkaw* 'kick', also appear with a directional initial. Consider (34) and (35) with the initials *izhi-* and *dago-*. As with manner-of-motion verbs, speaker judgments indicate that the boundedness of a cause-motion predicate depends on the initial: *izhi-* denotes a path, and *dago-* denotes a goal of motion. In (34), 'the rock' does not reach Thunder Bay, but in (35) it does.

(34) Ningii-izhiwebishkawaa asin Thunder Bay

nin-	gii-	iN-	web-	ishkaw	-aa	asin	Thunder Bay
1-	PST-	toward-	push.away-	act.with.foot.TA	-DIR	rock.NA	Thunder Bay

'I kicked the rock toward Thunder Bay.'

(35) Ningii-dagwebishkawaa asin Thunder Bay

nin-	gii-	dago-	web-	ishkaw	-aa	asin	Thunder Bay
1-	PST-	to-	push.away-	act.with.foot.TA	-DIR	rock.NA	Thunder Bay

'I kicked the rock to Thunder Bay.'

Since the initial plays the same role in both constructions, this cause-motion construction has a structure comparable to the one in (23). Thus, I assume that the initial realizes P_{dir} that is base-generated as a complement to the final. P_{dir} then moves head-wise to v, as (36) shows for (34). (For simplicity, the positions of the subject and object are omitted.)

(36) $[_{vP}$ $[_{v}$ $[_{Pdir}$ izhi] webishkawaa] $[_{PPdir}$ t_{izhi} $[_{PPloc}$ Thunder Bay]]]

To conclude this brief section, I have observed that the cause-motion construction in Ojibwe can be analyzed in a parallel fashion to the manner-of-motion construction.

Conclusion

In this paper, I have described and provided an analysis for the manner-of-motion construction in Ojibwe. I argued that manner-of-motion verbs take a directional PP complement, and that the directional P determines the telicity of the predicate. I further proposed that Ojibwe has complex PPs.

This analysis builds on the previous Algonquian literature (e.g., Hirose 2001; Mathieu 2008; and Slavin 2012) that proposes that word formation is syntactic. In line with Slavin, in particular, I argue that the verb stem in Ojibwe corresponds to the vP. This paper thus contributes to the growing body of literature of word formation and the nature of predication in Algonquian languages.

NOTES

1. The typical Algonquian verb stem consists of two derivational morphemes: an INITIAL is the left edge element that supplies lexical content, while a FINAL is at the far right edge of the stem and defines the stem's lexical category. A verb stem can be optionally modified by a bound preverbal (adverbial-like) modifier, traditionally called a PREVERB. The following abbreviations are used: 1 = first person; 3 = third person; AI = animate intransitive; DIR = direct; II = intransitive inanimate; LOC = locative; NA = noun animate; NI = noun inanimate; PST = past; TA = transitive animate; TI = transitive inanimate.
2. For expository purposes, I use the elements to the left of the "/" when referring to the directional element. Since the element *biiji-/biid-* seems to have the same meaning as *bi-* 'hither', I have placed them in the same cell. I do not make any claims regarding their morphological relationship or origin. Furthermore, note that *izhi-/in-* 'toward' has the underlying form /iN-/, where /N/ is a morpheme that surfaces as [zh] or [n].
3. See, for example, Goddard (1990) for a morphological analysis; see also Hirose (2001), Mathieu (2008), and Slavin (2012) for syntactic analyses.
4. The English translations in (5) are not meant to be literal. The verb stem does not contain an element that means 'go'. (However, see, for example, Zubizarreta and Oh [2007], who have argued that manner-of-motion verbs in English contain a covert *go*).
5. The *for an hour/in an hour* test (Dowty 1979) does not apply in Ojibwe. That is, Ojibwe does not distinguish between measure and interval adverbials.
6. In this paper, I assume that the subject is in Spec,vP, but nothing hinges on this matter.
7. The schematization in (23) assumes that words may be formed syntactically. Above, I showed that the element *eta* 'only' may scope over just the final. Although space reasons prohibit a full explanation of the scope facts, I offer a possibility here. I suggest that *eta* is merged with the structure by adjoining to v (as in (i) for (5a)). I argue that since *eta* is contained in v, it modifies just the final. However, I make two crucial assumptions. First, I assume that linearization and morpheme ordering phenomena are postsyntactic operations (Arregi and Nevins 2012). The terminal nodes Adv and v in (i) undergo metathesis in the postsyntactic component (as roughly shown in (ii)), and this process

derives the postverbal position of *eta*. Second, I follow Chomsky (1995) and assume that head movement occurs postsyntactically; otherwise, *eta* would be in a position to modify P_{dir} after head movement. The order of these two operations is not crucial, as far as I can see.

(i)

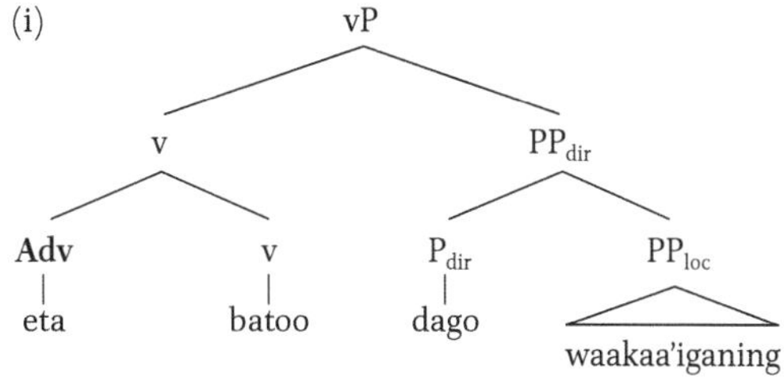

(ii) PF: **Adv** v → v **Adv**

8. See Rhodes (2005) for a historical analysis of relative roots. There, Rhodes argues for a post-positional structure of relative roots, whereby the relative root is morphophonologically reanalyzed as part of the verb. Under the current approach, the directional P (the initial) and v (the final) can only form a "word" when P is a complement to v. No such merger occurs if the directional P is a preverb.

   See also Baker (1988), who has proposed that applicative constructions are the result of preposition raising (that is, incorporation of P). While the present analysis is similar to Baker (1988) in that it proposes incorporation of a P head, there is one main difference: the P head that incorporates in (23) is a functional head, whereas Baker's P is lexical since it assigns a theta-role to its nominal complement.
9. See Landau (2010) for further discussion on obliques as PPs.
10. Since the function of *izhi-* here is unclear, I gloss it as "izhi."

REFERENCES

Arregi, Karlos, and Andrew Nevins. 2012. *Morphotactics: Basque Auxiliaries and the Structure of Spellout.* Dordrecht: Springer.

Baker, Mark C. 1988. *Incorporation: A Theory of Grammatical Function Changing*. Chicago: University of Chicago Press.

Beck, Sigrid, and William Snyder. 2001. The resultative parameter and restitutive again. In *Audiatur Vox Sapientiae: A Festschrift for Arnim von Stechow*, edited by Caroline Fery and Wolfgang Sternefeld, 48–69. Berlin: Akademie Verlag.

Bliss, Heather, Rose-Marie Déchaine, and Tomio Hirose. 2013a. Locative PPs in Blackfoot and Plains Cree. Paper read at CLA/ACL 2013, University of Victoria.

———. 2013b. A comparison of locative PPs in Blackfoot and Plains Cree. Paper read at the Forty-Fifth Algonquian Conference, University of Ottawa.

Chomsky, Noam. 1995. *The Minimalist Program.* Cambridge, MA: MIT Press.

Dowty, David. 1979. *Word Meaning and Montague Grammar.* Dordrecht: Reidel.

Folli, Raffaella, and Heidi Harley. 2006. On the licensing of causatives of directed motion: Waltzing Matilda all over. *Studia Linguistica* 60:121–155.

Jackendoff, Ray. 1990. *Semantic Structure.* Cambridge, MA: MIT Press.

Goddard, Ives. 1990. Primary and secondary stem derivation in Algonquian. *International Journal of American Linguistics* 56:449–483.

Halle, Morris, and Alec Marantz. 1993. Distributed morphology and the pieces of inflection. In *The View from Building 20: Essays in Linguistics in Honor of Sylvain Bromberger*, edited by Kenneth Hale and Samuel Jay Keyser, 111–176. Cambridge, MA: MIT Press.

Hirose, Tomio. 2001. Origins of predicates: Evidence from Plains Cree. PhD thesis, University of British Columbia.

Koopman, Hilda. 1997. Prepositions, postpositions, circumpositions, and particles: The structure of Dutch PPs. Unpublished manuscript, University of California, Los Angeles.

Krifka, Manfred. 1989. Nominal reference, temporal constitution and quantification in event semantics. In *Semantics and Contextual Expression*, edited by Renate Bartsch, Jonah van Bethem, and Peter van Emde Boas, 109–137. Dordrecht: Kluwer.

Landau, Idan. 2010. *The Locative Syntax of Experiencers.* Cambridge, MA: MIT Press.

LeSourd, Philip S. 2012. Prepositional phrases in Maliseet-Passamaquoddy. Paper read at WAIL 15, University of California, Santa Barbara.

Levin, Beth, and Malka Rappaport Hovav. 1995. *Unaccusativity: At the Syntax-Lexical Semantics Interface.* Cambridge, MA: MIT Press.

Mathieu, Éric. 2008. The syntax of abstract and concrete finals in Ojibwe. In *Proceedings of NELS 37*, edited by Emily Elfner and Martin Walkow, 101–114. BookSurge Publishing.

Oxford, Will. 2011. The syntax of Innu-aimun locatives. In *Proceedings of WSCLA 16: The Workshop on Structure and Constituency in Languages of the Americas*, edited by Alexis Black and Meagan Louie, 135–150. University of British Columbia, Vancouver.

Ramchand, Gillian. 2008. *Verb Meaning and the Lexicon: A First Phase Syntax.* Cambridge: Cambridge University Press.

Rhodes, Richard A. 2005. *Clause Structure, Core Arguments, and the Algonquian Relative Root Construction.* The 1998 Belcourt Lecture. Winnipeg: Voices of Rupert's Land.

———. 2010. Relative root complement: A unique grammatical relation in Algonquian syntax. In *Rara & Rarissima: Documenting the Fringes of Linguistic Diversity*, edited by Jan Wohlgemuth and Michael Cysouw, 305–324. Berlin: De Gruyter Mouton.

Slavin, Tanya. 2007. In search of the event argument: A semantic analysis of the preverb *ishi-* in Oji-Cree. In *Proceedings of SULA 4*. Amherst, MA: GLSA.

———. 2012. The syntax and semantics of stem composition in Ojicree. PhD thesis, University of Toronto.

Snyder, William. 2001. On the nature of syntactic variation: Evidence from complex predicates and complex word-formation. *Language* 77:324–342.

Svenonius, Peter. 2010. Spatial P in English. In *Mapping Spatial PPs* (*The Cartography of Syntactic Structures*), Vol. 6, edited by Guglielmo Cinque and Luigi Rizzi, 127–160. New York: Oxford University Press.

Tenny, Carol. 1994. Aspectual Roles and the Syntax-Semantics Interface. Dordrecht: Kluwer.

Valentine, J. Randolph. 2001. *Nishnaabemwin Reference Grammar*. Toronto: University of Toronto Press.

Zubizarreta, Maria Luisa, and Eunjeong Oh. 2007. *On the Syntactic Composition of Manner and Motion*. Cambridge, MA: MIT Press.

The Semantics of Blackfoot Arguments

Natalie Weber and Lisa Matthewson

This paper argues that Blackfoot transitive verb stem morphology reflects the semantic type of the complement. Semantically bivalent verbs surface with three different stem types: TRANSITIVE ANIMATE (TA), TRANSITIVE INANIMATE (TI), and ANIMATE INTRANSITIVE PLUS OBJECT (AI+O) (Bloomfield 1946; Frantz 2009). Our evidence that stem type encodes the semantic type of the complement includes the (in)ability of complements to "escape" a clause, and scope with respect to clause-mate quantifiers. Formally transitive (TA/TI) stems combine with choice functions of type e. Complements to formally intransitive (AI+O) stems are either predicates of type ⟨e,t⟩ or existential quantifiers of type ⟨⟨e,t⟩,t⟩. While predicates of type ⟨e,t⟩ are pseudoincorporated (Bliss 2013) and must scope under operators, existential quantifiers can have either wide or narrow scope. Blackfoot therefore encodes a distinction between saturated and unsaturated semantic complement types.

Unless otherwise noted, all data in this paper come from original fieldwork with

Special thanks to Beatrice Bullshields for her laughter and patience and for sharing her language. *Nitsíkohtaahsi'takihpinnaan!* Thanks to audiences at UBC, the Forty-Fifth Algonquian Conference, and SULA 8, and to Meagan Louie and two anonymous reviewers. This research was supported in part by SSHRC grant #410-2011-0431.

one female speaker of the Káínaa (Blood) dialect in her late sixties. Our methodology involves the standard techniques of translation tasks (in either direction), elicited production tasks based on explicitly described discourse contexts, and acceptability judgment tasks in which the speaker judges the acceptability of Blackfoot sentences in particular discourse contexts. See Matthewson (2004) for further details of methodology.

Transitive Verb Stems in Blackfoot

The three types of stem for semantically transitive verbs are shown in (1)–(3): transitive animate (TA), transitive inanimate (TI), and animate intransitive plus object (AI+O), respectively (Bloomfield 1946; Frantz 2009).[1]

(1) naowatsiw [amo mamii/*akoopis]

na-**oowat**-yii-wa	[amo-yi	mamii-yi/	*akoopis-yi]
PST-**eat.TA**-DIR-PRX	DEM-OBV	fish.AN-OBV/	*soup.IN-OBV

'She/he ate this fish.' (Ritter and Rosen 2010:134)

(2) naowatoom [ani akoopis/*mamii]

na-**oowatoo**-m-wa	[ann-yi	akoopis-yi/	*mamii-yi]
PST-**eat.TI**-DIR-PRX	DEM-OBV	soup.IN-OBV/	*fish.AN-OBV

'She/he ate that soup.' (Ritter and Rosen 2010:134)

(3) naoyiw (mamii/akoopis)

na-**ooyi**-wa	(mamii/	akoopis)
PST-**eat.AI**-PRX	(fish.AN/	soup.IN)

'She/he ate (fish/soup).' (Ritter and Rosen 2010:134)

These verb stems differ in the animacy of the complements they may take; subjects of transitive verbs in Blackfoot must always be animate (Frantz 2009). TA verbs occur with objects of animate gender, such as *mamii* 'fish' in (1), but cannot occur with objects of inanimate gender, such as *akoopis* 'soup'.[2] Conversely, the object of TI verbs must be inanimate, as in (2). AI+O verbs allow complements of either gender, as in (3).

The three stem types also differ in their morphosyntax. TA and TI verbs are formally transitive in that they contain direct/inverse morphology, often called a THEME SIGN (Bloomfield 1946; Frantz 2009). The form of the theme sign depends on the person and proximate/obviate status of both the subject and object (Bliss 2005). Examples (4) and (5) differ minimally: the object of (4) is third person, and the object of (5) is first person. This affects the form of the theme suffix, showing that the object is indexed on TA/TI verbs.

(4) kitsíínowaa
kit-iino-**aa**-wa
2-see.TA-**DIR**-PRX
'You saw him/her.'

(5) kitsíínookį̥
kit-iino-**oki**
2-see.TA-**INV**
'You saw me.'

AI+O verbs are semantically bivalent but formally intransitive: the object is not indexed on the verb with a theme sign, as seen in (3). They have the same morphology as semantically monovalent verbs with animate subjects (AI verbs), such as *sspitaa* 'tall' in (6).

(6) ííksspitaa
iik-isspitaa-wa
VX-tall.AI-PRX
'She/he is tall.'

The formation of new TA, TI, and AI+O stems is extremely productive. While the form of many stems is not predictable, novel stems are often productively formed by our consultant using the derivational suffixes *-at* (TA), *-atoo* (TI), and *-aki* (AI+O) (see also Armoskaite 2011). Therefore almost all bivalent stems have three surface forms.

Previous Analyses

The literature provides two ideas about what drives the choice between verb stems, a syntactic account (Ritter and Rosen 2010) and a syntax-semantics account (Bliss 2013). We discuss each previous analysis in the following two subsections.

Syntactic Explanation

The syntactic account relies on the observation that TA/TI verbs allow different types of complements than AI+O verbs do (Frantz 2009; Ritter and Rosen 2010). TA and TI stems occur with DP complements, in which the nominal is preceded by a demonstrative, while AI+O stems occur with morphologically bare NPs or with null complements. Ritter and Rosen (2010) argue that TA and TI stems license DP objects while AI+O stems do not. Their generalizations are summarized in Table 1.

New data in Bliss (2012, 2013) show that bare plural NPs (NPs with plural morphology that lack a demonstrative) can also occur with AI+O verbs,[3] showing that the allowed complement types are more varied than previously assumed. We will show below that complement types are not in complementary distribution between TA/TI and AI+O verb stems. We argue that a syntactic explanation of stem types cannot be upheld, because NPs modified by a numeral can occur with all three stem types.

Pseudoincorporation Explanation

Bliss (2013) shows that bare NP complements to AI+O verbs exhibit several semantic differences from DP complements to TA/TI verbs. She shows that bare NPs are tightly bound to the verb (they remain *v*′-internal), number-neutral,[4] and nonspecific in the sense of Enç (1991), and that they have obligatory narrow scope under quantifiers and other operators. Based on these criteria, she argues that bare NP complements are pseudoincorporated in the sense of Massam (2001). Bliss (2013) also notes that bare plurals may occur as complements to AI+O verbs, but that these are semantically and syntactically distinct from bare NPs. Bare plurals are not number neutral. They are also a slightly larger morphosyntactic unit and contain a suffix that marks plurality and (in)animacy.

Bliss assumes that bare plurals are also pseudoincorporated, and suggests that all AI+O complements combine with the verb via Restrict (Chung and Ladusaw

TABLE 1. Morphosyntactic Correlations between Verb Stem and Complement Type

TYPE OF COMPLEMENT	TA/TI STEMS	AI+O STEMS
DP	✓	✗
Bare NP	✗	✓
Null Complement	✗	✓

2004). This predicts that bare plurals will take narrow scope under quantifiers and other operators. We show below that this prediction is not borne out, and that unlike bare NPs, bare plurals may take either wide or narrow scope with respect to clause-mate quantifiers.

In the next section we present a fuller account of the complement types allowed by TA/TI versus AI+O stems. After that, we turn to the semantic properties of the complements.

Distribution of Complement Types

We investigate a fuller range of post-verbal complement types than discussed in Ritter and Rosen (2010) and Bliss (2013), including 'certain' NPs, bare plurals, and NPs modified by a numeral.[5] DPs and 'certain' NPs include a demonstrative, while the other complement types do not. The word translated as 'certain' by our consultant is built on a demonstrative root (*ann-*), but differs from other demonstratives in morphological complexity (for example, it includes the morpheme *-hka* INVS) and semantics. 'Certain' NPs can designate specific indefinites in out-of-the-blue contexts (such as the beginning of a narrative) while other DPs cannot, as shown in (7) and (8). In (7) the speaker is discussing a particular mouse he or she has in mind but which the hearer does not know about. Example (8) contains an ordinary DP, but is only licit in out of the blue contexts if the speaker can point to the mouse.

(7) Matónni nitsíínoaa [anááhkayi kánaisskiina]

matonni	nit-iino-aa-wa	[**ann**-wa-hka=ayi	kánaisskiina-wa]
yesterday	1-see.TA-DIR-PRX	**DEM**-PRX-INVS=OBV.SG	mouse.AN-PRX

'Yesterday I saw a (certain) mouse.'

(8) #Matónni nitsíínoaa [óma kánaisskiina]
matonni nit-iino-aa-wa [**om**-wa kánaisskiina-wa]
yesterday 1-see.TA-DIR-PRX **DEM**-PRX mouse.AN-PRX
#'Yesterday I saw that mouse.'
Speaker's comment: you can only say *óma* if the mouse is in the room with you and you are pointing at it.

We found that 'certain' NPs occur as complements to TA and TI verbs, but never to AI+O verbs. This is shown in (9), versus (10), for the verb 'see'.

(9) iinoyííyaa [aniskayi píita]
iino-yii-yi=aawa [**ann**-yi-hka=ayi píita-yi]
see.TA-DIR-PL=PRX.PL **DEM-OBV**-INVS=OBV.SG eagle.AN-OBV
'They saw a certain eagle.'

(10) *iyáápiiya [aniskayi píita]
iyaapi-yi=aawa [**ann**-yi-hka=ayi píita-yi]
see.AI-PL=PRX.PL **DEM-OBV**-INVS=OBV.SG eagle.AN-OBV
Intended: 'They saw an eagle.'

Similarly, a 'certain' NP can occur as the complement to the TI verb *iihkiitatoo* 'bake' in (11), but not as the complement to the AI+O counterpart *iihkiitaa* 'bake' in (12).

(11) iihkíítatoomya [aniíhkayi napayín]
iihkiitatoo-m-yi=aawa [**ann**-yi-hka=ayi napayin-yi]
bake.TI-DIR-PL=PRX.PL **DEM-OBV**-INVS=OBV.SG bread.IN-OBV
'They baked a certain bread.'

(12) *iihkíítaa [aniíhkayi napayín]
iihkiitaa-yi=aawa [**ann**-yi-hka=ayi napayin-yi]
bake.AI-PL=PRX.PL **DEM-OBV**-INVS=OBV.SG bread.IN-OBV
Intended: 'They baked a certain bread.'

We also confirmed Bliss's (2013) observation that bare plurals can occur as complements to AI+O verbs but not to TA or TI verbs, as demonstrated in (13) and (14). We also provide examples with TI and AI+O stems for 'read' in (15) and (16).

(13) *iinoyííya [píítaiks]

iino-yii-yi=aawa	[piitaa-iksi]
see.TA-DIR-PL=PRX.PL	eagle-AN.PL

Intended: 'They saw eagles.'

(14) iyáápiya [píítaiks]

iyaapi-yi=aawa	[piitaa-iksi]
see.AI-PL=PRX.PL	eagle-AN.PL

'They saw eagles.'

(15) *iikstóómya [sináákia'tsists]

iikstoo-m-yi=aawa	[sinaakia'tsis–istsi]
read.TI-DIR-PL=PRX.PL	book-IN.PL

Intended: 'They read books.'

(16) iikstákiiya [sináákia'tsists]

iikstaki-yi=aawa	[sinaakia'tsis-istsi]
read.AI-PL=PRX.PL	book-IN.PL

'They read books.'

We also investigated NPs modified by a numeral but no demonstrative (NUMERAL NPs), which were not included in previous studies. Numeral NPs can appear with both TA/TI verbs and AI+O verbs, as shown in (17) and (18).

(17) á'pistotsimya [nióókskayi itáísóyo'pists]

a'pistotsi-m-yi=aawa	[niookska-yi	itaisooyo'p-istsi]
build.TI-DIR-PL=PRX.PL	three.IN-PL	table-IN.PL

'They built three tables.'

(18) á'pistotakiiya [nióókskayi itáísóyo'pists]

a'pistotaki-yi=aawa	[niookska-yi	itaisooyo'p-ists]
build.AI-PL=PRX.PL	three.IN-PL	table-IN.PL

'They built three tables.'

TABLE 2. Distribution of Complement Types

COMPLEMENT TYPE	TA/TI STEMS	AI+O STEMS
DP	✓	✗
'Certain' NP	✓	✗
Bare NP	✗	✓
Bare plural NP	✗	✓
Null complement	✗	✓
Numeral NP	✓	✓

The distribution of types of complements is summarized in Table 2. AI+O verbs can never take a DP complement. TA/TI stems can appear with DP complements (including 'certain' NPs) or with Numeral NPs. Without further assumptions, a purely syntactic explanation cannot account for the fact that Numeral NPs are compatible with all stem types. Our proposal that the choice of stem type is sensitive to semantic, not syntactic, criteria predicts that when Numeral NPs occur with TA/TI stems, they should exhibit different semantic attributes than when they occur as complements to AI+O stems. We turn to the evidence for this in the next section.

Verb Stem Reflects Semantic Type

Our proposal is that complements to TA and TI verbs are of type e, while AI+O complements are of a nonreferential semantic type: either quantificational (type $\langle\langle e,t\rangle,t\rangle$) or predicative (type $\langle e,t\rangle$). Complements to TA/TI verbs introduce free-variable choice functions, and combine with the verb via Functional Application.

We give two types of evidence for our proposal. First, we show that TA/TI complements display exceptionally wide "scope," even scoping outside clause boundaries. This behavior is a hallmark of referential elements, including specific indefinites (Fodor and Sag 1982). Complements to AI+O verbs cannot escape clause boundaries. Second, we show that TA/TI complements never scope below a quantifier within the same clause, except in cases of PSEUDOSCOPE (Kratzer 1998). Bare NP complements to AI+O verbs, on the other hand, must take narrow scope with respect to a clause-mate quantifier, which is predicted for arguments of type

⟨e,t⟩. Finally, we show that bare plural and Numeral NP complements to AI+O verbs can scope either above or below a clause-mate quantifier.

Exceptional Wide-Scope Behavior

Quantifiers occur as prefixes on the verb and can associate semantically with DP subjects or objects within their clause. This is shown in (19) with a TI verb.

(19) Nitohkanáóhpommatoo'pinnaaniaawa
nit-**ohkana**-ohpommatoo-'p-innaan-yi=aawa
1-**all**-buy.TI-DIR-1PL-PL=PRX.PL
'We all bought them.' OR 'We bought all of them.' (Frantz 2009:85)

However, quantifiers are clause-bound in conjunct clauses (embedded clauses marked with the clause-typing suffix *-hs* CNJ; Déchaine and Wiltschko 2014). In (20), *ayak-* 'both' presupposes that the argument it quantifies over contains only two entities. Embedded *ayak-* can only associate with clause-mate arguments, not with matrix clause arguments. These data indicate that conjunct clauses are scope islands in Blackfoot.

(20) nitsíksstaahpinnaan [kitááhkayaksiistapoohsoaayi]
nit-ik-sstaa-hpinnaan [kit-aahk-**ayak**-iistap-oo-hs-oaa-yi]
1-DEG-want.AI-1PL 2-might-**both**-away-go-CNJ-2PL-OBV
✓'We want you both to go away.' *Context*: There are three of us and two of you.
#'We both want you to go away.' *Context*: There are two of us and three of you.
(adapted from Bliss 2012:12)

We now investigate the conjunct-clause-escaping properties of complements to verbs of various stem types. We show that complements to TA/TI verbs can "escape" semantic islands, while complements to AI+O verbs cannot. As discussed by Fodor and Sag (1982), among others, island-escaping behavior—and in particular island-escaping behavior to take only WIDEST, not INTERMEDIATE, scope—suggests that the relevant noun phrases are of type e. These phrases appear to take widest scope, but in reality are scopeless because they are directly referential. The three relevant readings to investigate—widest, intermediate, and narrowest—are illustrated for an English example in (21).

(21) Those girls all want [to buy **a dog**].
Widest: $\exists y(\mathbf{dog}(y))$ [$\forall x(\text{girl}(x))$ [x wants [x buys y]]]
Intermediate: $\forall x(\text{girl}(x))$ [$\exists y(\mathbf{dog}(y))$ [x wants [x buys y]]]
Narrowest: $\forall x(\text{girl}(x))$ [x wants [$\exists y(\mathbf{dog}(y))$ [x buys y]]]

Example (22) shows a DP complement to a TA verb within an embedded conjunct clause. It only has the widest scope reading, as we expect under our analysis of TA complements as type e.

(22) ómiksi aakííkoaiks ikohkanáísstaya [omááhkohpommataahsa ómi imita]
om-iksi aakiikoan-iksi ik-ohkana-issta-yi=aawa
DEM-AN.PL GIRL-AN.PL VX-all-want.AI-PL=PRX.PL

[o-m-aahk-ohpommat-aa-hsi=aawa **om**-yi imita-yi]
3-3-might-buy.**TA**-DIR-CNJ=PRX.PL **DEM**-OBV dog.AN-OBV
'Those girls all want to buy that dog.'

✓Widest: for one particular dog x, all the girls want to buy x
#Intermediate: for each girl, there is a different dog which she wants to buy
#Narrowest: all the girls want to buy a dog, any dog

This widest-only behavior is not limited to DP complements, but is true for all allowed complement types to TA and TI verbs (for example, DPs, 'certain' NPs, and Numeral NPs). For space reasons, we do not include all the relevant examples here, but see Weber and Matthewson (2014) for a fuller data set.

In contrast, AI+O complements in embedded clauses CANNOT escape a conjunct clause. In example (23), the only possible reading is one where each of the girls has the desire to buy a dog, but none of them have a particular dog in mind.

(23) ómiksi aakííkoaiks íkohkanaisstaya [omááhkohpommaahsa imita]
om-iksi aakiikoan-iksi ik-ohkana-issta-yi=aawa
DEM-AN.PL GIRL-AN.PL VX-all-want.AI-PL=PRX.PL

[o-m-aahk-ohpommaa-hsi=aawa imita]
3-3-might-buy.AI-CNJ=PRX.PL dog.AN
'Those girls all want to buy a dog.'

#Widest: for one particular dog x, all the girls want to buy x
#Intermediate: for each girl, there is a different dog that she wants to buy
✓Narrowest: all the girls want to buy a dog, any dog

Similarly, bare plural and Numeral NP complements within AI+O conjunct clauses must take narrowest scope, as shown in (24). Recall that Numeral NPs may also appear as complements to TA/TI verbs, where they display widest-only scope. The different behavior of Numeral NPs as complements to TA/TI versus AI+O verb stems is one of our strongest arguments in favor of a semantic analysis.

(24) ómiksi aakííkoaiks ikohkanáísstaya [omááhkohpommaahsa (nióókskami) imitáíks]
om-iksi aakiikoan-iksi ik-ohkana-issta-yi=aawa
DEM-AN.PL girl-AN.PL DEG-all-want.AI-PL=PRX.PL

[o-m-aahk-ohpommaa-hsi=aawa (**niookskam**-yi) imita-**iksi**]
3-3-might-buy.AI-CNJ=PRX.PL (**three.AN**-PL) dog-**AN.PL**
'Those girls all want to buy (three) dogs.'

#Widest: there is one particular set of (3) dogs that all the girls want to buy
#Intermediate: for each girl, there is a different set of (3) dogs she wants to buy
✓Narrowest: all the girls want to buy (3) dogs, any (3) dogs

The exceptional scope data are summarized in Table 3. All complements to TA/TI verbs are interpreted as if they took widest scope, but the absence of intermediate readings shows that these complement types are in reality scopeless (cf.

TABLE 3. Island-Escaping Properties of Complements to Different Verb Stems

STEM TYPE	COMPLEMENT	SCOPE?
TA/TI	DP	widest
TA/TI	'certain' NP	widest
TA/TI	Numeral NP	widest
AI+O	bare NP	narrowest
AI+O	bare plural	narrowest
AI+O	Numeral NP	narrowest

Fodor and Sag 1982). Bare NP, bare plural, and Numeral NP complements to AI+O verbs, on the other hand, are clause-bound, which shows they are NOT of type e.

An important point is that Numeral NPs behave differently depending on whether they are complements to TA/TI verbs or AI+O verbs. This shows that the choice of verb stem reflects semantic properties of the complement, not syntactic ones. The choice between TA/TI and AI+O verbs reflects the semantic type of the complement (type e or not type e). In the next section we provide more semantic evidence for this proposal.

Clause-Internal Scoping Data

In this section we examine the scoping behavior of complements with respect to clause-mate quantifiers. We show that TA/TI complements always take wide scope with respect to quantifiers, which is expected if they are of type e. Complements to AI+O verbs show two different behaviors: bare NPs always take narrow scope, while bare plurals and plurals modified by a numeral can take either wide or narrow scope. We use the strong quantifiers *ayak-* 'both', *a'tsoot-* 'both', and *iihkana-* 'all' in the examples below, which always occur as verbal prefixes. Weak quantifiers such as 'many' may occur either as verbal prefixes or as a separate modifier, but we have not considered these in this paper.

The TA/TI data are shown in (25)–(27), with an animate DP, an inanimate 'certain' NP, and a Numeral NP. The results are summarized in Table 4.

(25) áyákohpommatsiiya [ómi isttoán]

ayak-ohpommat-yii-yi=aawa	[**om**-yi	isttoan-yi]
both-buy.TA-DIR-PL=PRX.PL	**DEM-OBV**	knife.AN-OBV

They both bought this knife.'

✓They bought this same knife (together).
#They bought one knife each.

(26) á'tsootokstoomya [aníhkayi sináákia'tsis]

a'tsoot-okstoo-m-yi=aawa	[**ann**-yi-hka=ayi	sinaakia'tsis]
both-read.TI-DIR-PL=PRX.PL	**DEM-OBV**-INVS=OBV.SG	book.IN

'They both read a certain book.'

✓They read the same book.
#They each read a different book.

TABLE 4. Scope of Different TA/TI Complements with Respect to Quantifiers

COMPLEMENT	WIDE SCOPE?	NARROW SCOPE?
DP	✓	✗
'Certain' NP	✓	✗
Numeral NP	✓	✗

(27) áyaká'pistotsimya [nióókskayi itáísóyo'pists]
ayak-a'pistots-m-yi=aawa [**niookska**-yi itaisooyo'p-istsi]
both-BUILD.TI-DIR-PL=PRX.PL **three**-PL table-IN.PL
'They both built three tables.'

✓They both worked on the same three tables.
#Piitaaki made two and Saako made one. (Three tables total.)
#They each made three tables. (Six tables total.)

On the other hand, bare NP complements to AI+O verbs must take narrow scope. This is illustrated with an animate complement in (28) and an inanimate in (29).

(28) iihkanááyaapiiya [píita]
iihkana-yaapi-yi=aawa [píita]
all-see.AI-PL=PRX.PL eagle.AN
'They all saw an eagle.'

#Three birdwatchers all saw the same eagle.
✓Three birdwatchers split up and they each saw a different eagle.

(29) iihkanáókstakiiya [sinaákia'tsis]
iihkana-okstaki-yi=aawa [sinaakia'tsis]
all-read.AI-PL=PRX.PL book.IN
'They all read a book.'

#They all read the exact same book.
✓Each of them read a different book.

Bare plural nouns may either scope high or low, as demonstrated in (30) and (31).

(30) iihkanááyaapiiya [píítaiks]
iihkana-yaapi-yi=aawa [piitaa-**iksi**]
all-see.AI-PL=PRX.PL eagle-**AN.PL**
'They all saw eagles.'

✓Three birdwatchers are together and they saw eagles.
✓Three birdwatchers split up and they each saw different eagles.

(31) áyakohpommayaa [sópa'tsists]
ayak-ohpommaa-yi=aawa [sopa'tsis-**istsi**]
both-BUY.AI-PL=PRX.PL chair-**IN.PL**
'They both bought some chairs.'

✓The shopowner dishonestly (re)sold the same set of chairs to two people.
✓Two people each bought some chairs separately.

Numeral NP complements to AI+O verbs also scope high or low, as in (32) and (33).

(32) anááhk píítaaki ki anááhk sááko áyaka'pistotakiiya [nióókskayi itáísóyo'pists]
ann-wa-hka píítaa-aakii ki ann-wa-hka sááko
DEM-PRX-INVS eagle-woman CONJ DEM-PRX-INVS saako

ayak-a'pistotaki-yi=aawa [**niookska**-yi itaisooyo'p-istsi]
both-build.AI-PL=PRX.PL **three.**IN-PL table-IN.PL
'Piitaaki and Saako both built three tables.'

✓They both worked on the same three tables.
✓They each made three tables. (Six tables total.)

(33) nitohkanáóhpommaahpinnaan [nióókska sináákia'tsists]
nit-ohkana-ohpommaa-hp-innaan [**niookska**-yi sinaakia'tsis-istsi]
1-all-buy.AI-IND-1Pl **three.**IN-PL book-IN.PL
'We all bought three books.'

✓We pooled our money to buy three books.
✓We each bought three books.

The AI+O complement scoping facts are summarized in Table 5. We confirmed Bliss's (2013) observation that bare NPs must scope under quantifiers. However, bare plurals and Numeral NPs cannot be pseudoincorporated in the same manner as bare NPs, contra Bliss (2013), because they do not obligatorily take narrow scope under quantifiers.

In the next two sections we present our analysis of these facts.

TABLE 5. Scope of Different AI+O Complements with Respect to Quantifiers

COMPLEMENT	WIDE SCOPE?	NARROW SCOPE?
Bare NP	✗	✓
Bare Plural	✓	✓
Numeral NP	✓	✓

TA/TI Complements Are Wide-Scope Choice Functions

We argue that all complements to TA and TI verbs introduce choice-function variables. The choice function applies to the set denoted by the nominal predicate and returns one individual from that set (Reinhart 1997). The entire DP is thus of type e, denoting one (possibly plural) individual. Following Kratzer (1998), we assume that the choice functions are left free. This predicts that the relevant noun phrases can escape from islands and display clause-internal widest-scope behavior, just as we showed is the case for Blackfoot TA/TI complements. The analysis is illustrated in (35) for the sentence in (34) (repeated from (26)). We assume that the 'certain' demonstrative introduces a choice function variable, and the verbal stem morphology presupposes that the complement is of type e.

(34) á'tsootokstoomya [aníhkayi sináákia'tsis]

a'tsoot-okstoo-m-yi=aawa	[**ann**-yi-hka=ayi	sinaakia'tsis]
both-read.TI-DIR-PL=PRX.PL	**DEM-OBV**-INVS=OBV.SG	book.IN

'They both read a certain book.'

✓They read the same book.
#They each read a different book.

(35) [[á'tsootokstoomya pro_3 aníhkayi$_4$ sináákia'tsis]]^g is defined only if $|g(3)| = 2$.
If defined, [[á'tsootokstoomya pro$_3$ aníhkayi$_4$ sináákia'tsis]]^g
$= \forall x\ [x \in g(3) \rightarrow \text{read}\ (x, g(4)(\text{book}))]$

Sentence (35) asserts that they each read the element that is chosen from the set of books by the contextually salient choice function. This correctly predicts that they both read the same book.

Our analysis makes a further prediction, again inherited from the analysis of Kratzer (1998) (and its variant in Matthewson 1999, used for similar facts in St'át'imcets): if there is a bound pronoun inside the relevant complement, apparent narrow scope will arise (Kratzer's pseudoscope). This is because there can be a different choice function for each individual. This prediction is borne out, as shown in (36)–(37). Sentence (36) asserts that each girl *x* is holding the pen which is chosen from the set of *x*'s pens by the choice function. Since there is a different set of *x*'s pens for each value of *x*, there can be two different pens.[6]

(36) ómiksi nráátsitapiks aakííkoaiks (áyaká)áyinniiya (ómiksi)
otó'ohtaisinaaki'ihpowai(ks)

om-iksi	naat-itapi-iksi	aakiikoan-iksi
DEM-AN.PL	two-person-AN.PL	girl.AN.PL

(ayak-)a-yinn-yii-yi=aawa	(om-iksi)
(both-)IPFV-hold.TA-DIR-PL=PRX.PL	(DEM-AN.PL)

ot-ohtaisinaakiyihp-owaa-yi/-iksi
3-pen-3PL-OBV(SG)/-AN.PL
'They are holding **their own** pen(s).'
Nonwidest scope available: for each girl *x*, *x* is holding *x*'s pen(s)

(37) [[ómiksi náátsitapiks aakííkoaiks (áyak) áyinniiya pro_3
(ómiksi$_4$) otó'ohtaisinaaki'ihpowai(ks)]]^g
$= \forall x[x \in g(3) \rightarrow \text{hold}(x, g(4)(x\text{'s pen(s)}))]$

Further cases of "pseudoscope" are given in Weber and Matthewson (2014). This pattern, whereby indefinite noun phrases display widest-scope effects which are mitigated by bound variable pronouns, provides strong support for a free-variable choice function analysis of Blackfoot TA/TI complements.

AI+O Complements Are Nonreferential, but Not All Predicative

Recall that unlike TA/TI complements, AI+O complements cannot escape semantic islands. We can therefore conclude that no AI+O complements are of type e. But because complements to AI+O verbs show two different behaviors with respect to scoping around quantifiers, we propose that AI+O complements come in two types. Morphologically bare NPs, which must take narrow scope with respect to quantifiers, are pseudoincorporated and are of type ⟨e,t⟩. They compose with the verb via Restrict, and Existential Closure then applies (Bliss 2013; Chung and Ladusaw 2004). On the other hand, plural AI+O complements may scope either above or below quantifiers. This is explained by analyzing plural complements as existential quantifiers (of type ⟨⟨e,t⟩,t⟩). This also correctly predicts that plural NPs cannot escape the clause to take exceptionally wide scope. For Numeral NPs (the one type of complement that is grammatical with both types of verb stem), our analysis correctly predicts differential scope behavior, depending on whether the Numeral NP appears as complement to a TA/TI verb or an AI+O verb.

Conclusion

In this paper we have argued that the choice of Blackfoot verb stem is semantically, not syntactically, driven. A primary piece of evidence for the proposal comes from Numeral NPs, which can occur as complements to both TA/TI and AI+O verbs, but with different semantic behavior. Blackfoot overtly encodes referential objects (via TA/TI stem morphology) versus nonreferential objects (via AI+O morphology). We note that a similar distinction of complement types is maintained in other Algonquian languages via two parallel series of inflectional morphology: the ABSOLUTE inflection (used with indefinite objects), and the OBJECTIVE (used with definite objects or null pronouns; Goddard 2007 and sources therein). While reflexes of both inflectional paradigms exist in Blackfoot, the absolute/objective contrast is no longer productive. Instead, the distinction between referential and nonreferential complement types is expressed via stem morphology.

We also showed that complements to AI+O verbs are semantically non-uniform, and that only bare NP complements are pseudoincorporated (contra Bliss 2013). Furthermore, the two proposed semantic types for AI+O complements correlate in a plausible way with the content of the complements themselves. It is unsurprising from a cross-linguistic perspective that it is the bare NPs that are pseudoincorporated. Objects with typical pseudoincorporated properties (such as obligatory narrow scope) are frequently number-neutral, just like Blackfoot bare NPs but unlike Blackfoot bare plurals and Numeral NPs (Chung and Ladusaw 2004; Dayal 2011; Farkas and de Swart 2003; van Geenhoven 1998).

A number of issues remain for future research. One question concerns whether AI+O complements are discourse transparent (can be anaphorically referred back to in subsequent sentences). The literature on pseudoincorporation shows that there is cross-linguistic variation with respect to whether an incorporated noun is discourse transparent (e.g., Mithun 1984). Research suggests that the ability of pseudoincorporated nouns to allow anaphoric reference depends in part on whether the language allows both singular and plural incorporated nominals, whether the anaphor is covert or overt, and whether the sentence is telic or atelic (Dayal 2011; Farkas and de Swart 2003). Future research should explore where Blackfoot fits in this typology with respect to anaphora.

NOTES

1. In our data, we use the orthographic conventions of Frantz (1978, 2009), except that we overtly mark devoicing of word-final vowels with the IPA diacritic X̥. Examples from other sources include the original transcription and free translation, but we have sometimes amended the gloss line for consistency. Abbreviations that are not in the Leipzig Glossing Rules: 1, 2, 3 = first, second, third person; AI = animate intransitive; AN = animate; CNJ = conjunct order; CONJ = conjunction; DEG = degree marker; DIR = direct; II = inanimate intransitive; INVS = invisible; INV = inverse; IN = inanimate, MEANS = means/instrumental; OBV = obviative; PRX = proximate; TA = transitive animate; TI = transitive inanimate.
2. Animacy in Blackfoot is grammatical. The (in)animacy of a noun usually corresponds with real-world (non)sentience, but a subset of nonsentient referents are grammatically animate, such as *pokón* 'ball', *íssk* 'pail', and *isttoán* 'knife' (Bliss 2005; Frantz 2009).
3. This seems to be a recent change. Frantz (personal communication to Heather Bliss; Bliss

2013, n. 181) says that older data show bare plurals are not allowed as AI+O complements.

4. Bare NPs may not be number-neutral for our consultant; she typically rejects bare NPs in plural contexts. Investigation of number-neutrality goes beyond the scope of this paper.
5. Complements may also appear preverbally, with concurrent differences in verbal agreement and focus. We restrict our investigation here to postverbal complements.
6. The pens in (36) can be marked by the singular suffix *-yi* if each girl is only holding a single pen. However, the plural suffix *-iksi* is also valid or even preferred in this context. This morphological plurality may be a dependent plural effect (de Mey 1981).

REFERENCES

Armoskaite, Solveiga. 2011. The destiny of roots in Blackfoot and Lithuanian. PhD thesis, University of British Columbia.

Bliss, Heather. 2005. Formalizing point-of-view: The role of sentience in Blackfoot's direct/inverse system. MA thesis, University of Calgary.

———. 2012. A split DP analysis of Blackfoot nominal expressions. In *Proceedings of the 2012 Canadian Linguistic Association*, edited by P. Cajax. Waterloo, ON: Wilfred Laurier.

———. 2013. The Blackfoot configurationality conspiracy: Parallels and differences in clausal and nominal structures. PhD thesis, University of British Columbia.

Bloomfield, Leonard. 1946. Algonquian. *Linguistic Structures of Native America*, edited by Harry Hoijer et al., 85–29. Viking Fund Publications in Anthropology 6. New York.

Chung, Sandra, and William A. Ladusaw. 2004. *Restriction and Saturation*. Cambridge, MA: MIT Press.

Dayal, Veneeta. 2011. Hindi pseudo-incorporation. *Natural Language & Linguistic Theory* 29:123–167.

Déchaine, Rose-Marie, and Martina Wiltschko. 2014. Micro-variation in agreement, clause-typing and finiteness: Comparative evidence from Plains Cree and Blackfoot. In *Papers of the Forty-Second Algonquian Conference*, edited by J. Randolph Valentine and Monica Macaulay, 69–101. Albany, NY: SUNY Press.

de Mey, Sjaak. 1981. The dependant plural and the analysis of tense. In *Proceedings of NELS 11*, edited by V. Burke and J. Pustejowsky. Amherst, MA: GLSA.

Enç, Mürvet. 1991. The semantics of specificity. *Linguistic Inquiry* 22:1–25.

Farkas, Donka, and Henriëtte de Swart 2003. *The Semantics of Incorporation*. Stanford, CA: CSLI Publications.

Fodor, Janet Dean, and Ivan Sag 1982. Referential and quantificational indefinites. *Linguistics and Philosophy* 5:355–398.

Frantz, Douglas G. 1978. Abstractness of phonology and Blackfoot orthography design. In *Approaches to Language, Anthropological Issues*, edited by William C, McCormack and Stephen A. Wurm, 307–325. Berlin: Mouton.

———. 2009. *Blackfoot Grammar.* Toronto: University of Toronto Press.

Goddard, Ives. 2007. Reconstruction and history of the Independent Indicative. In *Papers of the Thirty-Eighth Algonquian Conference*, edited by H. C. Wolfart, 207–271. University of Manitoba.

Kratzer, Angelika. 1998. Scope or pseudoscope? Are there wide-scope indefinites? In *Events in Grammar*, edited by Susan Rothstein, 163–196. Dordrecht: Kluwer Academic Publishers.

Massam, Diane. 2001. Pseudo noun incorporation in Niuean. *Natural Language & Linguistic Theory* 27:379–426.

Matthewson, Lisa. 1999. On the interpretation of wide-scope indefinites. *Natural Language Semantics* 7:79–134.

———. 2004. On the methodology of semantic fieldwork. *International Journal of American Linguistics* 70:369–415.

Mithun, Marianne. 1984. The evolution of noun incorporation. *Language* 60: 847–894.

Reinhart, Tanya. 1997. Quantifier scope: How labor is divided between QR and choice functions. *Linguistics and Philosophy* 20:335–397.

Ritter, Elizabeth, and Sarah Thomas Rosen. 2010. Animacy in Blackfoot: Implications for event structure and clause structure. In *Lexical Semantics, Syntax, and Event Structure*, edited by Malka Rappaport Hovav, Edit Doron, and Ivy Sichel, 124–152. New York: Oxford University Press.

Van Geenhoven, Veerle. 1998. *Semantic Incorporation and Indefinite Descriptions*. Palo Alto, CA: CSLI Publications.

Weber, Natalie, and Lisa Matthewson. 2014. Reflections of complement type: The view from Blackfoot. In *MIT Working Papers in Linguistics*, edited by Luka Crnič and Uli Sauerland.

CONTRIBUTORS

Solveiga Armoskaite is a visiting assistant professor at the University of Rochester. Her specialty is morphosyntax, especially the typological and comparative aspects. She has worked on various issues of categorization in Blackfoot, Cree (Algonquian), Finnish (Finno-Ugric), Lithuanian (Baltic), Russian (Slavic), and Turkish (Turkic).

George F. Aubin is a professor emeritus of French and linguistics at Assumption College in Worcester, Massachusetts, where he earned his B.A. and M.A. He also has a Ph.D. from Brown University and did a postdoc at MIT. He has forty-three years of teaching experience at the college/university level, primarily at Assumption College, but he has also taught at Carleton University and at the Université d'Ottawa in Canada. His fieldwork was done primarily with Algonquin speakers in Golden Lake, Ontario.

Vincent Collette is associate professor of linguistics at First Nations University of Canada. He holds a degree in anthropology and a Ph.D. in linguistics from Laval University. He works on the morphology and semantics of East Cree (Algonquian) and Occitan (Romance). He is also interested in historical semantics and the ethnohistory of Native populations.

Amy Dahlstrom is associate professor of linguistics at the University of Chicago. Her research deals with issues of morphology, syntax, and information structure in Meskwaki and Plains Cree.

Michael David Hamilton is a Mellon Diversity Postdoctoral Fellow in the Department of Linguistics at Cornell University. He received his Ph.D. in 2015 from the Department of Linguistics at McGill University.

Meredith Johnson received her Ph.D. in linguistics from the University of Wisconsin–Madison in 2015.

Marie-Odile Junker is a professor in the School of Linguistics and Language Studies at Carleton University. She is cross-appointed to the Cognitive Science Institute and the French Department. Her research interests include language documentation with a specialization in Aboriginal languages (East Cree, Innu, and the Algonquian language family in general), information and communication technologies for language preservation, general linguistics, lexicography, cognitive semantics, cross-cultural communication, empowerment research, and French.

Sarah Lundquist is a linguistics Ph.D. student at the University of Wisconsin–Madison. Her primary research interests lie in the morphosyntax of Menominee and other languages native to Wisconsin. She is also passionate about endangered language documentation and revitalization.

Monica Macaulay is professor of linguistics at the University of Wisconsin–Madison. She specializes in the morphology of American Indian languages, including Mixtec, Karuk, and Menominee. She is also the coeditor of the Papers of the Algonquian Conference and is president of the Endangered Language Fund.

Lisa Matthewson earned her Ph.D. at the University of British Columbia. She is the author of *Determiner Systems and Quantificational Strategies: Evidence from Salish*, which was a cowinner of the Prize for Outstanding Dissertation in Language, Logic and Computation, European Association for Logic, Language and Information/FoLLI. She is interested in cross-linguistic variation in semantics and pragmatics, and what variation (or the lack of it) tells us about Universal Grammar. She has been doing fieldwork on St'át'imcets (Lillooet Salish) since 1992, and on Gitksan (Tsimshianic) since 2010. She has worked on a range of areas in semantics and the syntax/semantics interface, including determiners, quantifiers, adverbs, tense, aspect, modals, evidentials, mood, discourse particles, and presuppositions. She is also interested in the methodology of semantic fieldwork and in endangered language preservation and oral history. She is involved in community language preservation initiatives, including contributing to the First Voices website for Northern St'át'imcets.

Gerald P. McKinley is a medical anthropologist based in the Department of Pathology and Laboratory Medicine, Schulich School of Medicine and Dentistry, Western University. Dr. McKinley is teaching faculty in the Schulich Interfaculty Program in Public Health. His research focuses on the social determinants of mental health and First Nations youth suicide prevention in Ontario.

Sarah E. Murray is an assistant professor in the Department of Linguistics at Cornell University and a graduate field member in American Indian studies, cognitive science, linguistics, and philosophy. In 2010 she received a Ph.D. in linguistics with a Certificate in Cognitive Science from Rutgers University. Her primary interests are formal semantics and pragmatics, philosophy of language, fieldwork, and understudied languages.

Richard A. Rhodes has centered his work on topics relating to American Indian languages, particularly those of the Algonquian family. He has worked on the Ottawa dialect of Ojibwe, on Métchif, and on Sayula Popoluca, a Mixe-Zoquean language of southern Mexico. He has written extensively on the descriptive syntax and syntactic typology of Ojibwe, on the historical linguistics of Métchif, and on lexical semantics and lexicography in American Indian languages. His current research focuses on the intersection of language, history, and geography.

Bryan Rosen received his Ph.D. in linguistics from the University of Wisconsin–Madison in 2015.

Conor McDonough Quinn teaches linguistic field methods courses at the University of Southern Maine Department of Linguistics.

Natalie Weber is a graduate student in linguistics at the University of British Columbia. She is interested in phonology and the interfaces between phonology and other components of grammar. Her dissertation explores the relationship between word-internal prosodic and syntactic structure in polysynthetic languages. She focuses on Blackfoot, an Algonquian language spoken in Alberta and northern Montana. She is investigating phonological phenomena that hold across spans smaller than a word.